BOXING'S
GREATEST
CONTROVERSIES

BOXING'S
GREATEST
CONTROVERSIES

BLUNDERS, BLOOD FEUDS, AND MOB CORRUPTION

LOUIS JOSHUA EISEN

DUNDURN
PRESS

Publisher: Meghan Macdonald | Acquiring editor: Kwame Scott Fraser/Julia Kim
Editor: Kwame Scott Fraser
Cover designer: Karen Alexiou
Cover image: *Fight for the World's Championship, Tommy Burns and Jack Johnson, in the ring at the stadium, Rushcutters Bay, N.S.W., Saturday, December 26, 1908* (National Library of Australia)

Library and Archives Canada Cataloguing in Publication

Title: Boxing's greatest controversies : blunders, blood feuds, and mob corruption / Louis Joshua Eisen.
Names: Eisen, Louis Joshua, author.
Description: Includes bibliographical references.
Identifiers: Canadiana (print) 20240457374 | Canadiana (ebook) 20240457382 | ISBN 9781459754867 (softcover) | ISBN 9781459754874 (PDF) | ISBN 9781459754881 (EPUB)
Subjects: LCSH: Boxing matches—Corrupt practices. | LCSH: Boxing matches—Moral and ethical aspects. | LCSH: Boxing matches—History. | LCSH: Boxing—Corrupt practices. | LCSH: Boxing—Moral and ethical aspects. | LCSH: Boxing—History.
Classification: LCC GV1136.5 .E47 2025 | DDC 796.8309—dc23

We acknowledge the support of the Canada Council for the Arts and the Ontario Arts Council for our publishing program. We also acknowledge the financial support of the Government of Ontario, through the Ontario Book Publishing Tax Credit and Ontario Creates, and the Government of Canada.

Care has been taken to trace the ownership of copyright material used in this book. The author and the publisher welcome any information enabling them to rectify any references or credits in subsequent editions.

The publisher is not responsible for websites or their content unless they are owned by the publisher.

Printed and bound in Canada.

Dundurn Press
1382 Queen Street East
Toronto, Ontario, Canada M4L 1C9
dundurn.com, @dundurnpress

This book is respectfully dedicated to Dr. Abraham Eisen and Angelo Dundee, who influenced my life for the better and whom I think about every day. I am grateful every day for their wisdom and advice.

CONTENTS

INTRODUCTION

During the mild spring and brutally hot summer of 2004, the movie *Cinderella Man*, a fictionalized account of the life of former world heavyweight champion James J. Braddock, was filmed in Toronto, Ontario, Canada. Directed by Ron Howard and starring Russell Crowe, the film chronicles Braddock's life during the Great Depression.

I was privileged to be cast in the movie, in the role of Ray Arcel. Arcel was one of the greatest trainers in boxing history. I spent the first two weeks of April sitting with my hero, mentor, and surrogate father, Angelo Dundee, watching old black-and-white films of famous fights. I had actually met Angelo thirty-one years earlier, in Toronto. On September 22, 1973, my father, Stan, and I went down to Maple Leaf Gardens in Toronto to watch Canada's Clyde Gray challenge Angelo's fighter, champion José Nápoles, for the undisputed world welterweight crown. Nápoles was a typical Angelo Dundee–type fighter — very skilled and technically flawless in the ring.

My dad and I rooted for Gray because he was Canadian. Gray never quite got untracked that day. Nápoles emerged with a well-deserved unanimous fifteen-round decision win. After the fight was over, we waited around to meet Angelo. He walked out a short time later to greet many people — some of them he knew, many of them were strangers. When it was my turn, my father told him that I was a huge fan of his and that Muhammad Ali was my hero. To me, Ali was more than just the greatest prizefighter ever. He was God. Lots of kids back then had pictures of Farrah Fawcett on their bedroom walls. I had Ali.

The first thing Angelo asked me was, "What are your favourite subjects in school?" I replied, "English and history." He smiled. I told Angelo that I wanted to be a professional boxer. He strongly advised me against it. He said that unless my pugilistic skills were special, it would be best to forget about becoming a fighter. I was crestfallen. (Years later, he told me that my head was so big, the other guy could hit me without leaving his corner.) He then added, "That doesn't mean you are done with boxing. You said your favourite subjects in school were English and history. You can always combine them and write about boxing." I liked that idea a lot. Angelo was always unfailingly positive and optimistic.

So, thirty-one years later, I find myself sitting with Angelo Dundee at a movie studio in downtown Toronto, watching films of famous fights. Angelo had been present at many of these fights, and he had known most of the fighters involved in each bout. He had wonderful comments and asides about each match. When it came to James J. Braddock fighting Max Baer, Angelo told me a wonderful story. He recalled how, back in the 1960s, he had brought Muhammad Ali to New Jersey to meet Braddock. He laughed when he said that Braddock told Ali he was throwing his jab incorrectly. Braddock advised Ali to turn his fist on its side, knuckles facing left, when throwing his jab. Ali was, as always, very kind and polite, and thanked Braddock for his misguided advice. Angelo firmly believed — and he was right — that you can always learn something from watching and meeting older fighters.

About the second Tunney-Dempsey fight, he exclaimed, "The ref was owned by the Mob." We watched the Clay-Liston bout. Angelo's eyes sparkled. It was almost like the film of the fight had transported him back in time to that historic moment. Angelo stated often, "Styles make fights. Also, Liston was older than dirt. The Big Guy's speed and lateral movement negated Liston's power. It threw off his rhythm." He rarely if ever referred to Muhammad Ali by his name — he almost always called him the "Big Guy."

His comments about the Ali-Liston rematch were very telling as well. (In his first bout with Liston, he was named Cassius Clay. After the bout he legally changed his name to Muhammad Ali. When we filmed *Cinderella Man*, he had been known as Muhammad Ali for forty years.) Angelo remarked, "Whenever Liston threw his jab, his head was always out over his lead foot. He was off-balance. I told the Big Guy to slip Liston's jab, slide a half-inch to his right and then whack him with a counter right hand. We practised that in the gym every day. He used that move on a lot of guys, including Foreman. We called it slip, slide, bang!"

We watched many controversial fights together, such as the tragic third bout between Emile Griffith and Benny "Kid" Paret. Watching this fight visibly saddened Angelo. His shoulders slumped. He shook his head in disgust. "It was his manager, Manuel Alfaro, that got Paret killed. Paret was a shot fighter after his loss to Fullmer. It's always the fight before that causes the damage when a fighter dies. I told Alfaro that he should retire Paret, because he could really get hurt if he fought again. Do you know what he told me? 'If he dies, I go to Cuba and find another boy.'"

While watching Leonard-Durán I, Angelo vividly recalled how Durán got under Ray's skin. According to Angelo, Ray fought Durán's fight rather than fighting his own. He quoted one of his mentors, the great Charley Goldman, who once said, "No one ever invents their own game just to be beaten at it!" In other words, make your opponent fight your fight. In Leonard-Durán II, Leonard imposed his will upon Durán. He took his heart away. Angelo mentioned that Leonard was mentally and physically ready months before the fight. "Ray outboxed that sucker. If Durán had not quit, Ray would have knocked him out."

Boxing's appeal is eternal and primal and artistic all at the same time. Boxing has always had a strong hold on the public's emotional purse strings. Great fighters act as surrogates for their fans — gallant warriors fighting our battles against our enemies, regardless of whomever they may be facing in the ring. Each great fight from the past tells a story. Such stories live on forever in the hearts of true fight fans. Boxing aficionados still vehemently argue today about who won fights that took place over one hundred years ago. This is the lasting hold that boxing exerts over its fan base. Boxing's appeal is that it merges yesterday and today into the same time. The fight might have occurred in the past, but emotions regarding its outcome remain the same as when it originally took place. Controversy is as old as boxing itself. Angelo Dundee said that controversial fights will keep people talking about boxing every day, and that is a very good thing.

CHAPTER 1

PETER COCKRAN VS. BILL DARTS*

Fight: Peter Cockran (or variants, with the later "Corcoran" hardly ever used at the time) vs. Bill Darts
Weight Class: Heavyweight (although they would not have been described as heavyweights at that time)
Date: May 27, 1772
Location: Epsom Downs, England
Outcome: First-round win for Cockran
Referee: Broughton's Rules stated there should be two umpires outside the ring, and a third umpire to be selected by them only if they could not agree about a dispute. There was no information given in contemporary reports regarding the umpires.

---------------- **Background** ----------------

Modern boxing began in Great Britain between the late seventeenth and early eighteenth centuries. England's long eighteenth century, bookended

---

* The author is extremely grateful to noted historian and author Tony Gee, the world's foremost authority on British bare-knuckle boxing history, for providing new information, his helpful advice, and his generosity. It goes without saying that any mistakes found in this chapter are entirely of my own making.

by the Glorious Revolution of 1688 and the end of the Napoleonic Wars in 1815, produced many great fighters such as Jack Broughton, Daniel Mendoza, and Jem Belcher, names that still resonate with boxing historians today. This colourful prizefighting history is rife with many controversies dating back to the early 1700s. Surely, the most consistently prevalent of all controversies in eighteenth-century boxing was the thorny issue of fixed fights. There were plenty of fights during this time that were heavily rumoured to have been rigged, including bouts involving Broughton's conqueror, Jack Slack.

Undoubtedly some of those eighteenth-century fights were fixed; however, even with the use of today's hi-tech research engines, it is still

Boxing in the eighteenth and early nineteenth century.

practically impossible to determine definitively which bouts from that era involved prearranged outcomes. Unfortunately for prizefighting historians of today, boxing coverage by newspapers back then was sparse at best.

The fight between Bill Darts and Peter Cockran took place in 1772. It was a landmark event in boxing history as it seems to have been the first fight that can more positively be verified as having been rigged. Certainly, there are enough contemporary references for us to be quietly confident about this, so we do not have to rely on the word of later, often-inaccurate sources. Boxing historian Tony Gee points out a particular phraseology in the reporting, which could be construed to mean a fix was relatively common in Georgian Britain. Historian Dennis Brailsford actually describes such wording as the "time-honoured phrase of the age" — newspaper comments made following the event are far more difficult to explain away. Nobody involved with the fight admitted anything. As reports from that time are open to interpretation, it is comments made in newspapers following the fight that are really significant.

There are many boxing aficionados who assume that fixed fights were exclusive only to the twentieth century, specifically under the violent auspices of gangsters Owney "The Killer" Madden, Frankie Carbo, Blinky Palermo, and their multitude of feral henchmen. But sociopaths such as Madden, Carbo, and Palermo, as we will see, were not the first underworld figures to control boxing and fix fights. There is no doubt that fixed bouts, where the outcome of the bout is decided prior to both combatants entering the ring, are as much a part of boxing history as the left jab and the right cross.

The two participants in the bout covered in this chapter, Bill Darts and Peter Cockran, were not engaged in a battle but rather in what seems to have been a poorly scripted and poorly acted fraud. The beneficiaries of this fraud were the gamblers who were in on the fix. The losers, of course, were, as always, the spectators and, in a short time, the fighters themselves.

Suffice it to say, notorious British gamblers and bare-knuckle boxers were conspiring to fix fights nearly two centuries before Messrs. Madden, Carbo, Palermo, and their violent underworld ilk came along. Fixed fights seem as common during the eighteenth century as they were during the twentieth century. The salient difference is that it is almost impossible to prove conclusively that an eighteenth-century fight had been rigged due to the opacity of time and few if any primary sources.

During the 1700s, plenty of British bare-knuckle boxing bouts were rumoured to have been rigged. Undoubtedly some were, but it was not until 1772 that more conclusive proof emerged via one fight in particular — the Cockran-Darts imbroglio was indeed a match whose outcome had been chosen well in advance of the actual fight.

Bill Darts — The Dyer

Bill Darts, often referred to as The Dyer, was a fighter respected by his peers and fistic enthusiasts alike, who often clamoured to see him fight. That is until he deliberately went into the tank against Cockran. He appears to have been a tough fighter with grit and courage, and with power in both hands. He loved to stand toe-to-toe in ring centre and trade blows with his opponents, confident that his punching power would prevail. That is not to say that he was technically deficient; he possessed good balance in the ring, which helped him achieve maximum leverage with his punches. Darts's path to his fight with Cockran was, as we shall see, an eventful one. Below are some examples of his prior encounters.

Following Darts's ascent to the upper echelons of English boxing, there was a tough-as-nails fighter who hailed from an area known as the West Country, named Isaac Doggett, who seems to have been a well-respected fighter and was said to possess formidable power, thereby forcing his opponents to approach him with caution. Darts, eager to show his superiority over such a reputedly strong man, could not travel to Doggett's hometown fast enough, ostensibly to be beaten senseless, as Doggett's supporters rather mistakenly expected.

As often happens in boxing, the ensuing contest did not quite go the way Doggett's supporters had envisioned. Doggett's success had come against ordinary fighters. He had yet to face a skilled professional opponent the calibre of Darts. Darts was reported to have demonstrated his superiority after an even start, with the *Bath Chronicle* stating that the contest, on (as Gee has ascertained) December 19, 1770, ended when Doggett's supporters broke into the ring after a battle of nearly forty minutes to prevent their man from

Boxing as it appeared on an elevated stage in the late eighteenth and early nineteenth century.

being defeated. It was a hard-fought battle. After the ring was broken into, Darts was later declared the winner.[1] Doggett subsequently denied that he lost in a letter to the *Bath Chronicle*.

Regardless of one's opinion of Darts, any man that willingly enters his rival's stronghold and demonstrates superiority over his more powerful foe is a man possessed of immeasurable self-confidence, unflagging courage, and undoubtable grace under pressure. Pierce Egan's (1772–1849) comments in *Boxiana* about the Darts-Doggett fight were written with audience titillation in mind above any sense of journalistic distance, as he was prone to colourful and exaggerated dramatizations. "A West-country Bargeman (Doggett), celebrated for strength, challenged Bill Darts, after his successful contest with Juchau, for one hundred pounds. Doggett was the hero of the country, and, from his great prowess, flattered himself he could make an easy conquest of Darts; — but, in the field of battle, he experienced so many severe *darts* from his antagonist, that he was quickly slain. Doggett acknowledged that he [Darts] was the *worst customer* he had ever met with."[2]

Many boxers in the eighteenth century were known by their respective trades (or where they were born.) Thus, a fighter could be named, to give fictitious examples, Jones the Printer or Brown the Gravedigger or Thomas the Bargeman, which leads us to Swansey the Butcher. As the story goes,

Swansey was able to convince (or fool, depending on your vantage point) several backers to put up the sum of fifty guineas, to allow him a chance to face the seemingly unbeatable Darts. Or, put another way, to permit him a prime opportunity to allow Darts to use him for target practice. Swansey was apparently typical of many of the lower orders who fancied themselves fighters, plenty of whom, for some odd reason, turned out to be butchers by profession. Occasionally, such men, while watching a superior battler, were able to convince themselves that they had a chance to beat an elite-level, skilled prizefighter.

They were usually quickly disabused of this foolhardy notion once their fight with the elite prizefighter got underway. Some delusional fight enthusiasts believed that any man engaged in a profession requiring strength, hard work, and courage would be a prime candidate to defeat a skilled professional pugilist.

This is perhaps one reason for boxing's immense popularity in Britain at that time. Maybe even more surprising is that these novices were on occasion allowed to pursue their dreams, which were almost always shattered by their much more experienced opponent's flashing, highly skilled fists. Boxing has always appealed to the everyday working man or tradesman, because it is the only sport where someone with little education and few connections could make some money through the toil and sweat of their own labours.

Getting a fight with a top pugilist as accomplished as Bill Darts was, in essence, an opportunity for the common labourer or tradesman to win the lottery. It could also be construed as a death wish, as such men had virtually no chance of defeating a talented and experienced prizefighter. For Swansey the Butcher, it seems his wish came painfully true, as Darts wasted no time administering a vicious beating, opening numerous cuts on the Butcher's face and knocking him down many times on a painful, blood-soaked day in Epping Forest, October 13, 1767.

It would be fair to say that Swansey the Butcher wound up looking like one of his own cuts of meat that hung from his shop window, such was the ferocity of the beating he received. Discretion always being the much better part of valour, Swansey seemed to have wisely retreated to the comfort of

The fight between Jack Slack and Jack Broughton on April 11, 1750. Since no sketches exist from boxing's "Dark Period," this drawing exists as a close approximation of how the Darts-Cockran fight appeared, on an elevated (outdoor) stage, to spectators at Epsom Downs.

his shop while smartly avoiding a rematch. Whether or not Swansey ever fought again is unknown.

Egan's *Boxiana* gives several inaccurate descriptions of Darts's fights and contains many mistakes. Additionally, author Henry Downes Miles lists Darts as the champion of England from 1764–71; however, no contemporary newspapers seem to have made any claims to his holding of this title (let alone world titles, which were very much in the future). Darts is thought to have been known in his era at least in part for a brutal brawl with Tom Juchau, reputedly claimed (according to Miles) to have taken place in May of 1766 and held at Guildford, Surrey.[3] Information regarding this fight (including time, place, and outcome) has not been possible to confirm.[4] Boxing historians have not thus far found a Darts-Juchau report in any extant contemporary newspapers before, at the time of, or after this fight supposedly took place.

In truth, we do not know if Miles's report on the bout in *Pugilistica* was accurate to any degree, especially since it was written many years after the fight is said to have occurred. However, Miles could have seen contemporary sources that no longer exist. Certainly, according to Gee, unproved fights do not necessarily mean that an event did not take place. It might just have not been reported as such (since coverage was poor at the time), sources might not now survive, or there might be contemporary accounts that no one has yet located.

According to Miles, "One of the most remarkable of his [Darts's] battles was with Tom Juchau, at Guildford, Surrey, in May, 1766. It was a famous fight for forty minutes, when Juchau was beaten out of time." Gee explains that the term "beaten out of time" means that the fighter was not able to get to the scratch within the then-stipulated thirty seconds. (When Broughton's Rules were superseded by the "New Rules" of 1838, the time was extended to thirty-eight seconds — thirty seconds plus an extra eight to get to the scratch unaided.) Gee makes an important distinction here when he suggests that this phrase should not be stated as "knocked out," as "has been used in some secondary sources when describing bare-knuckle contests, as knocked out implies glove fights under the Marquess of Queensberry rules. However, fully 'knocked out of time' would be correct."[5]

The stakes, as stated by Miles, were one thousand guineas, which was a huge amount in the 1700s (even in the next century, prizefights were normally for a lot less money) for any man doing forty minutes of work, albeit rather bloody, painful, bruising, permanently scarring work.

It is perhaps worth drawing a distinction at this point between regular fights, held on the ground, and stage fights, held on a raised platform or stage. Some fighters of that era are listed as having participated in their first fight on stage. As Gee has pointed out, this does not necessarily mean they were boxing novices. It simply means that they were taking part in their first fight on an elevated platform, or stage, but could well have had experience in matches fought on the ground.

Specially built stages were constructed primarily for important fights, such as when two elite-level combatants faced each other. Prizefights held on a stage typically attracted many more spectators, not least because their view of the action was unobstructed and the contest was usually a significant one. It should be noted, however, that "bums on seats" was not usually an aim in this period, as in most cases there was no gate money. Previously, with the contests that occurred at Broughton's Amphitheatre, for instance, tickets were bought very much like today; therefore, the more spectators there were, the more profitable the event. However, with the closing of the amphitheatres and the sport being forced "underground" and occurring outdoors, regular promoters (like James Figg, James Stokes, George Taylor, and Jack Broughton) disappeared, and obtaining money from potential spectators became problematic.

Bill Darts was like most top fighters of his era in his willingness to fight any man who had the courage to get in the ring with him. But fighters from that era were not infrequently limited in how often they could fight, due to injuries they suffered — specifically badly damaged knuckles and fingers. Darts was considered to be a fighter of the first rank because of the men he had handily defeated. In fact, among the boxing cognoscenti, the mere suggestion that a novice such as Peter Cockran might give Darts any trouble in the ring seemed to be nothing more than a foolish suggestion.

Peter Cockran

Some biographical references to Irish-born bare-knuckle boxer Peter Cockran start along the lines of "Boxer known for rigged fights." This description is short, brief, and most unfortunately, accurate with regards to his fight with Darts. Rumours persisted for years after he retired that he willingly participated in a handful of fixed fights. Whether he did engage in more than one rigged bout is open to conjecture, but that one fixed match was enough to forever tarnish his reputation. Egan claimed that Cockran was born in Athoye, County Carlow, Ireland. Yet this place does not seem to have existed and it is more likely to have been Athy, County Kildare (which is near the Carlow border). There is no doubt that Cockran was very strong and carried fight-ending power in both hands. Nevertheless, he seems to have been little more than a walk-in, face-first brawler.

Cockran won his legitimate matches mostly with brute strength, perseverance, and seemingly inexhaustible stamina. He was reportedly willing to take many shots just to get in one of his own, which has always proven to be a career-shortening strategy. Cockran employed this undisciplined brawling style to make up for his overall lack of ring finesse and technique. He had a reputation as a fighter who could be bought by gamblers, which, ultimately, appears to have destroyed his career and his life. The stain from participating in a rigged fight always leaves a lasting taint on a boxer's reputation.

Contrary to some unverified claims, Cockran does not seem to have been the first Irish bare-knuckle boxer to have staked a claim to being a champion of England. Certainly, like Darts, there does not appear to be any newspaper evidence from the time that he held this title. Cockran's defeat of Darts merely brought him a faux victory and career-defining infamy.

It is unlikely that Cockran realized at the time that being involved in such a sleazy event would forever be a black mark on his name. Most likely, he thought the furor from engaging in a fixed contest would eventually die down. Sadly, the tumult regarding his fight with Darts never seems to have abated for either man. Remember, it was Darts and not Cockran who received money for losing on purpose. Although Cockran was, from the outset, part of the nefarious scheme to defraud the public in attendance, all he received from the fight was the disdain of his peers and the undying shame of having participated in such an ill-advised undertaking.

The first anyone heard of Cockran was, according to Egan, when it was rumoured that he had fled Ireland for the supposedly safer pastures of England, after murdering a man in a violent, drunken dispute about a woman. As it was Egan who detailed this lurid tale of depravity, we are unable to claim, with any degree of veracity, that it even took place — the account was written at least four decades after it supposedly occurred.

Cockran had obviously thin skin and seems to have been constitutionally incapable of letting even the slightest slur against his character pass unavenged. According to Miles in *Pugilistica*, and Egan in *Boxiana*, Cockran eventually found his way to Birmingham, whereupon he inadvertently engaged a butcher, who also happened to be a local prizefighter, in a fight over what Cockran considered an exorbitant price for a leg of mutton. This purported fight was not planned and came about as a result of the rude treatment Cockran and his friend supposedly received from the butcher. The story is almost certainly apocryphal.

Cockran found employment in London, doing the arduous job of coal-heaving. At that time, London had more jobs to offer than just about any other British city; however, many were not easy jobs, and the pay was nothing about which to brag. Not too long after, Cockran was taken by a press gang. Press gangs were bands of armed men led by the king's officers who crimped unsuspecting bystanders into service in the navy during the eighteenth and early nineteenth centuries. They were, in effect, little more than kidnappers and were even known to carry off a bridegroom and congregation from the church door.

There is a dubious account, from Egan once again, that while in the British navy, Cockran apparently amazed his fellow shipmates by performing incredible feats of strength. It was also in the navy where he picked up the rudiments of boxing. After his short stint in the navy, he was discharged and resumed his nascent boxing career. Cockran then made a terrible career move by allowing notorious gambler Dennis O'Kelly to guide his burgeoning pugilistic career. In time, O'Kelly appeared to be the reason for Cockran's downfall, both professionally and, seemingly, personally. O'Kelly also did considerable damage to Darts and British boxing in general. Prizefighting in Britain had some lean years, at least partly due to the chicanery of O'Kelly. This was during the "Dark Period" of British boxing, when the sport had been essentially pushed underground with the closure of the amphitheatres. Cockran's ring style resembled a runaway train — he preferred to try and run over his ring rivals, like a steamroller. He rarely, if ever, went down deliberately without a knockdown blow to end the round, as many other fighters of the day often did until it was deemed a foul in the New Rules of 1838. Cockran never seems to have developed much of a defence and ended up absorbing more punishment than was necessary.

During the bare-knuckle era of boxing in Britain, well-heeled gamblers plotted with prizefighters, encouraging them to engage in fixed fights by offering them bribes to throw a bout. Unbeknownst to the spectators, these gamblers were able to convince boxers who were betting favourites to deliberately lose to opponents who were declared huge underdogs by the oddsmakers, giving the gamblers an opportunity to place large bets on said underdogs. Unlike today, fighters customarily received no fight fees. Fights back then were generally "winner take all" affairs. Any money obtained by the loser was usually received from a "whip-round" (a collection of money donated by fans for the loser of a bout); the generosity of their backers; and later in the bare-knuckle period, a benefit if they performed well.[6] The loser would likely receive nothing for a very poor performance, so any bribes made to them would have to be at least worthwhile — although a loser could clean up with bets.

Every time a heavily favoured prizefighter lost, the gamblers enjoyed a huge pay-off. Those unaware of what had been arranged were the losers as they unknowingly lost money in these rigged encounters. Even the higher classes could be duped as well, hence their withdrawal from the sport when the situation became too unsporting. "Set-ups," as they were then on occasion known, created by English gamblers, formed the essential blueprint for fixed fights, which has lasted for over two hundred and fifty years.

Most prizefighters in the eighteenth century, like plenty of boxers today, made little money; therefore, such paydays were often not enough to feed their families, clothe their children, and pay their rent and other bills. There were definitely some exceptions. Tom Johnson and Daniel Mendoza, for instance, earned extremely well, although both ended up losing everything through high living, gambling, or other causes. In the eighteenth century, extremely few proponents of the Manly Art of Self-Defense were able to make a living solely as prizefighters. Even elite-level pugilists frequently practised other trades and saw prizefighting as a way of adding some extra income to their otherwise meagre earnings.

Many boxing enthusiasts in the 1700s were commoners, although there were often members of the well-heeled aristocracy in attendance, and even on rare occasions royalty, including the Prince of Wales, later to become King George IV of England. Some fighters had upper-class patrons. Commoners still made up the bulk of the spectators, though. Whatever the classes in attendance, the love of gambling was common. And fixers were skilled when it came to exploiting a fighter's financial needs.

Whatever the reason, these warriors were often poorly educated, if at all, and as such, probably felt they had no other option than to go along with the gamblers. There is a common misconception here that Darts and Cockran would not have understood the gravity of their illicit actions. That is not entirely true. It's probable they thought that any fuss arising from their misdeeds would soon be forgotten. They lacked the foresight to see the irreparable long-term damage such underhanded dealings would have on their respective ring careers. They most likely thought that many other fighters were engaging in rigged contests and getting away with it, so why shouldn't they do the same?

The one thing that eighteenth-century gamblers had in common with twentieth-century mobsters was that they both turned fight fixing into an exclusive and self-enriching racket. Prizefighters always benefitted the least from engaging in rigged fights. Usually only the gamblers and fixers really benefitted from fixed bouts. All the fighters received was lasting disrepute and some chump change.

Prizefighting during the early eighteenth century in Great Britain would not be recognizable to boxing fans today, with fighters at liberty to engage in all manner of behaviours that would now result in instant disqualification. But help in cleaning up bare-knuckle boxing, courtesy of the immortal boxer John (Jack) Broughton, was on the way. Bare-knuckle prizefighting was improved substantially with the advent and implementation of Broughton's Rules (1743). Rudimentary as they were, this was a huge turning point in boxing history. While they most certainly did not go far enough, they were, in their time, a good start. They were the first attempt to introduce a sense of order and decorum to boxing — although it seems the priority was clarification for betting purposes.

Then, some ninety-five years later, the New Rules of 1838 replaced Broughton's Rules, and in so doing, cleaned up boxing further. They introduced measures that remain in effect for professional boxing to this day, such as specifically outlawing butting, gouging, scratching, biting, and kicking.

Although the New Rules were sometimes referred to as the London Prize Ring Rules, it should be noted that these rules were never originally known as London Prize Ring Rules, and later in the century this term was generally used abroad but not favoured quite as much as in their country of origin.[7] Modifications were made in 1853 and 1866. It should also be noted that hitting a man when he was down was already outlawed in Broughton's Rules. It is from such humble and harsh beginnings, and the introduction of these two sets of rules, that modern boxing eventually developed into the sport we know and love today.

The big downside, of course, is that there has never been a set of rules implemented in boxing, at any time in its storied history, that could prevent rigged matches from occurring.

When the result of a fight was predetermined, rumours of the fix would, on occasion, spread like wildfire through the enormous crowds. Another way to verify when a fight was fixed, of course, was by looking at any sudden changes in the odds for a prizefight, just prior to fight time.

Gee has proven that much of what has been taken as fact about Peter Cockran and Bill Darts was written erroneously and then passed down through the years, becoming fossilized like a fly in amber in the minds of succeeding generations of fight historians and boxing enthusiasts. However, whatever the accuracy of some secondary source material, we can be confident that some enthusiasts and other pugilists attending various fights back then would have felt that they were watching bouts whose outcomes had been predetermined.

The appearance of and rumours surrounding such improprieties proved deleterious to boxing's popularity until the 1780s, when the revival occurred. Perhaps what is most remarkable about the prize ring in the eighteenth and nineteenth centuries is that even with such fixed bouts rumoured to be taking place, large crowds still turned out for them consistently in the United Kingdom. These crowds often consisted of hard-drinking spectators whose wages were small, and with families often too large to support. Thus, they needed an outlet to vent their personal frustrations, and boxing provided one such outlet. Much like fight fans today, boxing enthusiasts back then lived vicariously through the ring triumphs of their favourite battlers.

These fight enthusiasts usually had to walk extraordinarily long distances just to watch a prizefight. Violence often erupted among the large crowds in attendance. Enthusiasts could be robbed while walking to or from a prizefight, and particularly during the event itself, by common thieves and drunkards. Suffice it to say, boxing spectators back then were a hardy lot, willing to risk their personal safety just to view a boxing match.

To try and make some extra money, these commoners would bet their hard-earned wages on boxing matches. When a fight was fixed, it was these innocent commoners who suffered the most, losing money with which they could ill afford to part. Many of them were no doubt left destitute and disappointed due to the vile machinations of self-serving professional gamblers. It was not until the 1770s that a particular fight occurred where most newspapers reporting the event seemed to have agreed that the fix was in. Of course, we are speaking about the Bill Darts–Peter Cockran fight, held at Epsom Downs in 1772. Incidentally, it should be noted that in his research on that era, Gee discovered that Cockran was hardly ever referred to in print by the surname Corcoran, despite later being known as such. Indeed, most contemporary print references to him give his surname as either Cockran or Cochran.

The Darts-Cockran bout was not an isolated incident in its time. It was merely one of what historians believe were a significant number of fights to have been fixed during the Dark Period. However, not all fights then considered suspect were fixed, but enough of them were to cause the popularity of prizefighting throughout Britain to wane considerably at that time.

Surprisingly, Egan seems to have been keen to convince his readers that the Darts-Cockran fight was on the level, which certainly appears to be demonstrably false. Miles, in contrast, was certain about the fix occurring and called Egan's account "one of the funniest pieces of historical perversion on record." Maybe Egan's viewpoint is not so surprising in retrospect. Egan's marked bias with regard to Irish fighters is significant here. In addition, Egan likely would have derived his article from second- and third-hand sources.

The Cockran-Darts Bout

Thanks to Gee's comprehensive research, several mysteries regarding the fight have finally been put to rest, such as the aforementioned misspelling of the Irishman's name and the true date of the fight. Also, some historians through the years have taken to incorrectly referring to Darts in too familiar terms, as "Billy." Gee points out that early references usually refer to Darts's first name as Bill (if they did at all). He does not appear to have been referred to by the more colloquial moniker Billy by any eighteenth-century publications (although occasionally by the more formal William).

The Darts-Cockran fight is usually listed (in *Pugilistica*, for instance) as having taken place on May 18, 1771, which is untrue. Gee was able to show irrefutably that the actual date of the contest was May 27, 1772. How do we know that there were not actually two different fights a year apart? As Gee has pointed out, it would be stretching credulity to think that there occurred two such bouts involving the same combatants, where a very brief contest took place at the same location in the same month and where the underdog quickly disposed of the favourite in a fight considered by most as a fix.

Furthermore, and perhaps even more significantly, Gee adds that the winner was described in, for instance, *Aris's Birmingham Gazette* of June 1, 1772, as "one Cotrell, which is unlikely to have been the case if he had already previously beaten Darts, as he would then have been very well known."[8] Gee cites *Bingley's Journal* of May 30 to June 6, 1772, as afterward making a reference to the fact that "it is thought that the battle between Darts, the Dyer, and Cockering, the Irishman, fought a few days since at Epsom, was all sham"[9] (and there was a similar report in the *Public Advertiser* of June 5, 1772).[10] These, together with subsequent mentions he has found — such as, for instance, the considerable sum of money the loser was reported to have obtained in side bets (*Newcastle Courant*, June 20, 1772)[11] — significantly strengthen the argument should there be any doubt about a fix being perpetrated.[12]

<hr />

Fix!

Round one began, and it soon must have been obvious that the fight had been rigged. Miles noted in *Pugilistica*, "After a little sparring, Corcoran gave Darts a blow on the side of the head, which drove him against the rail of the stage, when he immediately gave in."[13]

Cockran was believed to have scored his biggest career win up to that time. He enjoyed some ring success, although one or two of his other fights were said to have been fixed, and for the next few years, and following tradition, he ran his own pub. However, due to his predetermined fight with Darts, his subsequent fights can be said to have occurred under a dark shadow of suspicion. The last contest Gee has found for Cockran occurred in 1778.

Controversy

The controversy inherent in the Cockran-Darts fight is that the outcome of the bout was predetermined and the participants willingly engaged in defrauding the public of their hard-earned money. The fact that they did so without any apparent thought given to the lasting damage they could do to themselves and their sport makes their actions that much more shameful.

The fight is reported to have ended very quickly (two minutes). There are more than enough contemporary references to justify considering the Darts-Cockran fight a sham — of that there can be little doubt. But there remain several pertinent questions regarding this fight: Why was the fight fixed? Who was responsible for it? And finally, who stood to benefit the most from the predetermined outcome?

The Decision

Dennis O'Kelly, a notorious, inveterate gambler, adventurer, and un-repentant rogue, was the "sport" who arranged for the upcoming Darts-Cockran fight to be fixed. Although O'Kelly was the primary instigator in what can be considered the first satisfactorily recorded instance of a boxing match with a predetermined outcome, he would not have been able to pull this off without the help of other gamblers and, of course, the bout's participants.

Why was the fight fixed? Well, like all fixed fights, it was done to enrich the gamblers involved, whose avarice usually went unabated. The money received by Darts can be said to have been little more than a pittance compared to the financial windfall reaped by O'Kelly and his dastardly confederates (although Darts did benefit by betting on his opponent to win).

Cockran was a big underdog, as this seems to have been his very first boxing match held on an elevated stage, as far as can be determined. Most people who wagered on the fight bet heavily on Darts to emerge victorious, based on his experience and his previous career victories. Only O'Kelly and his cohorts bet huge sums of money on Cockran to win the bout. Why? Obviously, because they knew the outcome of the fight in advance. The gamblers put their insider knowledge to good use by wagering vast sums of money, at very long odds, on Cockran to win the prizefight. When the upset occurred, the gamblers raked in a mountain of money.

Taking no chances, O'Kelly is believed to have paid Darts either one hundred pounds or one hundred guineas to lose. To say that O'Kelly wagered on the fight implies that there was an element of chance as to the outcome. In effect, what O'Kelly did was analogous to insider stock trading. He manipulated the odds to favour himself and members of his gambling syndicate. As the fight got underway, it can be said that Darts performed his role of loser to the letter. In fact, he outdid himself. He purposely lost the fight in what appears to have been no longer than a couple of minutes.

The man who benefitted the most from this fistic travesty was, of course, O'Kelly — his winnings were said to be between one thousand and three thousand pounds. (The *Newcastle Courant* reported a "certain sporting Captain … cleared no less than 1500L. by the battle"). It was Darts who had to endure the endless shame; the stain of throwing the fight apparently stuck to him permanently, like indelible ink. It cost him his good name and his career.

As noted earlier, the actual length of the Darts-Cockran fight seems to have been two minutes. Of course, neither man was a skilled actor. They were no doubt told to get the fight over with as quickly as possible and would have been following their pre-fight orders, as given to them by the gambler who orchestrated the entire odious affair, O'Kelly. Although some in the crowd might have been fooled temporarily as to the veracity of the outcome, plenty would have been suspicious of it and felt that a hoax had just been perpetrated upon them.

Darts and Cockran probably thought they were simply doing what other fighters were also doing at that time; however, following the herd does not make such underhanded actions acceptable, even though fixed fights were pretty common during this Dark Period. It is a profound indictment of boxing that such frauds were perpetrated throughout the United Kingdom and, later, in the United States and around the world.

Significance

Unfortunately, the trend of fight fixing has continued for over two hundred years. In essence, by accepting the money from O'Kelly to go into the tank, Darts put a price on his very soul and, in the process, robbed boxing enthusiasts of their hard-earned betting money. Not surprisingly, Darts appears to have found it difficult to obtain fights after his contest with Cockran. Gee has located one previously unknown major fight for him (for one hundred guineas) at the beginning of 1774, against one Pennick (which might also be suspect, depending on the interpretation of the reporting, but seems to have been hard fought for a considerable time), but that is all.

According to Miles, Darts appears several times as a second during the early 1770s, notably in a fight between Sam Peters of Birmingham and Rossemus Gregory, an Irishman, in which Darts seconded Gregory but was said to have behaved so egregiously to save his man that Peters simply refused to fight on. Darts died in 1774, although it has been erroneously stated by various authors that he died in 1771 (before the Cockran fight took place!). Interestingly, Gee found mention in the previously cited *Bingley's Journal* of May 30 to June 6, 1772 (and similarly in the *Public Advertiser*), that Darts was actually "said to be dying of his bruises" from the Cockran fight, but several days afterward fought "a more powerful man than Cockering [a Cockran variant occasionally used] for a considerable sum, and was victorious, which ought to be a caution how people lay their money on such fellows."

As Gee has uncovered, the *London Chronicle* of August 18–20, 1774, the *Middlesex Journal*, and the *Evening Advertiser* of August 20–23, 1774, actually reported the death of the "noted bruiser named Darts," with the significant comment that "he seemed to be uneasy in mind some days before he died, on account of his having played booty in a battle that he fought some time ago."

It is often said that in October 1776, Cockran's tainted winning streak came to a rather ignominious end when he lost to Harry Sellers; however, there are two things wrong with this assertion. Firstly, as Gee has ascertained, the Cockran-Sellers contest was well reported for the time, and there can be little doubt that it actually occurred in June, not October, of 1776. Secondly, as Gee has discovered, Cockran was defeated the previous year in a less high-profile fight, which has not previously appeared on the Irishman's record. (This was against a Clare Market butcher named William Allen, who beat "Cockran, the famous bruiser" in Lincoln's Inn Fields, the latter having "never lost a battle before" — *Morning Post*, April 24, 1775.[14])

It has been claimed by various sources that the Cockran-Sellers fight was fixed, but no real evidence has come to light to support this claim. The rumour that it was a "cross" appears to have come, at least primarily, from second-hand claims many years after the fight happened. It was, it seems instead, to have been a severe battle. The inexperienced Sellers, though a prohibitive underdog, showed grit and determination while managing to pull off an upset victory over the seasoned Cockran in a match contemporary accounts have stated lasted anywhere between ten and twenty minutes. Most certainly the fight with Sellers appears to have been "on the level," if newspaper accounts are accurate, as all agreed that it was an extremely hard-fought affair, with mentions of Cockran being most severely cut.

The only contemporary clue Gee has located that points to the possibility of the contest having been fixed is that a year later, the *Morning Post* noted that Sellers was one of two fighters who declined a match with Cockran, considering themselves "incapable of contending with that undaunted *gymnastic* champion." Gee suggests that if the paper was correct about this, it does appear somewhat strange that Sellers would have responded in such a fashion, should he have in fact legitimately beaten Cockran previously.[15]

It is believed the claim of participating in fixed fights proved financially disastrous for Cockran, as customers eventually refused to patronize his tavern. Seemingly such a belief was pervasive enough to lose him much support, and thus his career and ultimately his main source of income, his tavern. However, there were various fights in which he certainly continued to draw spectators — for instance, approximately ten thousand, it was reported, came out for a fight with Sam Peters. Egan wrote of this once-proud warrior sinking into "beggary and contempt." Certainly, although Egan's claim might not have been recorded at the time, Gee has found several papers that reported in 1780, Cockran had fallen so low as to be committed on a charge of extorting money from publicans. There was the mention of the possibility of this culminating in the Irishman's execution, although this obviously did not occur, since Gee located a reference dated four years later that mentioned Cockran being taken into custody for having been the paid leader of ruffians at an election riot.[16]

Of course, of larger significance was that the Darts-Cockran fight confirmed, for the press and spectators alike, that prizefighting had no scruples when it came to openly deceiving the public. Many believed that if two boxers such as Darts and Cockran could so willingly participate in a fix, then it was therefore safe to assume that plenty of other fighters had followed the same path. Hence all prizefighters were at risk of being tainted with the same brush, some deservedly and some not. It took British boxing and its participants many years to recover.

CHAPTER 2

JOE GANS VS. TERRY MCGOVERN

Fight: Joe Gans vs. Terry McGovern
Weight Class: Catchweight of 133 lbs.
Date: December 13, 1900
Location: Lou Houseman's Tattersalls A.C., Chicago, Illinois
Outcome: McGovern by second-round knockout
Referee: George Siler

Background

During the late 1800s, African American men and women were being indiscriminately lynched for such indiscretions as not stepping off a sidewalk to allow a white man to pass, or looking a white woman in the eyes. Many African Americans were lynched for simply being in the wrong place at the wrong time, by white mobs looking to murder the first Black person they came across. The unhinged bloodthirstiness of these mobs was usually based on false rumours about perceived indiscretions committed by unfortunate African Americans.

The perpetrators of these despicable crimes were almost never brought to trial. And when a trial did occur, the jury was all white, and always ended up acquitting the miscreants who committed these unspeakable crimes. Racial prejudice, in all its virulent forms, was alive and well in the United States during the latter part of the late 1800s.

The epic ring victories of Joe Gans and other outstanding fighters of African descent need to be viewed against the uncivil backdrop of that specific era, if we are to fully understand the true and lasting scope of their groundbreaking achievements. Think about this: for George Dixon, Joe Gans, and "Barbados" Joe Walcott to challenge white men and soundly defeat them was, in its own way, an affirmation of their civil rights.

Frequently, ring decisions during that period were racially based, and as such went against African American fighters. This is why Gans and his brethren always endeavoured to knock their opponents out. Knockouts are definitive. Over thirty years after Gans retired from the ring, one of his former contemporaries, Hall of Fame trainer and former lightweight contender Jack Blackburn, advised his young charge, Joe Louis, to always let his right hand be his referee. Sam Langford employed the same strategy many years earlier. Blackburn impressed upon Louis that he needed to win every fight by knockout, because a decision would always go against a Black fighter. This was the cross, said Blackburn, that all African American fighters had to bear.

After a ring win, Gans, Dixon, Walcott, Jack Johnson, Langford, and many other fighters of colour often had to make their way back to their dressing rooms through openly hostile crowds wanting to do them harm.

Joe Gans

Joe Gans packed a lot of living into his thirty-five turbulent years. The Baltimore native rose from the humblest of beginnings to ascend to the very top of the boxing world. Known during his career as "The Old Master," he is considered today by many boxing historians to be the greatest fighter, pound for pound, that ever lived. Gans's boxing knowledge was vast and his technical ring skills were sublime. It was a good thing too, because Gans had to endure an endless tsunami of racist taunts, crooked management, biased referees, *and* a bigoted press corps throughout his stellar ring career. All Black fighters who dared to box white men were, like Dixon, Walcott, and Gans, risking their very lives. These brave Black warriors could easily have been killed on numerous occasions by rabidly hostile, gun-toting crowd members. A boxing ring was the only place on Earth back then where a fighter of African descent could face a white man on semi-equal terms.

Joe Gans was born Joseph Saifuss Butts in Baltimore, Maryland, on November 25, 1874, a mere nine years after the American Civil War ended and during the ultra-violent era of Reconstruction. Newspaper reporters later misprinted his adopted surname of Gant as Gans, and it stuck.[1] Gans was named after his father, baseball player Joseph Saifuss Butts. Unable to care for his infant son, Butts gave baby Joseph to a foster mother, Maria Jackson Gant. It was Gant who loved and cared for young Joe as if he were her own son. They formed a very close bond.[2] Gans adored his foster mother,

Joe Gans.

and her well-being was always uppermost in his mind. She instilled within him the values of hard work, honesty, determination, courage, and toughness. These were the values Gans unfailingly displayed throughout his glorious ring career.[3]

Maria Gant worked long, hard hours for scant pay to provide for Joe and herself. Gans never forgot the sacrifices she made on his behalf. If not for her unstinting belief in him, Gans might never have achieved his lofty status as a boxing immortal.[4] Gans and Maria lived in a violent, poverty-stricken area in the Greenwillow section of Baltimore known derisively as "The Bottom." Murders, rapes, and muggings in the Bottom were a daily occurrence. Even if you take boxing out of the equation, the mere fact that Gans survived into adulthood in such a dangerous neighbourhood was astonishing, as many young African American males who lived there were not so fortunate.

The life spans of African Americans were much shorter than those of white Americans in the late nineteenth century. Job prospects for African Americans were grim — career advancement in any profession was simply non-existent. Boxing was one of the few fields of endeavour where an African American could earn a living. African American prizefighters, especially ones as exceptionally talented as Gans, were vastly different from their white counterparts. Their pay was lower, they were preyed upon by corrupt managers, and they were entirely on their own within the boxing community. Their sense of isolation and loneliness must have been intense.

It was not unusual for Gans to receive death threats prior to or during his fights. This was true for Dixon and Walcott as well — in fact, it was the norm for most fighters of colour. Gans received thousands of letters from barely literate bigots threatening him with death just for daring to engage white men in battle. Gans took these threats seriously yet still managed to perform to the best of his abilities every time. He was unflappable in the ring. His inner resolve was unbreakable.

In the eras of Dixon, Walcott, Gans, and Langford, great Black fighters were forced to carry their white opponents for a certain number of rounds during a match if they hoped to get paid and, in some instances, even make it out of the arena alive. These metaphorical manacles forced Gans to allow

The immortal Joe Gans.

his white opponents to bloody his nose for at least seven or eight rounds before he was unbound from his figurative shackles and permitted to display
the full depth of his vast ring arsenal. Gans often had to endure humiliating stipulations just to convince an opponent to get in the ring with him,
such was the disparity in ring talent between him and many of his opponents. Considering the so-called handcuffs Gans was forced to wear through
many of his contests, his record of 101 knockouts over 147 career victories
is amazing.

One notable exception was his demolition of Frank Erne on May 12,
1902, at the International Athletic Club in Fort Erie, Ontario, to capture the
undisputed world lightweight crown. Mind you, Gans had already fought
Erne once before, so he knew exactly what to expect. Gans had decided before facing Erne for the second time to end matters quickly and decisively.
Erne was visibly terrified of Gans in their rematch. Gans, unfettered by
constraints, real or imaginative, took advantage of Erne's fear by dispatch-
ing him at the 1:40 mark of round one. Boxing historians often talk about
Benny Leonard and Roberto Durán as the greatest lightweight champions
of all time, but Gans deserves to be held in the same high esteem.

By the time of Gans's birth in 1874, African Americans had only been free for eleven years. In truth, they were free only in word and not in fact. It would take another one hundred years before any substantive changes were realized on behalf of civil rights for all African Americans. Gans well understood the peril that was possible when interacting with white people — for African Americans, every day was dangerous and potentially fatal. By the time he became a well-known boxer, Gans knew what to expect from the predatory white power brokers who controlled prizefighting. Gans was the first African American fighter to ever hold an undisputed world title. He blazed the trail for every Black fighter to follow, including Jack Johnson, Joe Louis, and Muhammad Ali.

The first Black man ever to hold a world boxing title was Canadian George Dixon, a friend and contemporary of Gans. Like Gans, Dixon had to endure an implacable wall of racism on his way to becoming a world champion in two different weight divisions. Dixon was treated slightly better than Gans, because he was a lighter-skinned Black man. *The Ring* magazine founder Nat Fleischer perpetuated the fiction that Dixon's father was a white British sailor, thus Dixon had white blood coursing through his veins. Dixon's parents were African Canadians. His ancestors were slaves who were transported to Nova Scotia during the war of 1812 on a British destroyer, along with up to thirteen other enslaved families, in return for providing the British navy with logistical information regarding American naval encampments.

Like Dixon, Gans possessed that rarest of ring skills, patience. Gans made time in the ring work for him by patiently waiting for his opponents to make mistakes he could quickly capitalize on, to turn a fight in his favour. Gans's ring smarts were off the charts. He was a gifted counterpuncher, although he was equally adept at going on the attack, and his ring poise stood out in an era where most boxers eagerly rushed at their rivals, face first, swinging wildly like rampaging bulls at Pamplona. Fighters who engaged in such foolhardy rushes against Gans usually ended up with very little to show for their efforts beyond broken, bloodied noses, fewer teeth, and hideous facial cuts.

Gans preferred to observe his opponents through the first several rounds of a match, making mental notes as to their various strengths, weaknesses, and flaws. He would then systematically take them apart, round by round, feint by feint, punch by punch, until they either quit, lost a decision, or, as in most cases, were knocked out. Gans's most potent weapon was his brain. His ability to think on his feet was unrivalled; he was quick, powerful, perfectly balanced, and possessed unparalleled ring vision. He controlled the geography of the ring, meaning he knew where he was in relation to the ropes and his opponent at all times. Gans used his full weight to exert maximum leverage on every punch, and he always had the perfect counter shot ready to fire in response to whatever shot his opponent sent his way. Suffice it to say, Gans was a huge problem for every man he faced. His ability and reputation were enough to intimidate most ring rivals.

Gans wielded his jab like Matisse wielded a paint brush. It was like a king cobra lashing out at its prey — he violently snapped back the heads of his opponents every time he landed his concussive jab. Gans expertly hid his powerful, fight-ending straight right hand behind his jab, so much so that his opponents rarely saw it coming. It's the punches you don't see that get you out of there. This is a common move for fighters today, but Gans was really the first to do that on a regular basis. He was a master at the art of feinting, putting his opponents into position to be hit. He was exceptional at using their own momentum against them, and in effect, forcing them to knock themselves out. Gans's ring skills left everyone privileged enough to have seen him in action in awe.

Even while admiring his magnificent ring skills, it is impossible to look at a photograph of Gans and not be overcome by the deep, penetrating sadness in his eyes. The sheer hopelessness etched into his face is unmistakable and moving. The virulent racism he experienced every day of his life certainly took a negative toll on his emotional well-being and undoubtedly helped shorten his life.

Gans first entered the ring in Baltimore in 1886, when he was a mere boy of twelve, in a common and degrading racist spectacle known as a battle royale. A battle royale included ten or more blindfolded African American boys in a ring with gloves on, throwing punches blindly at each other. The last boy standing was declared the winner. Such events were held throughout the nineteenth century, in both the North and the South, much to the amusement of white spectators who randomly threw coins into the ring to show their approval or disapproval.[5] On this night, in his very first ring appearance, Gans was named the winner — he was the last boy still upright. Gans's skills were such that he soon graduated from these humiliating affairs to legitimate prizefights.

Gans's very first recorded pro bout was actually a controlled sparring session against another African American fighter named Buck Myers, on October 23, 1893, at the Avon Club in Baltimore. It was the opening bout of a three-bout card and was of indeterminate length. Since it was a sparring match, it was declared a no-contest decision. No one that night could have known they were witnessing the professional ring debut of the greatest fighter that ever lived.

"Terrible" Terry McGovern

It's almost criminal that boxing fans today don't know more about the phenomenal ring exploits and incredible life of "Terrible" Terry McGovern. He was an elemental force of nature, a two-fisted twister inside the squared circle. He fought with an intense, animal-like ferocity never seen before or since in the ring, with the possible exception of Mike Tyson. McGovern shone very brightly and all too briefly, and then descended into the hell of early onset dementia pugilistica, no doubt caused by his face-first style of swapping leather. Those who were lucky enough to have seen him once remembered him forever. McGovern hit his opponents so hard and so often, they sometimes felt as if they were fighting two men at the same time.

McGovern went into the Gans fight as the reigning world featherweight champion. He'd captured the featherweight crown on January 9, 1900, via a brutal eight-round knockout over George Dixon at the Broadway Athletic Club in New York, in a bout that was originally scheduled for twenty-five rounds. Dixon was on the downward slope of a long and storied career, with almost eight hundred fights behind him. McGovern was just too young, too fast, and too strong for the already-faded Dixon.

McGovern was born John Terrence McGovern on March 9, 1880, in Johnstown, Pennsylvania, to Irish immigrants Ellen Munroe McGovern

"Terrible" Terry McGovern.

and Thomas McGovern. It was soon after Terry's birth that the McGovern family moved to Brooklyn, New York.[6] Terry's mother, Ellen, was married three times and had eleven children in all. Her first marriage produced four children, while her marriage to Thomas McGovern produced seven, two of whom never made it to adulthood. It was quite common back then for families to have many children precisely because the infant mortality rate was so high. They were praying that at least some of their kids would survive into adulthood.

McGovern's father died young, and his mother remarried to a man named Joseph Kenny, who has incorrectly been named as McGovern's birth father. He was, in fact, Ellen's third husband, and fourteen years her junior. Ellen McGovern needed the extra income Kenny added to their coffers, as well as the roof he helped keep over their heads. Like Gans, the McGoverns grew up in dire poverty. Sadly, Joseph also died at a young age, and Terry was forced to take odd jobs around Brooklyn to help keep his family solvent. These jobs involved long periods of gruelling work for extremely low wages, but McGovern never complained. He felt it was his solemn duty to help his family.

Around this time, in 1896, McGovern, just sixteen years of age, joined the local Greenwood Athletic Club of Brooklyn and fell in love with boxing. He took to pugilism as though to the manner born. He genuinely enjoyed fighting — he had found his calling. It wasn't long before he started to engage in three- and four-round bouts. With a large starving family to support, McGovern had no time to spend honing his craft in the amateur ranks. He would instead learn his craft against seasoned professional fighters.

McGovern held two undisputed, universally recognized world titles before facing Gans — bantamweight and featherweight — although not simultaneously. He was somewhat of a boxing prodigy, winning the world bantamweight title at nineteen and the world featherweight championship at twenty. McGovern stood five-foot-three with a reach of sixty-five inches. Gans stood approximately five-foot-six and a half with a reach of seventy-one inches. Gans was the bigger man in every measurable physical statistic.

Gans was also the smarter ring man and knew well how to turn his superiority in height and reach to his advantage. McGovern was not intimidated by Gans's superior physical attributes. McGovern was usually the smaller man in most of his fights, but he turned such disadvantages into pluses by fighting from an exaggerated crouch, bulling his opponent up against the ropes and crowding him while launching furious two-fisted assaults on his head and body. Bigger men needed room to punch effectively, and McGovern never gave it to them. This was the secret of his success. McGovern really was the epitome of the old saying, "the best defence is a good offence."

McGovern fought like a man attempting to claw his way out of hunger and poverty precisely because he was a man trying to claw his way out of hunger and poverty. He battled with a singular viciousness, putting every family tragedy, physical slight, and personal indignity he had ever suffered into every punch he threw. McGovern was the original "Mr. Bad Intentions." He won the world bantamweight title with a devastating knockout over British bantamweight champion Pedlar Palmer of England on September 12, 1899, at the Westchester Athletic Club in Tuckahoe, New York. An estimated crowd of ten thousand spectators watched McGovern obliterate Palmer in just 2:32 of the first round. It was his eighteenth knockout in thirty-six fights. The savagery of his attack and the quickness of his victory stunned the boxing world. McGovern had brilliantly reduced the sport to its bare essence — violence mixed with speed and fury.

McGovern sported a professional record of 53–2–4 when he entered the squared circle to do battle with Gans, who boasted an astonishing 94–6–14 pro ledger. Gans was the more experienced fighter, although McGovern's record of fifty-nine fights was no less exceptional. What McGovern lacked in technique, though, he more than made up for with naked aggression. The difference in physical size between Joe Gans and Terry McGovern is instantly noticeable in the films of the fight, and such details favoured Gans by a considerable degree. The difference in their respective ring styles and skill levels was also a stark reminder of how most people thought this fight would turn out. McGovern was the bull while Gans was the highly skilled matador. Their contrasting ring styles, in some respects, were emblematic of their different personalities.

Gans was poised and polite, and moved in the ring as if on gossamer wings; McGovern was impetuous, restless, and approached life like a conductorless train hurtling toward infinity. McGovern was a walk-in-and-throw slugger, whereas Gans was always prepared and exquisitely precise, like an assassin.

Controversy

The controversy about this fight does not involve whether or not the fight was fixed. We know beyond a scintilla of doubt that this fight was rigged. The first question that needs to be answered here is, why was it fixed? Secondly, who was to blame for the predetermined outcome? Thirdly, if the people present knew the fight they were about to witness was a tank job, why was it allowed to happen? Also, how did the fix affect the legacies of both Gans and McGovern? Finally, what was the immediate after-effect of the fix fiasco on professional boxing?

The Decision

It was well established over a century ago that the Gans-McGovern bout was not on the level. Even so, there are still naysayers that surprisingly disagree with this assertion; however, there is much evidence that proves conclusively that the outcome of the Gans-McGovern fight was predetermined, with the film of the bout substantiating its rigged outcome. It is worth remembering that the fight was scheduled for only six rounds. The contract stated that if McGovern could last the full six rounds, he would receive 75 percent of the agreed-upon purse and be declared the winner.[7]

It is readily apparent when watching the fight that Gans was certainly not trying to win. Although he was knocked down seven times (once in the first round and six times in round two), it is very difficult to find more than one or two flush shots that landed on his jaw by the smaller McGovern. Gans was able to easily ride out McGovern's head shots, thereby lessening their true impact. Gans went down mostly from shoves and glancing blows. He was bigger and more powerful than McGovern, and possessed enough strength to have forcefully clinched McGovern, had he chosen to do so. But he deliberately kept his big guns silent. In fact, Gans did not throw a single punch during the two rounds the fight lasted. He had absorbed harder punches from bigger men than McGovern without so much as blinking. For the uninitiated or the simply naive, it appeared that Gans was taking a fearful pasting from McGovern ... or was he?

Gans followed the script laid out for him by his despicable manager, Al Herford. In fact, once the fight was stopped by famed referee George Siler at the 2:05 mark of round two, Gans rose with no apparent lasting damage and smilingly shook McGovern's hand, as if nothing untoward had happened. We can only speculate on how deep the wounds were to Gans's enormous pride, for having to lay down against a man he knew he could have destroyed had the fight been on the level.

Could Gans have refused to take part in the fix? The short answer is no. Unfortunately for Gans, his manager, Al Herford, was one of pro boxing's biggest power brokers at the turn of the twentieth century. Gans needed Herford to secure him big money fights (which he did, but not before absconding with most of Gans's purse money) while he advanced up the lightweight ladder, hopefully toward another title shot at lightweight champion Frank Erne. The goal was always to get another shot at Erne's title.

Nine months before his notorious fight with McGovern, on March 23, 1900, Gans challenged reigning lightweight world titlist Erne at the Broadway Athletic Club in New York. Gans was forced to quit after the twelfth round due to an accidental head-butt by Erne, which opened up a deep and hideous cut over his left eye. Gans's corner was unable to stem the flow of blood, forcing him to retire from the contest — his left eye could have been permanently blinded had he continued on.

Every subsequent fight that Gans participated in was designed to help him get another shot at Erne and the title. That was the long-range plan, why Gans was ordered by Herford to tank the McGovern fight — to speed up the process of getting Erne to face Gans again, or so Herford thought. Did Gans disagree with throwing the fight? We don't know. He was likely not very happy about it, but at the same time, he was desperate to redeem himself against Erne. The reasoning behind the fix was that a loss to McGovern would theoretically make Erne more amenable to giving Gans another title shot, because such a defeat would indicate that Gans's boxing skills had significantly regressed. This specious theory is predicated on the notion that Erne was not smart enough to know the fight was a tank job. Unfortunately for both Herford and Gans, Erne was not stupid. The boxing community was tiny but interconnected — Erne had to have known that Gans deliberately threw the bout.

Herford knew he stood to make significantly more money in a betting coup from a fixed fight than from a straight bout, because Gans would have entered the ring as the heavy favourite against McGovern. Herford was powerful enough to have demanded the fight be fought on a legitimate basis during his initial discussions with Broadway impresario Sam Harris, McGovern's manager; however, Herford never even considered staging the

Gans-McGovern fight on the level. Herford and Harris no doubt thought that Gans and McGovern could easily pull off a faked fight without incurring any lasting repercussions to their ring reputations. Their plan was doomed to failure from the beginning as both Gans and McGovern were pugilists and not trained stage actors. Harris's background was in theatre, while Herford's entry into boxing was as the manager of the Eureka Athletic Club in Baltimore. He was one of the sleaziest managers that boxing ever produced.

In an ironic coda to the Gans-McGovern debacle, McGovern actually received credit for his (tainted) win from the boxing community, while Gans suffered an indelible blow to his career and ring legacy. The fix had temporarily stalled Gans's efforts to gain a (quick) rematch with Erne, but McGovern suffered no negative effects to his career for his participation in an obviously fixed fight. The African American was punished while the white man escaped any opprobrium for his fistic malfeasance. Losing deliberately to McGovern must have been particularly galling for Gans, especially after Erne still refused him a rematch. Gans was forced to wait an additional twenty-nine months and twenty fights before he caught up with Erne again. Gans, meanwhile, reaped nothing from the ruse except abuse and shame.

Gans was livid with Herford, since it was Gans and not Herford who had assumed all the risk and had the most to lose for deliberately losing a prizefight, referred to back then as "going into the tank." During that time period, an African American fighter throwing a fight was doing irreparable harm to his future career prospects. Racist fight fans already despised him because of his skin colour. Now, he was a cheater. Gans should never have gone through with the fight, although he likely had no choice in the matter. Anytime Gans tried to leave the employ of Herford, his manager made sure he was shut out of the boxing industry entirely. Unluckily for Gans, all boxing roads led to Herford.

Both Gans and McGovern were promised a purse of $7,500 each, plus 50 percent of the gate receipts. Lou Houseman, the promoter and owner of Tattersalls Athletic Club in Chicago, planned to make his money from the sale and distribution of the film of the fight. Of course, any income earned from fight films in that era depended on the length of the fight. This is why

Herford often had Gans carry his opponents — a longer fight guaranteed a bigger box office for the film. A two-round fight, where the bout was widely panned as a fix, had little to no chance of garnering any significant revenue. Herford promised Gans $45,000 for throwing the fight. In the end, Gans only received $4,500 for deliberately losing to McGovern. Herford shorted him $3,000 from his contracted purse, plus the extra $45,000 he had promised. This was par for the course — many Black pugilists bore the brunt of Herford's loathsome pilfering.[8]

Gans never held any animosity toward McGovern regarding the fix. The two were friends; McGovern genuinely thought he was doing Gans a favour. McGovern was radically different from most fighters of his era. He was friendly with various African American and Jewish fighters, such as bantamweight contender Charley Goldman, who idolized him. For some unknown reason, McGovern was immune from the bigotry so prevalent in his time, particularly in boxing circles. But while there existed a deep and abiding mutual respect between Gans and McGovern, this did not prevent them from perpetrating a terrible fraud on the Chicago sporting public.

There have always been claims that McGovern was not in on the fix. That seems highly unlikely. Gans, McGovern, Herford, and Harris were often seen together in public in the days and weeks leading up to the fight, no doubt discussing the predetermined outcome of their upcoming imbroglio. It is unlikely that McGovern was not intimately involved in the set-up, as it would have been almost impossible to prearrange the fight's outcome with Gans alone. McGovern's reputation was that of a hard-working, honest athlete, and his complicity in arranging the predetermined conclusion of his fight with Gans has never been proven one way or the other, but an educated guess, given the circumstances leading up to the fight, would suggest that he was indeed as guilty as Gans.

After the fight, in a world class display of chutzpah, Herford claimed disingenuously that the McGovern bout could not have been fixed specifically because it ended early. His fallacious reasoning was that it usually took Gans many rounds to warm up before he became aggressive enough to bring the attack to his opponents. This, of course, was patently untrue, as was evidenced by his aforementioned one-round blowout of Frank Erne over two years later. Herford conveniently omitted the fact that Gans often had been forced to carry many of his white opponents into later rounds as the true reason for his supposedly "slow" starts.

We will never know if McGovern experienced any guilt about participating in a fixed fight. He may very well have thought that it was a great way to earn extra money while at the same time doing a good friend a favour. Fight historians sometimes like to ascribe a 2025 sense of morality to fighters from that era. Today's sense of morality simply did not exist back then. A fight, fixed or otherwise, was a payday in 1900. McGovern had beaten many other good fighters quickly and easily (including an eighth-round knockout of the immortal world featherweight champion, George Dixon), so for the boxing public at large, anything within the realm of reason was considered a possibility in the prize ring.

However, there is a problem with such logic: Joe Gans was not just another good fighter. He was recognized in his own time as the greatest fighter in the world. He was considered by all boxing experts to be the most technically complete fighter of all time. Also, unlike Dixon, who was on the downside of his career when he faced McGovern, Gans was considered to be in his prime. Gans was a much bigger man with a better record and more ring experience. Something was obviously awry, according to veteran referee George Siler, who commented after the fight, "If Gans was really trying, I don't know much about the game."[9]

When the fight was first announced, Gans was a prohibitive favourite to defeat McGovern, as the chasm between their respective skill sets and size was thought to be too wide for McGovern to overcome with sheer physicality. Gans's ring expertise was considered far superior to the skills displayed by the crude, slugging McGovern. It is worth mentioning here that the Gans-McGovern bout was at a catchweight of 133 pounds. The lightweight limit was 135 pounds, whereas the featherweight limit then was 126 pounds. Gans was forced to weigh in at 133 pounds at 7:00 p.m. on fight night.[10] Since the bout was being contested at a catchweight, McGovern's featherweight title was not at stake. This was unfair to Gans, although it was a common stipulation in most of his fights, especially during his three battles with Oscar "Battling" Nelson. It is doubtful, however, that the catchweight adversely affected Gans. Their fight was contracted for only six rounds, which was ideal for the movie cameras. The Gans-McGovern fight contract further stipulated that Gans could only win by knockout before the sixth round, whereas McGovern only had to stay on his feet for the whole six rounds to be declared the victor. That would very quickly prove to be a moot point. Once again, such onerous stipulations involving African American fighters were quite common in that era. Ironically, the prospect of McGovern knocking out Gans was never discussed as it was considered an impossibility.

The sudden shifting of the odds to favour McGovern just moments before the fight was an obvious sign that the forthcoming fight was not on the level. Word spread quickly throughout the racially mixed crowd that the fight's outcome had already been decided. This triggered a surge of wagers on McGovern to win by an early knockout. Something smelled rotten in Chicago, and this time it was not the stockyards.[11]

To quell rumours of an impending fix, which would have hurt the gross gate receipts (and ultimately, sales of the subsequent fight film), Al Herford announced that he was betting $3,000 ($110,000 in 2025) of his own money on Gans to win. Of course, that amount was a mere drop in the bucket compared to what Herford stood to earn if he bet a substantial amount on McGovern to win by an early knockout. No proof exists that Herford bet any money on Gans, which is not surprising, given his duplicitous nature.

What helped to condemn Gans in the eyes of the world was that he looked magnificent in his previous fights before facing McGovern, and then appeared even more scintillating in his next twenty fights. His successes before and after the McGovern fight were a clear indication that their abbreviated Chicago melee was a hoax.

The audience in attendance knew immediately that the fight was a tank job and let their displeasure be loudly known. They furiously tried to get their money back from the bookies, but it was too late — the bookies had already stopped taking bets as they could no longer cover the large amounts of money being wagered on McGovern, and almost everyone had bet on him. The bookies took a huge bath on the fight. Herford, Harris, and McGovern had placed their bets on McGovern days before, so as to allay any fears that the bout was not on the up and up. The three men cashed in big time.

For a fighter like McGovern to bet on himself was not unusual for the time. Fighters often tried to increase their ring earnings by wagering their fight purses on themselves. Of course, the main difference here is that McGovern knew the outcome of the fight before he put his money down. Looking back, it was foolish of the cabal to think they could hide such fraud from the public. It would have been next to impossible to prevent word from leaking out that Herford had wagered large amounts of money on McGovern to win by an early knockout. This wasn't the first time Herford had staged a rigged match, and it wouldn't be the last; however, this was the one that stuck to him forever.

Herford's scheme was not only far-fetched, it was downright stupid. Herford reasoned that a dramatic loss by Gans would substantially increase his future fight purses — he assumed bigoted fight fans would pay more to see Gans lose. It was rather expedient of the avaricious Herford to ignore the fact that fighters' purses go down after a loss and not up. The fix ended up being a black mark on boxing, and on Gans's legacy. He would never live it down. Given that he likely had no say in the fix, it is probably unfair to judge him so harshly. The backlash from the fight further embittered Gans, driving a permanent wedge between him and Herford.

Significance

The real significance of the Gans-McGovern farce was that it resulted in world title fights being banned in Chicago for almost three full decades, until the second Dempsey-Tunney heavyweight title fight in 1927 (which, ironically, is considered the most controversial bout in boxing history). Low-level club fights were still permitted, however. This was a huge blow to boxing in the Midwest as Chicago produced many world champions who, because of the Gans-McGovern fiasco, were forced to pursue their pugilistic ambitions everywhere but in their home city.

Gans, who had been put in a terribly untenable situation by his manager, received the most infamy from the bout — from fans, the press, and the boxing community. Frank Erne was always rather leery of fighting Gans. Then again, most top fighters were apprehensive of facing Gans. He was a high-risk, low-reward proposition for any pugilist. But there was another factor involved, one that was contemptibly common in that era. As a white champion, Erne could have avoided Gans by drawing the colour line. The entire Gans-McGovern cockup and its fallout only provided Erne with another convenient excuse to avoid facing Gans again so soon after their original encounter.

Interestingly, McGovern easily crushed Erne by TKO on July 16, 1900, at Madison Square Garden. It is now believed that if Gans had not gone along with the ruse, Herford would have blackballed him from professional boxing permanently. Gans was up the proverbial creek without a paddle.

The McGovern fight was really the only blemish in Gans's Hall of Fame career. The fighter's greatest moment was his forty-two-round victory by disqualification over Nelson in their first battle. Gans was considered even more heroic in his subsequent two defeats by Nelson, especially since he was seriously ill at the time — he fought Nelson hard in every round, until his tuberculosis-ravaged body collapsed and he could go no further.

In 1900, Gans was so supreme in the ring that the only way he could be hit flush so often was if he allowed it. What would have happened had Gans flattened McGovern? Well, it is likely that he would have been worked over by thugs employed by Herford, and even banished from the sport. Herford did blackball Gans at various times, forcing the champ to come back into the fold on his hands and knees. If Gans had gone rogue and trounced McGovern, he certainly would never have received another crack at the world lightweight title.

Even after begrudgingly selling his soul to Herford, Gans fought under his mismanagement regularly. Gans believed in his heart that once he won the title, the dynamic of his relationship with Herford would change dramatically with the balance of power swinging in his direction. With the lightweight title firmly ensconced around his slender waist, Gans felt he could demand his rightful share of his purses from Herford. If Herford denied him, he would, as champion, possess the gravitas to hire someone else as his manager. But things never worked out that way for Gans. Herford's reign of terror was absolute.

Gans certainly brought some of his financial woes upon himself. His addictions to gambling and alcohol made him constantly in need of funds.

As hard as it is to accept, had he been paid the full amount promised in each of his fights, Gans would likely have imbibed and gambled it away. His compulsions to drink and gamble were no doubt his way of escaping the pernicious racism of the world he inhabited, as well the unending fraud perpetrated on him by boxing's unshakable criminal element.

It is profoundly sad that Gans was never able to find a manager whose skills and integrity outside of the ring were equivalent to his marvelous abilities inside the squared circle. In that era, honest managers were few and hard to come by. It was also extremely unlikely that anyone with honesty and integrity would ever be drawn to boxing as a vocation.

Al Herford is long forgotten now. He was just one of the many syphilitic charlatans who masqueraded as managers and promoters only to shamelessly exploit hundreds of African American prizefighters. Herford's dirty deeds and the delight he took in them earned him an exclusive position at the top of history's dung heap. He no doubt has much company there.

In the end, Gans and McGovern are remembered and celebrated to this very day for their Hall of Fame careers. That is as it should be. Their non-fight is a distant memory from another time. Only the film of their fight remains to tell the story. There are other films of both men in action — wonderful black-and-white films that showcase these magnificent warrior kings. Both men are still fondly remembered for their charismatic personalities, superlative talent, and enormous contributions to the sport of boxing. Most assuredly, they deserve nothing less.

CHAPTER 3

JACK JOHNSON VS. TOMMY BURNS

Fight: Jack Johnson vs. Tommy Burns
Weight Class: Heavyweight
Title at Stake: World heavyweight
Date: December 26, 1908
Location: Rushcutters Bay, Sydney, Australia
Outcome: Jack Johnson by unanimous decision
Referee: Hugh D. McIntosh

Background

During the tumultuous period between the late nineteenth and early twentieth century, many brilliant boxers of African descent (such as Canadians George Godfrey and Sam Langford, along with Peter Jackson, Joe Jeannette, and Sam McVey) were routinely denied world title shots in the heavyweight division. Only in the lighter weight classes were Black fighters permitted to challenge for world titles, albeit under very adverse conditions. The heavyweight division, then and now, has always been the most prestigious and profitable in all of boxing for any fighter not named Mayweather.

More than a few heavyweight title fights over the past 141 years have been billed as "The Fight of the Century." The fight between Jack Johnson and James J. Jeffries on July 4, 1910, was the first to be billed as such, and it certainly lived up to its billing. Johnson won every round by a wide margin before knocking out the badly beaten and terrified former heavyweight champion in the fifteenth and final frame of a scheduled forty-five-round bout.

The first bout between two undefeated world heavyweight champions, Muhammad Ali and Joe Frazier, on March 8, 1971, was also billed as the "Fight of the Century," and it not only lived up to the hype surrounding it but, in many ways, surpassed it. Like all truly great prizefights, the Johnson-Jeffries battle and the first Ali-Frazier bout captured a historic moment in time.

In every respect, the Tommy Burns–Jack Johnson world heavyweight title clash really was the first "Fight of the Century." This is due to its social and racial implications — it would be the very first chance for a man of African descent to fight for the heavyweight crown. Racial tensions throughout the United States were at a breaking point leading up to the match, and many white Americans were strongly against allowing any man of African descent to fight for the most important prize in all of sports.

The world heavyweight title, by design, had previously been the domain of white men. Many around the world were outraged by Burns allowing Johnson to challenge him for a title they felt firmly belonged in the arms of the white race. Men of African descent weren't even deemed worthy of consideration for the title. This is why there was so much criticism directed at Burns for giving Johnson a crack at the crown.

The tidal wave of racism levied against Johnson was, as always, rooted in fear and ignorance. Biased white politicians, clergymen, and media all over the world urged their millions of servile followers to believe the virulent racist claptrap that white people were born superior to people of African descent. These ignorant, hate-filled white leaders had been spewing such garbage and calling it the gospel truth for centuries. Of course, what really terrified white leaders was the distinct possibility that Johnson could win, thereby exposing their prejudices and lies.

The previous heavyweight champions, all of whom were white, were also not pleased with Johnson's title shot. John L. Sullivan, James J. Corbett, Bob

Fitzsimmons, James J. Jeffries, and Marvin Hart were all extremely prejudiced toward African Americans. Hart was even rumoured to have been a member of the KKK.

The title of "world" heavyweight champion did not truly mean what it implied until Jack Johnson assumed the throne on December 26, 1908, at Rushcutters Bay in Sydney, New South Wales, Australia, by fourteenth-round stoppage. Although the film that was later released to the public was edited, there can be no doubt that Burns had been knocked out as he was on the canvas when the police entered the ring to stop the fight.

Burns entered the fight as a six-to-four favourite. Obviously, the odds were racially inspired. A closer look at their respective careers reveals that Johnson had the better resumé going into their fight. Johnson had fought and defeated Sam Langford, Joe Jeannette, and Sam McVey, three men whom Burns assiduously avoided, and with good reason — they would have killed him. Burns had beaten some good heavyweights, but no one in

Canadian world heavyweight champion Tommy Burns.

the class of a Langford, Jeannette, or McVey. Burns was paid the enormous sum of $30,000 to face Johnson, which is equivalent to $1,003,659.78 in 2025. Some fans were outraged at the amount, but Burns's logic was sound. Johnson was the biggest threat to his title; therefore, he should get the biggest purse possible. Johnson earned $5,000, which in 2025 comes to $167,276.63.

The fallout from Johnson's stunning victory was far greater than the money either man received. Johnson considered his remuneration for the fight a personal insult, which it was. He took his fiscal anger out on the smaller Burns, punishing him unmercifully for fifteen one-sided rounds. Johnson could not have brutalized Burns any better had he been allowed the use of a baseball bat.

At the turn of the twentieth century, several world boxing champions were Canadian, which is astonishing for a country with such a small population. George "Little Chocolate" Dixon, Johnny Coulon, "Mysterious" Billy Smith, and, of course, Tommy Burns were just some of the great champions that emerged from Canada. Fellow Canadian Sam Langford is widely believed to be the greatest fighter never to have won a world title.

Tommy Burns garnered more press than any of these turn-of-the-century Canadian pugilistic greats except for Dixon and Langford. Why? Well, he held the most prestigious title in sports. Burns was an outgoing man who lived his life to the fullest and, like Johnson, always danced to a tune of his own making.

Tommy Burns

Tommy Burns fervently believed that he was born with a love for fighting the same way Mozart was born with a genius for music. Burns loved fisticuffs. He could never get enough fighting, in or out of the ring. He grew up in what was then considered frontier Canada, in southern Ontario, and was forced to endure a very rough and violent upbringing. Fighting was a way of life in small town Canada in the late nineteenth century.

Burns was born Noah Brusso on June 17, 1881, a mere fourteen years after Canada became a sovereign nation, in 1867. His parents were Frederick

Brusso, an Italian Canadian cabinetmaker, and Sophia Dankert, a German Canadian housewife.[1]

Noah Brusso was the first Canadian-born prizefighter to win the world heavyweight title. He was not, however, the first Canadian-born fighter to win a world boxing title. That honour belongs to the immortal African Canadian George Dixon, who won the bantamweight and featherweight world crowns and invented shadowboxing and the heavy bag. In his late teens, Brusso changed his name to Tommy Burns, to hide his chosen profession from his mother. Tommy Burns was from Hanover, Ontario, which is how he earned the sobriquet "The Little Giant of Hanover."

Burns stood slightly over five foot seven and is still the shortest man ever to hold the heavyweight crown. He was really a puffed-up middleweight (with heavyweight power). Today he would be considered a super middleweight. In fact, Burns turned down a shot at middleweight king Tommy Ryan in order to go after the more glamourous heavyweight belt (and more money) by taking on Hart.

Burns was well put together. He had huge shoulders and thick calves. He took great pride in always being in tremendous physical shape. He may have been built like a middleweight, but he had enough power in his fists to stretch any heavyweight for a ten count. Burns carried dynamite in both hands and knew how to get full leverage on all of his power shots.

But the sport in which he really excelled was lacrosse, which is the national sport of Canada. Back then, lacrosse was a very violent sport. When trouble broke out on a lacrosse pitch, it was usually Burns who stepped in — he'd settle scores with opposing players and rambunctious, drunken fans alike. Burns never took fighting personally, except for his fight with Johnson. He was pugnacious by nature, never letting any slight or slur on his character pass unanswered. Although Burns loved fighting, he had never even considered a career in professional boxing.

While playing lacrosse in Detroit, a sportswriter named Joe Jackson told Burns he should pursue boxing as a vocation. Burns was getting into fights everywhere he went — bars, restaurants, hotels. He was a magnet for rowdy ruffians desperate to engage him in street brawls. And Burns was always happy to oblige. Jackson suggested to him that rather than fight for free, why not do it professionally and get paid.[2]

Burns followed Jackson's advice and began to pursue in earnest a career in pugilism. Jackson referred Burns to former boxer and promoter Sam Biddle, a crusty old cur of a man. Biddle might have been a curmudgeon, but he knew his boxing, and he knew how to bring a fighter along. Under his tutelage, Burns quickly learned the craft of boxing and started to ascend the ranks of the heavyweight division.

Burns acquired the undisputed world heavyweight title from Kentuckian Marvin Hart on February 23, 1906, in Los Angeles, California, via a twenty-round unanimous decision. Ironically, Hart had been gifted a decision over Johnson the previous year, in San Francisco, in a fight clearly dominated by Johnson. Upon winning the title from Hart, Burns upset many people in the boxing community by emphatically stating that he would be a champion for all people, regardless of race, creed, or colour. In 1906, this was a revolutionary proclamation — it was practically a declaration of war on the racial status quo of that era. Needless to say, Burns's comment did not sit well with the boxing community or the boxing press.

In theory, this meant that Jack Johnson, the number one challenger for Burns's crown, and the best heavyweight on the planet for almost four years, would finally get his long-overdue shot at the celebrated world heavyweight belt. But this chance would not happen immediately. First, Burns wanted to make as much money as possible from the heavyweight crown by defending it against lesser opponents, before facing what would be his toughest test in Johnson.

Jack Johnson

Jack Johnson was born John Arthur Johnson on March 31, 1878, in Galveston, Texas, thirteen years after the end of the American Civil War. His parents, Henry and Tina (known as Tiny) Johnson, were formerly enslaved. Johnson was the third of nine children, and the first son. As a teenager, he enjoyed watching both amateur and professional boxing matches and sparring contests. He quickly fell in love with the sport and gradually developed

The magnificent Jack Johnson.

an unrelenting determination to learn and master the art of prizefighting.

Johnson was a very intelligent man. He was self-educated and his ring smarts were off the charts. He was able to glean important tidbits of information from veteran fighters he met along the way and instantly incorporate these nuggets of wisdom into his own arsenal, on his journey up the heavyweight ladder. With Johnson, once learned, a lesson stayed with him forever. Johnson made his professional prizefighting debut at the age of twenty in his hometown of Galveston, Texas, at Professor Bernau's Gymnasium on November 1, 1897, against Charley Brooks. He knocked Brooks out cold in the second round of a scheduled fifteen-round bout and was awarded the Texas State Middleweight Title.[3]

In Johnson's era, a boxing debut did not necessarily mean a fighter was engaging in his first professional fight. It usually indicated this was the fight in which a boxer would be showcased to the media for the first time.

Johnson likely had other professional fights prior to facing Brooks, because it was unheard of back then for a fighter to debut professionally in a fifteen-round bout. Most nascent pros first fought four-, six-, and eight-round fights before working their way up to the fifteen-round distance.

A fourth-round knockout loss to "Jewish" Joe Choynski on February 25, 1901, at Harmony Hall in Galveston, Texas, turned out to be the major turning point in Johnson's magnificent career. The fight was scheduled for twenty rounds. The veteran Choynski knocked Johnson unconscious in the third round. Choynski had set a trap for Johnson, into which the naive young man readily stepped. At the beginning of round three, Choynski held his hands very high, deliberately exposing his midsection. It was an old sucker move. Johnson leaned forward to jab Choynski's stomach, thereby exposing his head. Choynski immediately tagged Johnson with a brutal left hook behind his right ear, sending the future champion into dreamland.

After the fight, both men were arrested by the local constabulary for staging an illegal prizefight. Someone had neglected to pay off the police. Johnson and Choynski were only in jail for a month, but each day they put on boxing exhibitions for the jailers, the sheriff, and their fellow prisoners.[4] During these exhibitions, Choynski taught Johnson the science part of the Sweet Science. Johnson eagerly absorbed Choynski's pointers on tactics, strategy, and technique, and successfully applied them in his subsequent fights. Choynski told Johnson that with his considerable height and reach advantages, he should never get tagged with a flush shot. And except for the Jess Willard fight, he never did.

It was Choynski who turned Johnson into a deadly counterpuncher, educating him on how to use the entire ring to his advantage. It was Choynski who instructed Johnson on how to successfully use his opponents' momentum against them. After his loss to Choynski, Johnson became a much more complete and dangerous fighter. His rise to the top of the heavyweight division was meteoric, although he would have to wait a while for a title shot because of the racism endemic to the era in which he fought.

Johnson used his poleaxing jab to keep his opponents in perfect position to be hit with straight right hands and fight-ending uppercuts. He put Choynski's sage advice to good use with devastating effect. Fighters who recklessly ran at Johnson winging wide punches often woke up several hours later, groggy and confused with many teeth missing, asking what had happened.

Johnson is considered to be the greatest defensive heavyweight champion of all time. It was an odd decision for an African American pugilist to become a defence-first fighter back then. During Johnson's era, many African American fighters lost very questionable decisions to white fighters. This is why so many African American fighters became knockout artists — they desired to take the decision out of the referees' hands. Yet, in seventy-four fights, Johnson recorded only eleven knockouts. Incredibly, the racism of his times did not induce Johnson to alter his fighting style. He was confident enough in his own abilities that he could beat any man without having to go for a knockout.

Although Johnson well understood the racial implications of his fight with Burns, he never viewed the contest in such myopic terms. Johnson felt that viewing any occupation strictly on racial terms was self-limiting and demeaning. He was determined to be judged only by his ring success and the content of his character. While in Australia, Johnson paid a quiet visit to the grave of his hero, the great African Australian heavyweight (by way of the Virgin Islands) Peter Jackson. Johnson knew how Sullivan had drawn the colour line against Jackson, denying him a much-deserved shot at the heavyweight title. Sullivan did this out of fear, for Jackson was a bigger and infinitely more skilled heavyweight than Sullivan. The Boston Strong Boy knew he could not beat Jackson, even on his best day.

Jackson died at forty from tuberculosis, aggravated by alcoholism. Johnson no doubt had Jackson on his mind when he stepped into the ring to face Burns. Jackson's demise had hardened Johnson's resolve — this was his chance at stardom, and he intended to take full advantage of it. Johnson was a bigger picture man with a well-defined view of the world and his place in it. He was in prizefighting to make money. Period. He did not believe it was his job to stand up for the rights of all African Americans. Just navigating the treacherous shark-infested waters of professional boxing was more than tough enough for one lifetime, thank you very much.

Johnson never looked at life in purely racial terms. He was certainly aware that other people did, but that was their problem. Johnson was primarily concerned about receiving full financial remuneration for his ring efforts. He was combative when it came to money, and for good reason: boxing managers and promoters were crooks and not to be trusted. Johnson managed his own finances during his career and used various white managers only to negotiate contracts. He knew he would make big time money from future title defenses. Still, Johnson unhappily agreed to fight Burns for one-sixth of the champion's purse. His bitterness over his purse for fighting Burns never left him.

It was long rumoured that Johnson refused to make the walk to the ring unless the Australian promoter, Hugh D. McIntosh, gave him more money. Demanding more money immediately before a fight began was a tactic he employed often, but no promoter ever gave into these bullying tactics. Rumour has it that McIntosh put a loaded pistol to Johnson's head to induce him to begin his ring walk. If the story is true, it certainly worked.

By 1908, Johnson had chased Tommy Burns all over the world for almost two years, hounding him at every stop to give him a shot at the world heavyweight title. Burns ignored Johnson's challenges as long as he could, but the pressure he felt from fans and the media to give Johnson a shot at the crown was unrelenting. The long-held boxing fiscal strategy is to make the most money for the least amount of risk. That option no longer existed for the champion. There really was no other credible opponent for Burns to fight.

Johnson stabbed his manager Sam Fitzpatrick in the back after the Burns fight by firing him and never repaying the money Fitzpatrick had loaned him. Johnson was angry that Fitzpatrick had not earned him a better purse. But Fitzpatrick was in a delicate situation while negotiating on Johnson's behalf. The offer made to Johnson via Fitzpatrick, by promoter McIntosh, was a take-it-or-leave-it offer. If Johnson had turned down the offer, the promoter would have asked Sam Langford to face Burns. That would have been a historic event in and of itself, as it would have been the only time that two Canadian-born heavyweights had ever faced off for the undisputed world heavyweight title.

Although Johnson did not view the fight as a black-versus-white scenario, not everyone shared his sanguine view. In the minds of many white people, there was much more at stake than mere money or fame. Whites felt that it was Burns's solemn duty to uphold the supposed "glory" of the white race. Ironically, those same fans felt Burns should protect the "superiority" of the white race by refusing to fight Johnson. Burns ignored the naysayers — what good was holding the undisputed world heavyweight crown if you could not profit from it immeasurably?

Johnson was the only opponent who could bring Burns his biggest payday in the sport. In that sense, fighting Johnson was an easy financial decision. Burns was not in boxing to lose money; however, Burns mistakenly thought no promoter would meet his exorbitant price of thirty thousand dollars, thus allowing him to avoid facing Johnson altogether. This scheme backfired when McIntosh gladly agreed to foot the bill. Burns then had no choice but to defend his beloved title against the superior Johnson or look like a yellow cur for deciding otherwise.

Burns's well-known racist comments before, during, and after the fight were surprising but not out of character for the time. Prior to his contentious bout with Johnson, Burns had never displayed any outward signs of racism or hostility toward African Americans or African Canadians. Like many top white fighters, Burns had had Black sparring partners. Indeed he had fought six Black fighters before winning the world heavyweight title, all without any attendant hullabaloo. In fact, Burns was briefly married to a Black woman named Irene Peppers. Irene was the sister of one of Burns's opponents (and occasional sparring partners), Harry Peppers. Burns and Harry got along exceedingly well, and the two men became close friends. Irene was an absolutely stunning woman who turned heads everywhere she ventured.

Many educated and uneducated whites feared that a Johnson victory over Burns would disprove their ignorant and often violent racist beliefs of white supremacy. Johnson had no doubt heard this garbage many times before and was inured to it by this point in his career — he was too close to attainting his life's goal to allow anything to get in his way. He stayed above the racial fray. The uppermost thing on Johnson's mind was simply destroying Burns.

Unlike most prizefighters, Johnson well understood the business of boxing. The majority of fighters back then were uneducated and illiterate and placed far too much trust in their managers and promoters. Fighting in the squared circle and the business of boxing are two entirely separate but related entities. The amount of money an elite fighter receives has always come down to how many asses he puts in the seats. Johnson filled stadiums, mainly with spectators coming to see him get beat, much like Muhammad Ali would during his prime, almost sixty years later.

Although promoters made significantly more money than fighters during Johnson's day, they always complained about the fees Johnson demanded for his services. Johnson's monetary requests were not excessive if they were correlated to what his fights brought in at the box office. Rather, it was the manner in which he went about his fiscal requests that angered promoters. Johnson's pleas for more money were always made after he had signed his contract and usually on the day of the fight. He did the same thing during his vaudeville tours — he held promoters hostage in order to get additional funds. This tactic almost never worked. It also did not win him many friends or allies. Johnson felt that by holding promoters hostage to his whims, he would benefit financially. His reasoning made sense; it was his execution that lacked finesse. The fans indeed came to see Johnson and not the promoter; however, putting a gun figuratively to a promoter's head is never a sound business strategy. It only served to alienate prospective promoters from hiring him. In the end, Johnson became unbookable, and with only himself to blame.

There was another factor at play here regarding Johnson asking for more cash from McIntosh. Johnson was slightly past his prime when he beat Burns. Thus, he wanted to make as much dough as possible until his career clock ran out. He was smart to do so. Johnson knew that once he lost the title, his earning and bargaining power would rapidly diminish. Johnson, like every other heavyweight champion in history, including Tyson Fury, was intent on squeezing every last nickel possible from the heavyweight title. It was his turn to be the best fighter in the world, and he was going to enjoy the ride.

As well as being a brilliant fighter, Johnson, like Ali, knew how to unnerve his opponents in the ring. They were both masters at psychological warfare. Johnson endeavoured to get under the skin of his various opponents.

He knew an angry man is rarely successful in the ring. Fortunately for Johnson, getting under Burns's skin was as easy as saying hello, because Burns had a hair-trigger temper and was apt to explode at even the slightest provocation. Burns was a pugnacious character. It was part of his DNA.

Contrary to how some historians have portrayed him, Burns was not an unskilled boxing luddite. He knew the ins and outs of the sport and was a skilled ring technician. He even published a book, titled *Scientific Boxing and Self Defence.*[5] Burns smartly fought out of an exaggerated crouch, to make himself less of a target to his opponents. He fought with his left arm straight out (much in the manner of James Jeffries), using it as a rangefinder against his opponents. Burns found great success with this style; however, against Johnson, this strategy did not work. Burns tried all sorts of boxing tricks and moves, but in the end, Johnson was too big, too fast, too mobile, too strong, and most importantly, too smart for Burns. Burns had an uphill battle against Johnson from the moment the contract was signed.

Burns liked to be the aggressor. Johnson was the greatest counterpuncher that ever lived, and Burns's aggression would play right into his hands. Johnson would not have to go looking for Burns, which would make the fight even easier for him. But to the crowd's utter astonishment, when the bell clanged to begin round one, Johnson flipped the table on Burns by attacking him directly out of the gate. Burns had not prepared for such a possibility and was at a loss as to how to defend himself while moving backwards. He had never experienced a situation like this in his title reign and just stood there, stupefied like a little kid on his first day at school. Burns was used to being the aggressor, not the defender. He was physically incapable of moving Johnson backwards. Johnson was effortlessly physically dominating Burns less than thirty seconds into the fight! Being the smaller man, moving forward and getting inside Johnson's reach was strategically the smart move, but Burns never got the chance. Johnson overwhelmed Burns from the outset and never let up until the fight ended in the fourteenth round.

Johnson's hand speed was breathtaking. No one in attendance had ever seen a big man with such lightning-quick fists. Johnson systematically annihilated Burns in every way. He dropped a crouching Burns with a huge uppercut a mere five seconds into the bout, a knockdown from which Burns never recovered. Johnson broke Burns's jaw with either that first uppercut or another punch later in the round. Burns was broken and bleeding from that point on.

Burns had no answers for Johnson's prodigious arsenal of ring weaponry. He followed Johnson all over the ring while, continuously and unwisely, squaring up against the bigger man. He was severely concussed and confused. Johnson jabbed him to pieces while consistently nailing him with straight right hands and bone-rattling uppercuts, verbally taunting him the entire time. By the close of the opening round, the champion had been reduced to a blood-soaked punching bag. Burns possessed neither the skill nor the strength to change the one-sided trajectory of the fight.

The fight became particularly odious during the middle rounds when Burns, who obviously knew better, disgraced himself mightily by directing a chorus of shameful racist jibes toward Johnson. Stunningly, it never occurred to Burns that provoking Johnson would only worsen the beating.

This was the only time in his career that Burns was known to have lost his cool in the ring. That Burns lowered himself to such a base level is inexcusable. There has been an unsettling tendency recently to excuse the racism that existed in boxing during that era, simply because it took place a long time ago and was common to that period. Such an opinion does not hold water. It has never held water. Just because such racism happened over one hundred years ago does not in any way mitigate its egregiousness or the hurt it caused its countless victims. The bitter aftertaste of bigotry is never dissipated through the passage of time.

It's worth noting that the big breakthrough for boxers of African descent came when African Canadian George Dixon became the first Black man (and Canadian) to win a world title when he won the world bantamweight crown by knocking out Nunc Wallace in nineteen rounds on June 27, 1890, in Britain.[6] Barbados Joe Walcott became the second Black man to hold a world title by capturing the world welterweight crown via TKO over James "Rube" Ferns in Buffalo on December 18, 1901.[7] The third Black man to win a world title was the "Old Master," American Joe Gans. He won the world lightweight title by stopping Frank Erne in one round at Fort Erie, Ontario, on May 12, 1902.[8] These three giants of boxing had shown Black athletes the world over that anything was possible.

Jack Johnson was the fourth Black man to win a world boxing title when he soundly trounced Canadian Tommy Burns on Boxing Day, December 26, 1908, in Australia. Truth be told, except for a very dubious loss to Marvin Hart and a disqualification loss to fellow great Joe Jeannette, Johnson had been the best heavyweight in the world for quite some time. Johnson's capturing of the heavyweight title had a much bigger worldwide impact than the title victories of Dixon, Walcott, and Gans because the heavyweight crown was the most important title in all of sports. Also, for their own safety, Dixon, Walcott, and Gans were quiet, introverted men. Johnson was loud and bellicose. Compared to him, Ali was shy.

Interestingly, after he won the heavyweight crown, in one of prizefighting's most extraordinary ironies, Johnson drew the colour line. He refused to face Langford, Jeannette, or McVey ever again. More than any other man on Earth, Johnson knew how truly dangerous these men were inside the ring. Only once, on December 19, 1913, did Johnson defend his crown against an African American fighter, easily beating journeyman heavyweight and third-rate fighter Battling Jim Johnson by decision in Paris.

According to Langford's manager, Joe Woodman, Johnson had signed a contract to make his first title defence against Langford at the National Sporting Club (NSC) of London if he beat Burns. Johnson reneged on the deal because he wasn't eager to face such a high-risk opponent so soon after winning the title. He also believed that he deserved much more than the five thousand dollars offered to meet the dangerous Langford — Langford was the best heavyweight in the world at that time, next to Johnson.

Also, Johnson thought, and rightfully so, that it was insulting for the NSC to negotiate his purse on his behalf without consulting him. Johnson was right about deserving more money to face Langford. More important, however, is the fact that Johnson had signed a legal contract in good faith, which he blithely discarded. This was part of an unsettling pattern for which Johnson became known. Johnson clearly never considered the long-term negative effects such actions would eventually have on his boxing career. You can only alienate so many promoters before you run out of people willing to book you.

There was some logic behind Johnson's refusal to face Langford. Johnson knew that the public would pay substantially more money to see him face a white fighter rather than a fighter of African descent. In that sense, Johnson used the white public's racism against them by playing on their hopes of seeing a white fighter like James J. Jeffries or Stanley Ketchel defeat him. Johnson was making the white man pay handsomely for the privilege of being a bigot. Burns and Johnson were similar in one respect — they both saw the championship as a gateway to untold riches. Like it or not, the heavyweight title has always been a means for personal financial gain.

The former white heavyweight champions of the world, prior to Burns, were hypocrites as well as racists. If Johnson had been an inferior fighter, it is unlikely they would have been so vehemently opposed to his challenge. Another point to consider is, these former champions were, with the exception of Corbett, broke. It was Burns's large purse that annoyed them as much if not more so than Johnson's skin colour.

As brave and cocksure as Burns portrayed himself to the press and public, he had to know in his heart of hearts that he stood almost no chance of retaining his title against a ring master like Johnson. When you factor in the considerable size, speed, reach, and power advantages possessed by Johnson, Burns must have felt like he was walking into a meat grinder. Boxing had never seen a fighter like Johnson because there had never been a fighter like him before in the heavyweight division. Johnson was uniquely a creation of his own making.

The overconfidence of Burns and the white race ended only five seconds into the first round, when Johnson dropped Burns and then picked him up like a rag doll. The look of stunned incredulity on Burns's face seemed to indicate that he really believed all of the bigoted scuttlebutt regarding Johnson and other Black fighters. The racists who ran boxing back then believed all Black fighters had a yellow streak of cowardice. This belief was predicated more on hope than on actual evidence. Burns and everyone in attendance was painfully disabused of this ridiculous notion less than ten seconds into the fight.

Johnson could have stopped Burns at any time during the scheduled twenty-round fight, had he so wished. Johnson allowed the fight to last fourteen rounds, just to punish Burns for making him wait so long for his title shot. Johnson knew the fight was being filmed for later theatrical release, and he well understood that it would be considered the most remarkable event in sports history at the time. There were twenty thousand fans in the arena screaming for his death, while an additional thirty thousand fans awaited his demise outside the arena. On that afternoon, Sydney, Australia, was a simmering cauldron of racial hatred. For Johnson, it must have felt like he was attending the world's largest KKK rally — all that was missing was the burning cross. The vociferous audience, including American sailors docked in Australia, never once stopped hurling racial invectives at Johnson. This kind of aggressive bigoted reception was certainly nothing new to Johnson, although this was on a level never before witnessed. Johnson remained calm, proudly flashing his golden smile as he thoroughly dismantled the heavily outgunned Burns.

Controversy

The salient questions stemming from the Burns-Johnson bout are as follows: Did Johnson, by prior arrangement, agree to carry the champion Burns for at least fourteen rounds? Also, why didn't Burns just draw the colour line, like his predecessors, to avoid fighting Johnson? Additionally, why were so many (white) people around the world enraged by Burns's decision to give Johnson a shot at the title?

Was Tommy Burns literally terrified of facing Jack Johnson? Is it true that Burns did not win one round in his fight with Johnson? Finally, and perhaps most importantly, were the local police asked beforehand by McIntosh to stop the fight if Johnson was on the verge of scoring a knockout?

The Decision

It is evident in the film of the fight that Johnson could have knocked Burns out at any point, had he so desired. There were a host of moments where Johnson hit Burns hard enough to drop him but deliberately held him up just to punish him further. However, this does not mean that he carried Burns at the request of the promoter. Johnson was an exceptionally smart businessman, and he knew that the longer the fight went, the more money the film of it would earn at the box office. Johnson might have also thought that the white public specifically would not pay to see a Black man demolish a white man in one round. Such mismatches made for poor box office returns.

Johnson also had personal reasons for allowing Burns to go fourteen rounds. Johnson wanted to punish him for the vicious racial slurs Burns had hurled at him during the fight. In a much larger sense, Johnson wanted to make Burns pay for the racist comments and slights he had endured throughout his life. This would be no rushed affair. Johnson was going to take his time carving up Burns in front of the whole world.

Johnson's personal enmity toward Burns cannot be dismissed. For years after their battle, whenever the conversation turned to Burns, Johnson's tone immediately changed from relaxed to serious. This is why it must have come as a giant shock to Johnson, almost four decades after their history-changing battle, when Burns, by then an ordained minister, unreservedly and sincerely apologized to Johnson for the racist language he had employed during their fight. To his eternal credit, Johnson forgave Burns. Johnson displayed more grace and aplomb in accepting the apology than Burns had during their fight.

So, why did Burns not draw the colour line against Johnson, like his predecessors had? Burns did not draw the colour line for two specific reasons. Firstly, that is not who he was as a person. Secondly, and perhaps more importantly, a fight with Johnson offered him a substantially bigger financial reward than a bout with any other contemporary challenger. In other words, the amount of money Burns was being offered was higher than his allegiance to any racist protocol.

One thing that is instantly noticeable in the film of the fight is Johnson's complete lack of a sustained body attack. Johnson threw practically no body punches over the course of the fight. This was a deliberate move on the challenger's part. Johnson knew that both the promoter and the fans in attendance were rooting for Burns. He feared that if he threw any body punches, regardless of where they landed, he could be unfairly disqualified for low blows. He simply didn't want to risk the chance of a fraudulent ruling going against him.[9]

As if the disparity in skill and experience was not enough of a handicap, Burns also gave away five and a half inches and twenty-six pounds to Johnson.[10] The fight was a mismatch, and everyone knew it. Burns constantly screamed at Johnson to "Come on and fight like a white man!" Given the unmerciful pounding he was receiving, it seemed like more of a desperate plea than an actual insult.

This was the first big money fight in modern boxing. Burns was paid more money for a single fight than any previous fighter in history. For promoter McIntosh, the amount of money demanded by Burns was astronomical but well worth paying compared to what he stood to gross from the fight, the film of the fight, and the concession stands. Needless to say, McIntosh did very well financially from the Burns-Johnson scrap, which earned him tremendous dividends.

It is true that Johnson was upset with the sum he received. He believed he deserved more as the much better fighter; that the best fighter always deserved more money. Perhaps, but Burns had one large advantage over Johnson — he had the heavyweight belt around his waist. Such a thing gave him leverage at the bargaining table. McIntosh convinced Johnson that he would pay him more than thirty thousand dollars in his subsequent title defence, if he won the match. Johnson was unhappy with McIntosh's empty promises, but there was nothing he could do until the belt was firmly in his possession.

The persistent claim that Burns was terrified to face Johnson held some truth. Two years later, Jeffries would have to be coaxed into the ring with Johnson, under threat of not being paid, by promoter Tex Rickard. Johnson inspired fear in most of his opponents, and he smartly played on that fear to help him win many of his fights. Any heavyweight from that era (with the exceptions of Langford, Jeannette, and McVey) would have necessarily been stupid or ignorant not to fear Johnson.

Did Jack Johnson win every round by a very wide margin? Yes. Did Tommy Burns get his licks in? Yes, but it would be a lie to say he ever had Johnson in any kind of trouble. Burns landed some good hard punches on Johnson's body, but his success in that area was extremely limited. There was an unsubstantiated rumour that Burns somehow managed to break one of Johnson's ribs, though there is no evidence to support such a claim. Years later, Johnson said that if he had wanted to, he could have killed Burns with his fists, and that given Burns's noxious, racist comments, he would have been more than justified in doing so.[11] It would be hard to disagree with Johnson's assessment. Burns was indeed lucky that day to have only lost his title and not his life.

At the start of the fourteenth round, Jack Johnson came on like gang-busters, hitting Burns with every punch in his vast arsenal, putting his full weight and years of frustration into every blow. Burns hit the canvas with a resounding thud, which echoed throughout the stadium, if not the entire world. Referee McIntosh started his count. A ludicrous rumour was created that day — that the day before the fight, promoter McIntosh had asked police to enter the ring to stop the fight if it looked like Burns was about to be knocked out. This story circulated after the fight and is surely apocryphal. It is true that midway through the fourteenth round, with Burns lying concussed and bleeding on the canvas, the local constabulary entered the ring and stopped the fight before McIntosh could toll the final count of ten. This is why the fight was recorded as a decision win for Johnson, rather than as a knockout victory. The police, who were as racist as the fans, did not want to allow Johnson the satisfaction of scoring a knockout.

In retrospect, it wasn't necessary for McIntosh to ask the police to stop the slaughter. They did so of their own accord, in order to avert a full-scale riot. The Academy Award–winning documentary *Legendary Champions* claims that police shut off the cameras during the fourteenth round, to prevent the knockout of Burns from being caught on film. This is untrue. The cameramen were in a box atop a twenty-five-foot pole, way above the ring. There was no way the police could reach them. Burns was about to be counted out when the police entered the ring and stopped the count at nine, thus ending the fight. This was all caught on film, but the film was later edited to exclude that part.

Did Burns actually make Johnson wait a full two years before giving him a title shot? The answer is yes and no. Burns was desperately hoping someone would come along in the interim to defeat Johnson decisively, relieving him of that obligation. Secondly, Burns never truly believed a promoter would come forward to meet his outrageous asking price of thirty thousand dollars, thereby preventing him from ever having to fight Johnson. Thirdly, Burns wanted to make as much money as possible for as long as possible before facing Johnson.

Unfortunately for the champ, by the time Burns faced Johnson in 1908, there were no more talented white heavyweights for Burns to face. This was a problem inherited by Johnson when he defeated Burns for the title. Johnson had to fight an old and over-the-hill Jeffries and the much smaller middle-weight titlist Ketchel due to a dearth of competent white heavyweights.

Without a doubt, the most bizarre controversy surrounding the Burns-Johnson title clash is the claim made by Johnson's cornerman, Rudy Unholz (supposedly admitted to promoter and writer Otto Floto years later), that he and another Johnson cornerman hid under the ring during the thirteenth round, screaming loudly for the police to enter the ring and stop the fight, to save Burns from further punishment.[12]

This sounds like another one of Johnson's tall tales. The stadium was such a cauldron of cacophonous sound that it would have been impossible for the police or referee to hear anyone, most especially two men hiding *under* the ring. The story is surely fictional, especially because it came from Unholz, who loathed Burns. Unholz foamed at the mouth like a rabid dog at the mere mention of the name Tommy Burns. Also, someone in the crowd of over twenty thousand spectators surely would have seen two large men sneaking under the ring as the fight approached its climax.

Unholz's claim is laughable, because at the end of the thirteenth round, Burns's face was a mask of crimson gore. Both of his eyes were swollen shut and he had sustained a broken nose and jaw, and fractured ribs. In addition, he was swallowing a lot of his own blood. Burns's terrible state was the only encouragement the cops needed to stop the fight. They certainly did not require any urging from Johnson's cornermen.

At the conclusion of the match, the heavily concussed Burns protested that he was not hurt and, as champion, should be allowed the privilege of continuing to fight. The mere fact that Burns wanted to keep fighting perfectly demonstrates the sorry state he was in. Burns ridiculously claimed that Johnson was beginning to tire. The end was unequivocal. Burns was out cold on the canvas and being dragged back to his corner by his handlers.[13]

It was the promoter McIntosh who ordered the clip of Burns hitting the canvas edited out. If the film had not been edited in such a way, it would never have been allowed into the United States, Britain, Canada, or anywhere else. As it turns out, the United States Congress banned the film from public viewing. Sadly, it would be another sixty years before fight fans could finally view the fight.

Significance

On December 26, 1908, Jack Johnson became the first Black man in boxing history to win the undisputed, universally recognized world heavyweight title. This was a hugely significant victory for all African Americans. It also turned the social and cultural status quo upside down in the United States.

One writer stated that the white man's burden had now become his master. This was too much for white Americans and the United States government to accept. All of the inferiority theories regarding African Americans, which had been peddled by bigots throughout the United States and the world since the 1600s, had been irrevocably refuted on one bloody, painful afternoon in Australia.

Looking back, Johnson's one-sided demolition of Burns should not have come as a shock to knowledgeable fight fans. Burns was really nothing more than a puffed-up middleweight at best. He benefitted by coming along at a time when there was a scarcity of white talent in the heavyweight division. It is entirely fair to say that any one of Langford, Jeannette, or McVey would have handled Burns as easily as Johnson had.

Johnson was justifiably proud of his accomplishment. He had achieved his life's goal. In so doing, he had become a hero to Black people all over the world. Johnson's victory significantly raised the level of violent racist attacks directed at African Americans in the United States. Many misguided and uneducated whites feared that Johnson's beatdown of Burns would be viewed as a clarion call for all African Americans to cast off their white oppressors. African Americans were murdered throughout the U.S. on a daily basis for daring to celebrate or even read a newspaper detailing Johnson's beatdown of the hapless Burns in public.

In reality, what white America feared most was that Johnson was literate and well spoken. This put fear into the hearts of many white Americans, who for centuries had denied formal education to African Americans. In under forty-two minutes, Johnson put all of these malignant racist stereotypes to bed forever. He showed all Americans that here was a man (of colour) who could *not* be held back or dictated to. He would live his life professionally and publicly, according to his own desires. Ultimately, Johnson's victory showed the world that Black people were not only equal but also, in many cases, superior to whites in every capacity and field of endeavour. And for that, the world owes Johnson an eternal debt of gratitude.

CHAPTER 4

JESS WILLARD VS. JACK JOHNSON

Fight: Jess Willard vs. Jack Johnson
Weight Class: Heavyweight
Title at Stake: World heavyweight
Date: April 5, 1915
Location: Oriental Park, Havana, Cuba
Outcome: Willard knocks out Johnson in 26th round to win heavyweight title
Referee: Jack Welch

Background

It might be surprising to fight fans today, but any fighter six feet or taller back in the early part of the twentieth century was considered a giant. Thus, the six-foot-four Carl Morris was known as "The Sapulpa Giant," and the six-foot-six Fred Fulton was known as "The Rochester Plasterer."

The Johnson-Willard battle featured the six-foot-one Jack "Galveston Giant" Johnson versus the six-foot-seven Jess "Pottawatomie Giant" Willard, both of whom became towering figures in American history, but for vastly different reasons. By the time Johnson faced Willard, he was well past his prime at thirty-seven years of age. He had held the crown for seven years and was tired of the travails of being king — the heavyweight title had become an albatross around his neck. All Johnson really had left to fight for was pride. Willard never expressed any personal dislike for Johnson or for African Americans in general; however, he knew he was in Havana to restore the heavyweight crown to the white race. After he did so, he redrew the colour line. Although the impact from the Johnson-Willard bout was global, the outcome of their match resonated most vociferously in the United States. Their fight was as much about contemporary social and cultural mores as it was about boxing. The match took place during the First World War and must be viewed in the racial and social context of that time period. Willard's victory, along with Johnson's defeat, has had a lasting effect on American race relations from the moment the fight ended.

Jess Willard

Willard, the youngest of four brothers, was born on December 29, 1881, in Saint Clere, Kansas, two months after the death of his father, Myron, a former grocer, school principal, and postal employee. At his birth, his mother, Margaret Willard, found herself a widow with four mouths to feed. Several years later, Willard's family moved to the small town of Pottawatomie, Kansas.[1] Willard's family was dirt poor and often went to bed hungry and struggled to make ends meet.[2] Willard's formal schooling ended when he was twelve, after he threw a nasty, abusive teacher out of the first-floor classroom window. He was already well over six feet by that age. Willard and his brothers went to work to help support their family. This was not uncommon in the American Midwest back then.[3] Children felt it was their duty to help support their parents and siblings. Education was considered a luxury.

Like many itinerant farm workers in the 1890s and beyond, Willard wandered around the Midwest looking for steady work of any kind. He travelled to the state of Oklahoma in 1911, hoping to become a policeman. When that didn't work out, he inadvertently wandered into a gym and began his prizefighting career.[4] Willard was thirty years old, which even then was considered rather late to launch a prizefighting career. He viewed his tentative entry into boxing as more of a lark than a carefully planned career path. But his decision turned out to be a fortuitous move, as this was the era of the search for a "Great White Hope."

Promoters and trainers all over America and the world were frantically searching for a white heavyweight good enough to wrest the crown from the brow of the immortal Jack Johnson. Willard was actually just one of many unexceptional, oversized white boxers with minimal skill and big dreams. Willard's boxing debut came at the Sapulpa Air Dome in Sapulpa, Oklahoma, on February 15, 1911. It was anything but a success. Willard was disqualified at the 0:45 mark of round ten by referee Al Venn for throwing the equally inept Lewis Fink to the canvas.[5]

The fight with Fink was peculiar. It was scheduled for fifteen rounds. Willard was not even a novice fighter at this point. He had no amateur experience. The fight with Fink was more of a controlled sparring exhibition — Willard was not in any condition to go fifteen rounds and it showed. He did not know how to clinch or jab; he was unaware that a round lasted three minutes. Willard was so green that whenever a crowd member called his name, he actually turned to look. His height was his best defence in all of his fights. Even against Fink, when he turned to look at a spectator who had called his name, Fink was still unable to reach him.

The Galveston Giant

The incomparable Jack Johnson is still considered to be one of the top boxing geniuses of all time. Johnson's boxing debut differed drastically from that of Willard's. It was short but successful. He received $1.50 for his first-ever ring encounter, in Galveston, Texas, scoring a second-round knockout over Charles Brooks on November 1, 1897.[6] Willard was sixteen at the time.

Unlike Johnson, who'd been mentored by "Jewish" Joe Choynski, there was no such watershed moment in young Willard's boxing career. Willard received few tips or advice from veteran fighters. This was partly due to Willard's innate shyness. Willard was a loner by nature and did not make friends easily. It was his soft-spoken trainer, Walter Moynahan, who patiently taught Willard the rudiments of prizefighting, hour after hour, day by day in the gym. Willard was a great student of boxing. To go from being a novice fighter in 1911 to world heavyweight champion in 1915 may very well be the greatest boxing accomplishment of all time.

By the time Willard faced Johnson, he had twenty-nine pro bouts under his belt. His record in those twenty-nine fights consisted of twenty-two wins, five losses, and two draws. This was considered a very good record in that time period. Willard was improving steadily in every fight. His quick advancement up the heavyweight ranks was aided by boxing's desperate search for a white man who could beat Johnson.

Johnson had faced and beaten a far better class of opponents than Willard, though they shared some opponents in common. Johnson's record is also rather misleading. He entered the Willard bout with seventy-two fights under his belt — fifty-four wins, five losses, three no-contests, and a whopping ten draws. During Johnson's time, it was not uncommon for a fight to be ruled a draw (by mutual consent) if both men were still standing at the fight's conclusion. Such agreements tended to work against Johnson's best interest because he was often forced to carry some of his white opponents, which is why he had ten draws. Johnson easily beat Marvin Hart over twenty rounds on March 28, 1905, at Woodward's Pavilion in San Francisco. Unfortunately for Johnson, referee Alec Greggains, a virulent bigot, awarded the fight to Hart. Johnson was unmarked whereas Hart's face looked as if it had been put through a meat grinder. Such were the vagaries of racist boxing referees in the early twentieth century.

It is simply not possible to view Johnson as a separate entity from the racist paradigm of his time. Bigotry and America walked hand in hand, indivisible as a single unit, in every field of endeavour, yet Johnson persevered and won. This is why many fight aficionados find it difficult to accept that someone as seemingly inexperienced and unskilled as Willard could defeat one of the greatest champions ever to have lived. Such enthusiasts tend to ignore the fact that this has happened many times in boxing's history. It all comes down to timing.

Willard's appearance on the fistic horizon was brief but impactful. This was the singular achievement of his life. He did nothing after beating Johnson to further his career, choosing to stay idle for almost four years, save for his boring 1916 title defence against the highly skilled but mundane Frank Moran. He was then demolished by Jack Dempsey on July 4, 1919.

By 1915, Johnson was a tired, weary, homesick fighter living in Europe. His ring skills were fading as fast as his zest for boxing. He was certainly not the unbeatable champion who had demolished former heavyweight king James J. Jeffries in 1910. His heart was simply no longer in the game. This provided Willard with a small window of opportunity to pull off the upset of the century. It's to Willard's lasting credit that he took full advantage of this opportunity.

There was no denying that Willard's ring skills had improved tremendously since 1911, thanks to the hard work of his trainer, Moynahan, who felt that with a little help from the hot Havana sun, Willard could beat Johnson. And that is exactly what happened. Willard met the champion precisely when Johnson was ripe for defeat. By 1915, Johnson was no longer a boxing god, but rather a mere mortal. And, as Willard proved, mortals can be beaten.

Willard reaped the spoils from his victory over Johnson. Or did he? Willard loathed the stage tours that were de rigueur for every heavyweight champion of his era. He did not seek or like public attention, and he certainly had no love for prizefighting. For Willard, the heavyweight title proved to be more of a bother than a blessing.

Willard's and Johnson's paths intersected at a fortuitous moment in ring history. For Willard, the timing could not have been better. For Johnson, the circumstances could not have been worse. While Johnson was on the downside of his illustrious ring career, these were Willard's finest ring moments — although the first twenty rounds consisted of him absorbing severe punishment from his desperate opponent. In fact, almost everyone in attendance gave Johnson the first twenty rounds. The fight was scheduled for forty-five rounds in order to exhaust Johnson. In fact, according to referee Jack Welch, if the fight had been scheduled for just twenty rounds, Johnson would have easily retained the heavyweight crown on points alone.

It has often been claimed that Johnson entered the Willard fight out of shape. That is untrue. Johnson battled Willard on a very hot Havana afternoon for twenty-six punishing rounds. Given his age and the furnace-like conditions, Johnson had to have been in phenomenal shape to pull that off; however, it wasn't his physical condition that was lacking. The main impediment to victory for Johnson was that his ring skills had noticeably faded.

Even though he was the champion, Johnson had no leverage whatsoever in the fight negotiations as he had alienated everyone in boxing who could have helped him years before. In many ways, Johnson was the architect of his own ring demise.

It is difficult to fully encompass Johnson's true brilliance as a prizefighter in one sentence. Never has a single fighter had as much of a global impact as Johnson, with the exception of Muhammad Ali. There certainly were no prizefighters even remotely comparable to Johnson, prior to his ascent to the top of the heavyweight division. Johnson risked his life not only by defeating white men but also by publicly gloating about it after each bout.

Willard was not without his fans. Well-respected sportswriter George B. Underwood was an unabashed supporter of Willard and was very close with one of Willard's trainers, Tex O'Rourke. O'Rourke's life was worthy of a movie. At one time or another, he had been a Texas Ranger, a soldier of fortune, a boxer, a Wild West show performer, a sportswriter, a painter, a boxing trainer, and a radio host.[7] O'Rourke knew boxing, and he knew Willard. Underwood was a former Olympic athlete whose name and reputation carried much weight in the boxing world. He served as the boxing editor of the *New York World*, sports editor and columnist for the *Boston American*, and news editor for the *Boston Globe*.

Underwood was present when Willard arrived in the port of Havana. According to Underwood, "There was never a more handsome or menacing ring specimen to step off a boat than the Jess Willard who disembarked in Havana for the world's heavyweight championship fight with the champion Jack Johnson. Willard was in his physical prime and at his pugilistic peak then, and what a wonderful figure of a man he was! Tall as a pine, tough as hickory, arms like twin oaks, bronzed, ruddy, springy stepped, clear eyed, radiating health, strength and power — power personified."[8]

O'Rourke continued:

Willard's arrival in Havana made the betting odds look as if they had been struck by lightning. When he got off the boat we were told that Johnson was a one to four favorite. "I'll bet my last cent at those odds," declared Cherokee Tom Jones (one of Willard's handlers). "Come on. Fellows," he declared, "dig down and cover some of these 'Habla' Spinola boys' simoleons. We can't be more badly busted than we are, anyway." But by the time we got to the hotel, cleaned up and went out to put some money down on Willard the odds had shifted to evens. The Cuban bookmakers and their runner were on the pier when Willard landed and their first peek at the gigantic, bronzed, menacing white giant threw consternation into their ranks.

The Cuban sports got one look at Willard and the influx of money drove the odds from four to one to evens in less than two hours. Outside of a couple of sentimental bets none of us in the Willard camp bet any money on the fight. Our bank rolls were lean, very lean. At odds of 4 to 1 we would have risked every penny, but, at evens none of us cared to wager, inasmuch as we scarcely had money enough to get out of Cuba.[9]

Willard's team devised a simple strategy for success against Johnson. The experienced men who were in Willard's training camp on a daily basis thought that the longer the fight went, the better Willard's chances for victory. Willard had spies at Johnson's training camp. They knew Johnson's ring skills were eroding, and that over time, in such intense heat, he would become dehydrated and his stamina would falter. During his training sessions, Johnson's blows lacked their usual snap. His power was disappearing — his sparring partners had no problems absorbing his shots. This did not bode well for his chances of retaining the title. Johnson's strategy was not hard to fathom. He wanted to knock out Willard early, before the adverse weather conditions started to seriously sap his energy. In a strange twist, Johnson could not use Willard's momentum against him because Willard refused to come forward, thereby forcing Johnson to lead, which was a style with which he was not comfortable.

Johnson always preferred to fight from a distance, where he could utilize his devastating jab to great effect. He found it almost impossible to land any shots on Willard's head because Willard's reach was one inch shy of seven feet! The mathematics were not in Johnson's favour. Every time Johnson rushed Willard and banged him on the inside, Willard clinched Johnson tightly without even attempting to fight back. Only in the last few rounds did Willard start trading shots with Johnson. Willard's reach advantage was so prohibitive that whenever referee Welch separated both men from a clinch, Johnson was always careful to walk back far enough from Willard so as to be out of range of his jab.

O'Rourke's comments about the fight are borne out by the fight films; however, he is mistaken with his comment about Johnson accepting defeat by round fifteen. Johnson was ahead after the fifteenth round, and after twenty rounds of action, according to Welch. But from the fifteenth round on, Johnson began to tire noticeably. For the aging, gasping-for-air Johnson, those first fifteen rounds in the punishing afternoon heat of Havana were exhausting. He endured those conditions because great champions always endure.

Much has been made about the height differential between Willard and Johnson. Yes, it does fatigue a boxer to have to constantly punch up during a fight. Johnson got around this problem by employing a savage and unrelenting body attack on Willard. When Willard bent forward to protect his body, Johnson then tattooed Willard's head with straight right hands and punishing uppercuts. Willard took it all and came back for more. Johnson grew increasingly frustrated as Willard took his best shots with no ill effects. Willard entered the ring in shape, weighing approximately 238.5 pounds compared to Johnson's 225 pounds, which was too much poundage for his old legs to carry for forty-five rounds. Johnson's optimal ring weight was always around 208–212 pounds.

O'Rourke recalled the moment when Johnson shielded his eyes after being knocked down by Willard. (The scandal mongers invariably call to their aid that picture of Johnson on his back and with his arms raised apparently shielding his eyes from the sun, in support of their stories that the fight was not on the level but rather, a fake. I have six pictures of that knockout of Johnson by Willard at Havana, but in not a single one of those pictures does the shadow fall across his face.[10] The pictures offer positive proof that Johnson was not shielding his eyes from the sun. It is too bad that little George Monroe, who seconded Johnson, isn't alive to tell the world today what condition Johnson really was in as he was dragged to his corner mumbling incoherently, "Where am I? Where am I? What happened?") Upon being informed that he had been in a prizefight, a clearly disoriented Johnson took his regular fighting stance, as if to continue. His corner told him that he had been knocked out by Jess Willard and then carefully assisted the fallen champion as he gingerly stepped down from the ring steps and, in a larger sense, from his perch atop the boxing world, into history.

For the rest of his life, whenever his name was mentioned with the phrase "world heavyweight champion," the word "former" would always precede it. And for a man as proud as Johnson, that was a very hard pill to swallow. Willard had violently changed Johnson's championship status with one savage right-hand punch.

Willard had kayoed Johnson in a manner similar to James J. Corbett's knockout of John L. Sullivan. World heavyweight champions are supposed to go out on their gumshields, according to fistic tradition. This is a pattern that has continued right up until today. It was important for Willard's trainer, O'Rourke, to get the story out to the public concerning Willard's victory and Johnson's false claims after the fight.

O'Rourke told Underwood, in no uncertain terms:

> Johnson's story that he laid down to Willard can be torn to shreds. As the rumor mongers gave it to me, Johnson declared that he had agreed to lay down in the tenth, but went along a few rounds further to make it look good. Do you think for one minute Johnson would have taken the terrific punishment he took in the closing rounds unless he was trying his mightiest to avert defeat? Johnson's story, as brought to me, has it that Jack declares he told Tom

Flanagan at the end of the twenty-fifth round to get Mrs. Johnson out of the arena as he did not wish to have her see him humiliated in defeat or lose admiration for his great physical prowess.[11]

Although the basic premise of O'Rourke's story is true, he confused Tommy Flanagan with Jack Curley. After the end of round twenty-five, Johnson felt he could go no further. He asked Curley to escort his wife out of the arena. Johnson was physically and mentally exhausted. Johnson had the look of a beaten gladiator, and he did not want his wife to witness his public demise and humiliation. Curley chose to stay at ringside but directed international sports promoter Richard Kegin to escort Mrs. Johnson from the arena. Johnson's bruised and battered eyes followed his wife out of the arena and then refocused on Willard. It was a sad but poignant moment.

Government Assistance

The white promoters that controlled boxing had combined with the U.S. Attorney General's Office to hound Johnson into submission since the very moment he lifted the heavyweight crown from Tommy Burns in 1908. Johnson was never given a single moment's peace during his unprecedented title reign. He was considered a social and pugilistic pariah by the federal government, white America, and many of his own people.

As unpleasant as it is to hear, Johnson was often his own worst enemy. He habitually skipped out on large hotel and restaurant bills in many European countries. He borrowed large sums of money from various people, with no intention of ever paying them back. He had taken sizeable advances for various stage tours and then skipped out on the tours without paying back the advances.

Johnson had lived too lavishly while champion, spending money as fast as he got it and saving nothing for the future. Like many champions in their prime, he thought the huge paydays would last forever. He outspent his income during his career, which is a trap that Joe Louis would later repeat. By 1915, Jack Johnson had outlived his own era. He was a pugilistic

Willard towers over a beaten Johnson.

anachronism, a man out of time and place. Johnson's high-handed and self-serving method of dealing with boxing promoters had come back to haunt him. All during this time, Willard was working hard to improve his limited boxing skills.

It was Johnson's ouster from Britain by the Home Office that signalled the end of his era. When the First World War began in 1914, Johnson's world shrunk even further as he was unable to find anyone willing to promote a fight on his behalf. He was out of options as he could no longer earn any income from being world heavyweight champion. Johnson became desperate, his behaviour increasingly mercurial, which scared off any potential backers he may have enticed with his phenomenal ring skills only a few years before.

The only path to revenue for him was to defend the title in North America against a credible white contender, one not of his choosing. The problem was that there really weren't any outstanding white contenders. Willard was the best of a bad lot. Mind you, Willard didn't have to be the best white fighter in the world. He only had to be better than Johnson on one specific day.

This is why O'Rourke bristled at the suggestion that Johnson had gone into the tank against Willard. O'Rourke told Underwood, "If Johnson was not beaten fairly then why did he not 'stay' long enough to save his wife from the spectacle of Johnson being hammered and battered to a pulp? If Jack Johnson could have saved her that spectacle he would have done so. But he couldn't. Johnson held off Willard as long as he could that was all."[12]

O'Rourke was correct. If Johnson had planned to throw the fight, as he falsely claimed for years afterward, why then did he wait twenty-six rounds in such unbearable heat to do so?

O'Rourke remembered, "If the Johnson-Willard fight had been a pre-arranged affair all of us would have been on Easy Street. We could have made a fortune in the gambling. We left Havana for the United States about flat broke."[13]

O'Rourke's comments about a betting coup for Willard's backers are salient. If the fight was fixed, Johnson would have demanded his money up front, as a guarantee. Johnson was promised thirty thousand dollars plus one-third of the film rights for facing Willard. That never happened. Johnson received almost no money for his loss to Willard. Why? Well, some fans got in for free, and more to the point, he owed a lot of money to Jack Curley and a host of other people in the boxing world. Johnson knew he would likely not see a dime for the Willard fight. Willard, however, was promised 25 percent of the total receipts plus one-third of the film rights.[14] Willard engaged in twenty-eight prizefights during his career. He defended his crown once before retiring in his corner between rounds against Dempsey. He ignominiously shares both of those distinctions in common with Sonny Liston.

Although Johnson's skills were ineluctably fading when he fought Willard, it is quite likely that Johnson did not perceive Willard as much of a threat, and for good reason. Willard had limited boxing skills and had defeated no one of consequence. Johnson had seen him fight before and was decidedly not impressed. Willard possessed little to no hand speed, uneducated feet, and was very easy to hit. Johnson viewed Willard as just another inept White Hope.

Johnson thought that the relatively inexperienced and gangly Willard would tire quickly in the stifling 40°C heat of a Cuban afternoon. He believed Willard simply did not have the skills to keep up with him over any distance. What Johnson failed to factor in to the equation was Willard's incredible endurance and his extraordinary ability to absorb punishment. Willard could take it ... and take it ... and take it. Had Johnson been younger, the outcome may have been different. However, you can only fight a man when you fight him. Willard caught Johnson at the right time, and that, too, is an integral part of boxing.

Controversy

This fight produced three controversies. Firstly, did Jack Johnson purposely lose the fight and his world heavyweight title to Jess Willard in exchange for thirty thousand dollars plus one-third of the film rights and a chance to return to the United States without going to prison?[15]

Secondly, did Jack Curley (who also promoted the fight) negotiate with representatives of the United States government, including Secretary of State William Jennings Bryan, to try and induce them to overturn Johnson's bogus Mann Act criminal conviction?[16] Thirdly, did Johnson deliberately shield his eyes from the sun while referee Welch tolled the ten-count over him?

The Decision

The simple verdict here is that the fight was not rigged and that Johnson was legitimately knocked out by Willard. Johnson's claim that his fight with Willard was fixed is purely fiction — the film of the fight proves irrefutably that the bout was on the level. Johnson's claim that he went into the tank for money is absurd because Johnson acted as his own manager and trusted absolutely no one with his money, specifically Jack Curley, with whom he had an acrimonious falling out after his loss to Willard, all regarding the film rights of the Willard-Johnson fight.

Johnson trusted the U.S. government even less than he trusted Jack Curley. Johnson was more apt to believe in the tooth fairy than in any promise of leniency from the federal government regarding his Mann Act conviction. There was no sensible reason for him to believe that the government that railroaded him would now quash his conviction and overturn his sentence.

One thing to consider is that Johnson was so desperate for money that he may very well have believed anything Curley told him. Johnson was also anxious to return home to see his ailing mother; he wanted to believe that all would be forgiven and forgotten. If so, Johnson was delusional, and Curley had no qualms about preying upon that delusion. All of Johnson's creditors — and there were many, including Curley — wanted to get Johnson back in the ring at any cost, just to recoup some of their losses before his title reign ended. Johnson rarely treated boxing managers or promoters with any degree of civility or respect.

The real arbiter of the Johnson-Willard tilt is the film of the fight. Willard stretched Johnson with a vicious overhand right that would have felled a charging rhino. In fact, the end for Johnson began one round earlier, when Willard hit the champion with a hard, straight right hand to the heart in round twenty-five. Johnson's knees sagged noticeably from the force of the punch. Willard's thudding right hand to the heart took all of the remaining fight out of Johnson, who let out an audible gasp, shocking those in attendance. Johnson's eyes rolled to the back of his head and he gasped for air, somehow managing to stay on his feet.

Willard's co-trainer, O'Rourke, was correct about Johnson's incoherent mumbling after the fight. Johnson was severely concussed and dehydrated. He was confused, dizzy, dazed, and barely conscious. He did not know where he was or what had just happened to him. Those are the reactions of a fighter who has been knocked out. This brings us to Johnson's false claim that he was shielding his eyes from the sun.

The film clearly shows that Johnson was on the canvas for several seconds before he shielded his eyes. Johnson shielding his eyes was a reflexive reaction. The more salient point here is that while lying on the canvas, Johnson's legs were bent at the knees for a split second before they gave out completely and went limp. Johnson was out cold.

More importantly, given the onerous conditions under which they were fighting, if Johnson did throw the fight, why on earth did he wait twenty-six rounds to do so? It would have made much more sense to tank the fight in an earlier round rather than continue to absorb such heavy punishment. Willard wryly commented years later that if Johnson took a dive, why did he wait so damn long to do it? It was just as hot on his side of the ring, too. There is simply no credible evidence that Johnson took a dive. He was knocked out by the better fighter that day and was apparently too proud to admit it.

The thorny issue of Curley's supposed government inquiries to help Johnson attain a reduced sentence or an outright dismissal of his Mann Act conviction, in return for throwing the fight, is rather problematic. We know Curley tried to help Johnson. We don't know if his inquiries were sincere or perfunctory in nature. Ultimately, Curley's pleas to federal officials turned out to be more of a superficial nature. He was trying to get a sense of the government's mood toward Johnson. Nothing of substance came from these political machinations, and given how poorly Johnson had treated Curley throughout the years, it is surprising that Curley even made any efforts to help Johnson.

No government official would have been stupid enough to put any such proposed deal regarding Johnson on paper. By 1915, federal officials were not in any mood to make a deal with Johnson. Johnson had skipped bail after his conviction and fled to Canada before sailing to Europe. He had humiliated the U.S. government. In their eyes, he had to atone for his sins. Johnson was interested in pursuing a legal appeal of his conviction, but no American court was in the mood to hear such an appeal.

Everyone who knew Johnson intimately believed the Willard fight was on the level. Johnson's close friends said the problem with the fix theory was, even if it was true, there was no guarantee that Johnson would have played ball once he entered the ring. He was notorious for breaking deals — you never knew what he would do because of his mercurial nature and ego. Johnson was an extremely proud man, and the mere suggestion of laying down for a fighter that he did not respect would have irked him in the extreme. The actual film of the fight shows that he did not perform against Willard like a man who had agreed to lay down for his opponent. Rather, he made a tremendous effort, under very adverse conditions, to try and knock out Willard within the first twenty rounds.

Johnson's unjust Mann Act conviction was a blatant appeal to prejudice by the federal government. Still, it weighed very heavily on Johnson's mind. The case never should have come to trial. His inability to return to Chicago to see his mom began to have a deleterious effect on his psyche. Suffice it to say, by the time of the Willard fight, Johnson was a severely disillusioned man. The mere fact that he experienced such acute mental trauma without suffering a psychological break of some kind speaks volumes about his mental toughness and strength of character. Jack Johnson was tougher than Bessemer steel.

Johnson's claim that the fight with Willard was predetermined was, in fact, a paid confession he gave to future *Ring* magazine founder and editor Nat Fleischer for $250 in 1916. Johnson alleged that his wife waved a white hanky to let him know when to go down. Johnson's assertion is laughable. With the hot sun blazing in his eyes for twenty-five rounds, it would have been impossible for Johnson to recognize a waving white hanky. Johnson stated the bout was fixed because he needed the money. By claiming the Willard loss was a tank job, Johnson was contradicting himself. In the immediate aftermath of the fight, he gracefully admitted his defeat was on the level and even complimented Willard on his victory.[17] Johnson was a very vain man. Losing his title in such brutal fashion must have been a tremendous blow to his outsized ego. His physical scars would disappear, but his emotional wounds never healed.

Johnson eventually returned to the U.S., a full five years after his loss to Willard. He was forced to serve a year in jail, where he was a model prisoner — he was famous, which made him the centre of attention. It was when Johnson left prison that he encountered problems. He was yesterday's news, and that fact rankled him severely. Even in his forties, Johnson continued to clamour for a shot at the new heavyweight king, Jack Dempsey. But Johnson would never again be allowed to participate in boxing in any meaningful manner — boxing had seen enough of him. Johnson remained a boxing pariah until Muhammad Ali appeared on the scene and acknowledged him as one of his major influences.

Significance

The historical significance of the Johnson-Willard fight was felt throughout America for decades to come. In an era when some very outstanding Black heavyweights were routinely denied a shot at the title, Johnson, through his persistence, his ring victories, and his courting of the world press, smashed through the colour line to capture the heavyweight crown. It is important to remember that many people in the crowd during his fights were armed and could have shot him if they had so endeavoured. Johnson's preternatural calm demeanour in such situations, combined with his fight focus, remains astonishing to this day.

Johnson always had to fight the haters, the promoters, and the man in front of him. He did all that and still emerged victorious. After enduring such hardships, do you really think he would even consider throwing a title fight? Not a chance. In Willard, he unfortunately had come up against a stronger and fresher man. Johnson's era had been long, but it was over. Willard's era, however, was even shorter than Johnson's. He was merely a caretaker champion; he was the guy between Johnson and Dempsey. Willard's victory over Johnson is one of many incongruities in boxing history.

After Johnson's reign came to its ignominious end, the white cabal that controlled prizefighting colluded to never allow another Black man a shot at the world heavyweight title. Fortunately, they did not succeed. Jack Johnson gave his people, and indeed all people, hope — a precious commodity in any age. Johnson was much more than a symbol of physical strength to his people; he was a pillar of mental and emotional strength as well. Johnson proved that even in the face of implacable, systemic racism, any African American with tremendous skill and brains and determination could make it to the very top of their chosen profession. His ability to showcase his extraordinary boxing skills in a climate of prominent racial hostility is surely one of the greatest achievements of the twentieth century.

No wonder Ali loved him.

What can't be ignored, though, is that Johnson's successful reign as champion, along with his insistence on cavorting with and marrying white women, often prevented the very best African American fighters from fighting for world titles. The Johnson-Willard fight would be the last mixed-race heavyweight title fight for twenty-two years. Then, like the angel Gabriel descending from the heavens, came the immortal Joe Louis, still considered by boxing historians to be the greatest heavyweight champion ever.

Jess Willard has perhaps been judged too harshly by history. Willard trained his mind and body to achieve a single goal, which he accomplished magnificently.

Willard was understandably insulted when Johnson claimed their fight was fixed, but he later had no qualms about falsely claiming he lost to Jack Dempsey due to the challenger's mitts being loaded. Perhaps the best way to view Willard is this: After he beat Jack Johnson, nothing more was asked of him pugilistically, and nothing more was given. In the end, the Willard-Johnson world heavyweight title fight irrevocably changed the course of prizefighting and American history. Were these good or bad changes for boxing and America? That is for you to decide.

CHAPTER 5

JACK DEMPSEY VS. JESS WILLARD

Fight: Jack Dempsey vs. Jess Willard
Weight Class: Heavyweight
Title at Stake: World heavyweight
Date: July 4, 1919
Location: Toledo, Ohio
Outcome: Dempsey wins by third-round knockout
Referee: Ollie Pecord
Timekeeper: William Warren Barbour

Background

On July 4, 1919, at Bay View Park Arena in Toledo, Ohio, under sweltering 38°C skies, Jack Dempsey's unbridled ring savagery was on full display before 19,500 sweat-drenched fight fans, in a prizefighting performance for the ages. Dempsey ruthlessly lifted the undisputed world heavyweight title from the bloody and battered brow of Jess Willard, after Willard's corner threw in the towel at the beginning of round four, to signal their fighter's submission. On that day, Dempsey's fists were as punishing as the whipping winds of an Arctic winter and as glorious as a prairie sunset.

Dempsey–Willard pre-fight collage.

Dempsey was always unrestrained in the squared circle. He never exited the ring after a fight thinking, "I could have done more." In truth, Willard was tailor-made for Dempsey. His defensive boxing skills were pretty much non-existent. Willard really only ever employed three defensive manoeuvres. They consisted of clinching, leaning back, or just taking his opponent's punches. Incredibly, Willard foolishly stood directly in front of Dempsey, attempting to trade shots with the hungry challenger. To square up against Dempsey and trade punch for punch with him was akin to committing suicide with a sledgehammer. Also working against Willard were the ring dimensions, just twenty square feet. It was a puncher's ring — Willard, who was a counterpuncher, had nowhere to hide. When the fight began, however, Willard eschewed his counterpunching style, instead using the small ring to his advantage by coming forward and attacking Dempsey. No one had expected Willard to go on the attack early in the bout. Everyone was surprised at Willard's aggression, including Dempsey.

Dempsey had no problem avoiding Willard's rushes by utilizing his superior footwork and head movement. Willard landed long right hands on

Dempsey, but they had no effect on the young phenom as he rolled with each punch. Unbeknownst to Willard, Dempsey was already positioning him on the road to perdition. Dempsey was about to unleash the proverbial hounds of hell upon the head of the unsuspecting champion.

Just past the minute-and-a-half mark of the first round, after breaking from a clinch, Dempsey charged the champion. He landed a ferocious four-punch combination that culminated with a murderous left hook that exploded off Willard's jaw, sending him to the canvas for the first of seven knockdowns in the opening round. The concussive force of Dempsey's punch shattered Willard's jaw in thirteen places and knocked out at least ten of his teeth. Dempsey changed the bone structure of Willard's face with each successive blow. Willard never physically or mentally recovered from that first knockdown; the six knockdowns that followed were merely a postscript to the slaughter. Willard's right eye was swollen shut and the right side of his face was broken and gushing blood. The fact that he survived two more rounds is a tremendous testament to his intestinal fortitude.

After the fight, Willard looked like an old wooden house that had been devastated by a Midwestern storm of pure Dempsey. It's hard not to describe Dempsey in purely meteorological terms — he had more in common with a Category 5 hurricane than with any previous heavyweight champion. In his prime, no man alive could withstand Dempsey's relentless, feral assaults. It was almost as if his fists were being guided by some supernatural force. One scribe commented that Dempsey's left hook was equivalent in force to the extinction meteor that took out the dinosaurs. If Willard's jaw had not been broken, he would no doubt have agreed. Dempsey's name became synonymous with devastation. No fighter, regardless of their talent, ever relished the prospect of facing Dempsey in battle. Walking to the ring to face him must have felt as if you were being led to the gallows.

The Dempsey-Willard heavyweight title bout ushered in the modern era of big-time money in professional sports. Through no fault of his own, Dempsey also ushered in organized crime's involvement with prizefighting with his first million-dollar gate fight against George Carpentier in 1921. The Dempsey-Willard battle helped boxing firmly establish a foothold as legitimate, mainstream entertainment and big business in the twentieth century. Equally as important is when their fight occurred, 1919. The First World War had ended one year earlier, and America needed a major sporting event to help boost its morale. Thanks to the new medium of radio, a tectonic shift was occurring in how Americans enjoyed their favourite sports, especially boxing, baseball, and horse racing in the 1920s. Radio was immediate. You heard each event as it was happening. Fans could enjoy an instant connection to important fights in the comfort of their own homes. The Manassa Mauler was made for the medium — the young, charismatic Dempsey was as electric and exciting as radio itself.

Dempsey made your heart beat faster. Those few seconds prior to the start of a great world title fight, when you feel your heart speed up with anticipation ... Dempsey did that. He made boxing matter. Dempsey was a major catalyst of the new decade, known as the Roaring Twenties. He was unlike any athlete or celebrity who'd come before. He was always going for the kill, just like America itself.

After four years of Willard's colourless and mostly inactive reign as world champion, Dempsey was just what boxing and America were craving — nonstop action. Dempsey was an intoxicating breath of fresh air, a captivating presence for a provocative new decade, where even the most far-fetched achievements in any field of endeavour seemed entirely within reach.

Perhaps what is most remarkable about the Dempsey-Willard fight is that the boxing cognoscenti favoured Willard by a margin of six to five. They completely ignored the fact that Dempsey was coming off five straight wins (four of which came via spectacular knockouts), whereas Willard had engaged in only one lopsided yet boring win three years earlier, against Pittsburgh dentist and future film actor Frank Moran. Boxing historians must wonder how these supposedly veteran boxing scribes and bookies missed the obvious signs that Dempsey was ready and ravenous for his chance to capture the heavyweight title with his brine-hardened hands. The boxing press disregarded the obvious clues that indicated Willard was about to walk wholly unprepared into a human buzz saw. They also deliberately chose to ignore Dempsey's previous ring prowess. They had all covered Dempsey's phenomenal knockout streak of top tier heavyweight contenders.

Their belief that Willard's talent was equivalent to his tremendous height was incredibly foolish.

Dempsey was lethal against oversized fighters, and the writers knew it. Dempsey's previous successes pointed to the inescapable fact that Willard would be quickly annihilated by the man from Manassa, Colorado. The outcome of the Dempsey-Willard bout came as a surprise only to Willard and the sportswriters who refused to see it for what it was — a mismatch of epic proportions. The media was lazy and chose to promote Willard's non-existent reputation over Dempsey's spectacular rise to the top of the heavyweight division. Both the media and Willard were about to be exposed as frauds in humiliating fashion.

The film of the Dempsey-Willard fight is rather unsettling. It is at once wonderful and sickening. Willard absorbed what many fistic historians consider the worst beating a fighter has ever received in the prize ring. The beat-down of Willard was magnified by the fact that there was no neutral corner rule or standing eight count stipulation in existence at that time. Dempsey was allowed to stand directly over the helpless Willard, waiting for him to rise on six different occasions before mercilessly pounding him back down again. It's hard to escape the thought that Dempsey looked as if he was literally trying to kill Willard — his attacks looked more like an aggravated assault than a sporting match.

Incredibly, Willard entered the ring with seemingly not a care in the world, casually blowing kisses to his "multitude" of fans. Willard's acknowledgement of the crowd seemed perfunctory at best. He acted like a victorious champion before the fight had even begun. He was completely oblivious of Dempsey's presence in the ring. Dempsey, meanwhile, was pacing in his corner like a caged, feral tiger yearning for a fresh kill. He was already zoned-in to the moment at hand while Willard's mind was off in the clouds. Is it possible that Willard's ego was so bloated that he believed his towering presence alone was all that was required for victory? If so, he was about to be persuaded otherwise, in a most forceful fashion.

Dempsey's manager, Jack "Doc" Kearns, told him not to look at the six-foot-seven Willard during referee Ollie Pecord's pre-fight instructions. Kearns was worried that the six-foot-one Dempsey might be intimidated by Willard's gargantuan size. Dempsey said years later that he was indeed intimidated by Willard's size, but that is hard to believe. He had faced men as big as Willard before and annihilated them in savage fashion. No doubt Dempsey experienced the normal pre-fight jitters that all fighters go through. Such jitters only served to heighten his senses and make him fight even harder.

Styles Make Fights

Styles make fights, and this was never truer than in the Willard-Dempsey blowout. Willard was a counterpuncher who fought with his hands by his sides, whereas Dempsey liked to lead and always had his mitts in a position to strike. It was only a matter of time before Dempsey figured him out and lowered the boom. Willard, like most large fighters, exhibited poor balance and was incapable of fighting effectively while backing up.

There have been many epochal changes in style throughout modern boxing history. The great Daniel Mendoza in the late eighteenth and early nineteenth centuries became the first fighter to fully utilize head and shoulder feints and dazzling footwork. He realized it was silly to stand directly in front of a man and trade blows. Mendoza gave birth to an entirely new style of fighting that emphasized brains over brawn and mobility over slugging. He was a short man, perhaps five foot seven, and everyone he fought was much taller and stronger than him. He had to outsmart them to beat them.

American John L. Sullivan emerged in the late nineteenth century to popularize prizefighting worldwide. It was Sullivan's boisterous personality, along with his ability to back up his boasts with his canned-ham-sized fists, that imbued boxing with worldwide appeal. His unique style featured strength, power punching, and constant pressure. He was not a technically skilled pugilist. He was a crude, walk-in slugger with unfathomable strength — the last great bare-knuckle fighter. Sullivan lost his title to scientific boxing master James J. Corbett.

Corbett lost his title to a very smart boxer-puncher named Bob Fitzsimmons. Corbett was a big man and an intimidating figure in the ring. When his size was mentioned to Fitzsimmons, he uttered the now famous phrase, "The bigger they are, the harder they fall." Fitzsimmons proved that body punches are as damaging as head shots, if not more so. He won the title from Corbett with his famed solar plexus punch, forever after known in boxing circles as "The Fitzsimmons Shift."

Not long after, Jack Johnson, the first African American world heavy-weight champion, appeared on the scene and showed that defence was as much of a skill set as offence inside the squared circle. Johnson's skills were so advanced that he seemed to have been created by an alchemist. Willard succeeded Johnson. Willard's fame is based on two fights, only one of which he won. He was one of many "White Hopes," a phrase originated by sports-writer/promoter Otto Floto.[1]

All heavyweight champions prior to Dempsey, including Willard, were powerful but slow. They were plodding fighters, with the exception of Corbett and Johnson. Sullivan and James J. Jeffries were more comfortable on the attack. Fitzsimmons, Corbett, and Johnson were natural counter-punchers. Then a seismic shift occurred in heavyweight boxing, one named Jack Dempsey. Dempsey was aggression personified, a fighter perpetually in motion for a decade perpetually in motion.

Jess Willard deserves credit for ushering in an era of calm in the heavy-weight division. In both temperament and ring style, Willard was the polar opposite of Dempsey. Dempsey loved crowds and excitement, and craved action. Willard preferred his own company. Willard's aloofness elicited no feelings of excitement among the American sporting public. He didn't have much use for the boxing community either. Willard did not enjoy boxing. For him, it was a means to an end. The quickest possible way to make a buck.

After besting Johnson, Willard settled in for what looked like a long reign as king of the heavyweights. His handlers figured his size alone would be sufficient enough to deter even the most ardent contenders from chal-lenging him. His handlers figured wrong.

Jack Dempsey

Dempsey was born in the rough mining town of Manassa, Colorado, in 1895.[2] He learned boxing at a young age while working in various mining and hobo camps across the country. He switched camps often. He would go into each new camp or local bar and, with his high voice, challenge any man to a finish fight. His effeminate voice often elicited snickers from these hardnosed hobos. Customers would pass the hat around to collect money for the winner, and some large man would step forward to take Dempsey up on his offer. Dempsey issued this challenge to hundreds of men in hundreds of different mining towns and hobo jungles across America. He rarely lost; he disposed of these erstwhile rowdies quickly and efficiently. Dempsey even made it a habit to approach veteran fighters in each new town, asking them for advice on how to improve himself as a fighter.

To label Dempsey as nothing more than a face-first, walk-in slugger is to do him a great disservice. Dempsey had an exceptionally high ring IQ. Everything he did inside the ring was carefully calculated for maximum effect — nothing he did was by accident. He was as proficient defensively as he was offensively. His ability to think quickly on his feet during the parry and thrust of battle is what separated him from the rest of the pack. Compared to most heavyweights from that era, Dempsey was a highly skilled artisan.

It was Dempsey who went to the training camp of Joe Louis prior to his rematch with Max Schmeling and showed him how best to defeat the German slugger. Sure, Dempsey was intuitive inside the squared circle, but he always had his wits about him. He was the best finisher boxing ever produced. Dempsey was the personification of grace under pressure. He knew exactly what to do and how to survive when he got hurt in the ring. He knew how to block punches well on the inside and how to shut down an opponent's offence by crowding or clinching him, or hooking his arm and spinning him off balance.

Dempsey was every inch a thinking man's champion. He raised boxing to the level of fine art. In 1918, after hooking up with the wildly ambitious Kearns, Dempsey managed to catch the public's imagination with a string of eleven devastating first-round knockouts, in particular his eighteen-second demolition of the giant Fred Fulton, which led to his momentous challenge of Willard. Dempsey was becoming well known to the American sporting public due to the machinations of his peripatetic, well-connected manager

Kearns. The wily Kearns ensured that every dazzling Dempsey knockout was feature news in every paper across America — he was a master at using the press to bolster Dempsey's career and popularity. Neither the press nor the public had ever witnessed such an array of beautifully brutal knockouts before Dempsey's arrival on the national scene.

Dempsey's fame started to open up other revenue streams for him to exploit. Whereas other than prizefighting, Willard had failed at every business enterprise he had undertaken. In fact, Willard and his young wife and family had to move often because they could not pay the debts owed on their failed undertakings in the various towns in which they lived. Willard happened into boxing quite by accident. He possessed no amateur boxing pedigree and entertained no fantasies regarding prizefighting. Even someone with an education as limited as Willard's could see how most prizefighters ended up: broke, battered, and indigent. He knew it was a brutal sport run by scoundrels whose only concern was enhancing their own financial positions at the expense of their (often naive) prizefighters.

Willard did have some physical assets that helped him in the ring. He possessed prodigious natural strength for one. Apparently when Willard was once riding his cotton wagon, it tipped over on the road, spilling its large load of almost seven hundred pounds of baled cotton but leaving Willard completely unscathed. To the utter amazement of everyone present, Willard was able to right the overturned wagon with his hands and then calmly reload the baled cotton back onto the wagon.[3]

Willard genuinely did not know the true extent of his own strength, which is why he supposedly never really went all out in the ring, fearing he might kill one of his opponents.[4] Willard had in fact killed one of his previous foes, John "Bull" Young, on August 22, 1913, in Vernon, California, for which he was arrested, charged, and later acquitted. Young likely died from an accumulation of punishment received over a series of tough bouts; nevertheless, his death tormented Willard for the rest of his life. Young's death changed Willard both in and out of the ring, which is not surprising. Willard became more reticent to mix it up in many of his fights, preferring to win by a dull decision rather than by knockout. He also started to withdraw inside himself.

Willard was a gentleman and unfailingly polite and courteous to everyone he met. That was his nature. He did, however, possess a healthy ego and believed wholeheartedly, after he won the heavyweight title, that the loss of his title was not even in the realm of possibility. In his defence, all champions must think that way if they are to enter the ring and do battle victoriously. Like most tall fighters, Willard's balance was never very good. Dempsey, meanwhile, displayed perfect balance, which is why his punches carried such incredible force. Willard's ring style was similar in approach to that of Jeffries. He preferred to stick his huge, telephone pole of a left arm straight out to ward off his opponent's rushes. Willard was caught in a stylistic time warp, fighting in the old mode of boxing common to the champions who preceded him.

Dempsey was very much a modernist in a boxing sense. He came forward bobbing and weaving, his chin tucked tightly into his left shoulder for protection. Dempsey's game plan for each fight in which he engaged never varied. It involved three simple steps: 1. find opponent; 2. corner opponent; 3. destroy opponent. Dempsey was not interested in the feeling-out process that occurs in most bouts, as that required patience, of which Dempsey had none. He was like a caged lion. He wanted to make a quick kill, lick his chops, and then anxiously look for his next meal.

Unfortunately for Willard, his poleaxing left jab did not work against Dempsey. Dempsey knew how to smoothly slip an opponent's jab and then shift an inch to either side, to launch one of his explosive hooks. It was his nuclear-fuelled left hook that lifted the crown that had once benighted the head of Willard. Dempsey possessed the greatest left hook in boxing history. His blowout of Willard is perhaps the most definitive knockout in boxing history.

Willard and Dempsey did have several things in common. They were both from the Midwest and they both drew the colour line after winning the heavyweight strap. It's probably more accurate to say that Dempsey was willing to face fighters of African descent, such as Canadian Larry Gains and American Harry Wills, but he was prevented from doing so by his manager, Kearns. In fact, Dempsey was banned from fighting in New York after signing a contract to face Wills and then backing out of the fight at the last moment. Even in the 1920s, drawing the colour line was considered a sign of racial and moral pride when in fact it was really an overt sign of racism and cowardice.

While Dempsey was rising through the heavyweight ranks, Willard spent his time earning a living performing rodeo tricks in various Wild West shows. Willard would have been much happier working in rodeos, where he felt more at home than in the prize ring. The Wild West gigs did not last long, though, as Willard was not a draw due to his indifferent demeanour. He certainly enjoyed making money off of his title, but he did not enjoy defending it, which is probably why he is so lightly regarded today among the pantheon of heavyweight champions.

Willard may not have been an exceptionally skilled prizefighter, but he possessed a truly devastating left jab, a crushing straight right hand, and such height that fight fans almost viewed him as a circus attraction. He was not uneducated in the Sweet Science — what he lacked was a natural feel for the sport. He did possess tremendous stamina, however, and an unusual ability to absorb gobs of punishment. Willard, like Tyson Fury years later, was very adept at leaning on his opponents with his massive girth, to gradually wear them down.

Willard was primarily a counterpuncher. That is how he felt most comfortable. If an opponent slipped Willard's long jab and closed the distance on him, he would shoot out his straight right hand to deter them from doing so again. For the most part, Willard would blunt his opponent's attack by clinching. But Willard's ring tactics did not work against Dempsey because the challenger was so much more skilled than the champion. When the skill of both fighters is equal, then the winner of the match is determined by which fighter can better impose his will on the other. That was not the case here. Willard's skills were basic at best. He was out of his league skill-wise against Dempsey.

Dempsey fought Willard from an exaggerated crouch, making himself an even smaller target at which to aim. This was a very smart move — it is exceedingly difficult to hit a shorter guy who is constantly moving from side to side. It requires a level of timing foreign to some of the most skilled boxers. To be sure, promoter Tex Rickard was not a fan of Jess Willard.

Willard was always difficult to deal with professionally, and he was a dud at the box office. The arena in Toledo held forty thousand people, but only 19,500 showed up. No one wanted to pay good money to see the lumbering Willard defend the heavyweight title in yet another boring fight. As such, the heavyweight division experienced a financial downturn during Willard's reign. This negatively impacted boxing's other divisions. Willard believed his status as champion automatically entitled him to million-dollar paydays. He did not understand that such paydays went to fighters who filled arenas. In Cuba, the fans came to see Johnson get beat rather than to watch Willard fight. Willard never caught the imagination of the American sporting public.

Interestingly, before settling on Dempsey, Willard's brain trust had trouble coming up with a credible opponent for him to fight. The champion's handlers feared Willard's large frame would deter even the bravest of fighters from coming forward. Dempsey was not a small man. He stood six foot one and weighed 186 pounds. Willard's team openly laughed when Dempsey was first suggested as an opponent. Needless to say, this did not sit well with the rustic challenger. Willard was looking past Dempsey and not at the young Coloradan's stunning, recent ring triumphs. Willard deliberately sloughed off Dempsey as a credible threat to his heavyweight supremacy.

There is no doubt that Willard underestimated Dempsey. Part of this misjudgement can be chalked up to hubris — Willard thought he could scare Dempsey with his size. But Dempsey called his bluff. If heart and determination could be solely measured by height, Dempsey would have stood ten feet tall. Dempsey had been very active in the ring leading up to his world title shot. His timing was honed to a fine edge. Willard, on the other hand, had been off for three years. Ironically, when Gene Tunney lifted the title from Dempsey in 1926, Dempsey was coming off a three-year layoff. For a champion to retain his title, he must fight often to keep his skills sharp. Willard had been idle too long. He was smug, overconfident, and pompous — the precursors to defeat.

Willard's team missed the obvious. Dempsey feasted on taller opponents like Morris and Fulton, and Willard certainly fit that bill. Tall heavyweights tend to be slow, lumbering, and frequently off-balance. They are only comfortable when fighting from a distance. By crowding them from the opening bell, Dempsey effectively negated their height and reach advantages. He forced them out of their comfort zones by making them fight on the inside. To be surprised by an opponent's strategy is understandable, but to be wilfully ignorant of their previous fights is inexcusable. This is when fatalities happen in boxing, and Willard was lucky to have escaped with his life.

Willard outweighed Dempsey by fifty-eight pounds and boasted a six-inch height advantage.[5] Dempsey felt he had to take Willard out quickly before Willard did the same to him. The vast disparity in physical size between the two warriors made promoter Rickard force Dempsey, at Willard's insistence, to sign a waiver indemnifying Rickard and Willard should Willard kill him in the ring. This episode only served to antagonize Dempsey. Looking back, it was Willard who should have signed the waiver. Everyone in attendance picked Willard to win for one reason — his size. After he lost the title, Willard falsely claimed for years that Dempsey's gloves were loaded. His wounded ego could not accept the fact that a smaller man, regardless of his superior skill set, could defeat him in such devastatingly brutal fashion. It seems Willard's ego was the only thing bigger than his body. He never came to grips with the fact that Dempsey beat his brains in because Dempsey was the better fighter.

Some champions deal with loss well, others go to pieces. Willard was simply unable to accept his defeat gracefully.

Willard earned his world champion stripes by rising from that first crushing knockdown. In the eyes of the fight community, he became more of a champion in his loss to Dempsey than in his victory over Johnson. Willard rose from seven vicious knockdowns in the first round in his mismatch with Dempsey. Any fighter who can do that deserves to be called a world champion.

Controversy

There are several long-standing controversies regarding this fight. Did the timekeeper deliberately end the first round early to prevent Dempsey from scoring a first-round knockout, thereby preventing gamblers (who had

Dempsey demolishing
Willard.

largely bet on Willard) from losing their money? The more well-known controversy is, did Jack Dempsey deliberately harden his fists before putting on
his gloves, by soaking his hand wraps in plaster of Paris? Finally, why did
Dempsey's manager, Kearns, tell everyone years later that Dempsey's gloves
were loaded?

The Decision

The rumour that Dempsey's wraps were loaded has lasted for over one hundred years. It is simply a fiction perpetuated by the vengeful and active
imagination of Jack Kearns, who stated that Dempsey's hands had been
soaked in plaster of Paris, thus giving them the consistency of bricks. Kearns
only made these claims years after Dempsey dropped him as his manager

and whenever he was in dire need of money, which was most of the time. In order to ensure that each fighter's hands are taped according to the rules in effect, it has long been the custom to allow a member of each fighter's team into the opposite fighter's dressing room. Dempsey's hands were taped in full view of, and examined thoroughly by, Walter Moynahan, Willard's trainer and chief second. Moynahan also observed Dempsey gloving up in the ring. Moynahan said after the fight that Dempsey's hands were legally wrapped and that they had not been soaked in plaster of Paris or any substance at any time, in the dressing room or in the ring. In fact, there exists a short film clip of Dempsey having his hands gloved up prior to the fight. There are existing photos clearly showing Dempsey entering the ring, just moments prior to his fight with Willard, with his hands legally wrapped in gauze and tape.

Moynahan asserted that Dempsey's hand wraps were kosher. He added that the problem wasn't with Dempsey's wraps but rather Willard's ego, which refused to let him accept such a one-sided defeat. The Dempsey-Willard bout was completely on the up and up, despite the farcical and unproven claims of Kearns and Willard. It is worth noting that Hall of Fame trainer Angelo Dundee once told me, if Dempsey's hands had been soaked in plaster of Paris, they would have broken the very first time he threw a punch, if he could have even lifted them at all.

Dempsey's hands were as tough as a catcher's mitt because, from a young age, he soaked them in beef brine daily, to toughen up his skin. Getting hit by Dempsey was akin to getting clocked in the head by a baseball bat. He did not need to load up his gloves or cheat in any way because he was an authentically devastating knockout puncher. His exceptional balance enabled him to achieve full leverage on all of his shots. It's likely that Willard thought Dempsey's hands were loaded because they were using only five-ounce gloves. Dempsey's wrapped, leather-hardened hands inside five-ounce gloves probably felt to Willard like a brick house had collapsed upon him.

Why did Kearns make the scurrilous claim that Dempsey's wraps were loaded to *Sports Illustrated* magazine in 1964?[6] He needed the money. Kearns was an alcoholic, inveterate gambler, and always in desperate need of funds. Dempsey had long ago grown tired of giving Kearns money to cover his mounting gambling losses — money that Kearns never repaid. Kearns had long been taking more from Dempsey's fight purses than they had contractually agreed upon. Understandably, this infuriated Dempsey.

Dempsey's wife, Hollywood actress Estelle Taylor, also forced Dempsey's hand in getting rid of Kearns, but in all fairness, Kearns was solely responsible for his split with Dempsey. Kearns was wholly incapable of controlling his gambling and alcohol addictions. He self-righteously believed any money Dempsey earned was for his (Kearns's) own personal use. Kearns launched mean-spirited verbal attacks on Taylor in front of Dempsey. He was lucky Dempsey didn't wring his neck. In Kearns's booze-addled mind, Taylor was getting in the way of his continued financial scamming of Dempsey.

For Kearns, the last straw was when Rickard started to pay Dempsey directly after his fights, which was the smart thing to do. Dempsey would then write a cheque for the exact amount owed to Kearns. Kearns hated this arrangement for obvious reasons.

Dempsey was none too pleased when he discovered (supposedly right before the opening bell) that Kearns had bet ten thousand dollars of his nineteen-thousand-dollar purse at odds of ten to one that he would knock out Willard in the first round. After expenses and Kearns's managerial cut, Dempsey fought Willard practically for free, because the fight officially ended after the third round and not the first frame. This is why it was not surprising that Dempsey fired Kearns. How much could Dempsey be expected to take from a scoundrel like that? He still needed Kearns's boxing acumen, but he could no longer tolerate his fiscal irresponsibility, not to mention the constant verbal abuse of his wife.

The destruction Dempsey wrought on Willard was almost Biblical in proportion. It was Willard, not Dempsey, who was forced to fight for his life. This was not supposed to happen, which is why everyone was shocked by the quick and dramatic outcome. Once Willard quit on his stool after the third round, rumours about the fight started to appear. One such rumour claimed that timekeeper William Warren Barbour was told to ring the bell before the first round ended, ostensibly by gamblers with large bets on Willard, to deny the Manassa Mauler a first-round knockout. It was also claimed that these hotshot gamblers wanted to deny Kearns the huge financial windfall he would have reaped if Dempsey had ended the bout in the first three minutes.

There exists no evidence to prove such a claim, but there is evidence to show how this rumour started.

The first round ended ten seconds early because when the bell rang to start round one, no one heard it — one of the workmen tasked with making the ring had neglected to attach the wire to the bell. Barbour had to use a marine whistle instead to alert the fighters to begin the fight. Finally, in utter frustration, he stood up and screamed at both fighters, "Go ahead!"[7] However, Barbour had started his stopwatch when the inoperative bell misfired rather than when he blew the whistle, ten seconds later. He should have restarted his stopwatch when the fight actually began. Barbour's error cost Dempsey a very valuable ten seconds in the round, thus denying him a legitimate first-round knockout. The round did indeed end early, but only because of a simple mistake by the timekeeper rather than pressure from gamblers. Thus, Dempsey did knock out Willard in the first round but was never given credit for it officially.

Significance

The phrase Dempsey-Willard is as American as Lewis and Clark. It is almost impossible to mention one without mentioning the other. Dempsey needed Willard to paint his masterpiece and to launch himself onto the world stage. Willard needed Dempsey to remain eternally relevant. Like Lewis and Clark, Dempsey-Willard appear still as a single entity in the hearts and minds of all boxing historians.

The Dempsey-Willard heavyweight title fight ushered in an era of monumental financial prosperity and excitement in prizefighting. Thanks to mass coverage of boxing on radio and in newspapers worldwide, heavyweight title bouts were enjoyed live all over the planet. This significantly increased the sport's global popularity, and the purses of the fighters involved. The Dempsey-Willard clash was the fight that forever defined in the American consciousness the image of Dempsey as the Manassa Mauler.

With the ascension of Dempsey to the heavyweight throne, boxing became the most popular sport in the world. It had finally managed to overcome its Wild West past to become a giant cash cow for all those involved.

Dempsey's spectacular win and alliterative nickname typified the new, unbridled, modern 1920s American capitalist spirit, where anything was possible and might always made right.

The Dempsey-Willard fight broke with pugilistic tradition. Willard became the first world heavyweight champion to relinquish his crown while sitting in his corner between rounds rather than lying unconscious on the canvas or losing by decision. (This would not happen again until forty-five years later, when Sonny Liston, while sitting on his stool, meekly surrendered the heavyweight title to Cassius Clay in 1964.)

Dempsey headlined the first four million-dollar gates in boxing history. He brought the upper crust of society — including women, business titans, and Hollywood stars — to the fights on a regular basis. He also brought out the lower crust, too: mobsters, pimps, prostitutes, and bootleggers. Simply put, Dempsey's phenomenal punching power and charismatic personality put asses in the seats, which is what prizefighting is all about. Dempsey filled stadiums in the United States and living rooms around the world, where entire families would gather around their radios to listen to his fights.

Dempsey's appeal was universal in nature. After winning the title, he enjoyed tremendous crowds of admiring fans when visiting England, France, Argentina, Canada, Spain, Italy, and Germany. His fan base was rabid and loyal and worldwide in scope. Everybody loves a knockout artist. Dempsey's physical prowess became part of the English language. Whenever someone was seen trying to pick a fight, invariably a bystander would yell out, "Who do you think you are, Jack Dempsey?"

Willard had two more fights after his title loss to Dempsey. Both were comeback fights and occurred in 1923, four years after his loss to Dempsey. Willard scored an eleventh-round technical knockout over journeyman Floyd Johnson on May 12, 1923, at Yankee Stadium.[8] Two months later, on July 12, also at Yankee Stadium, hulking Argentinean heavyweight Luis Ángel Firpo hastened Willard's retirement plans by knocking him to the canvas where referee Harry Lewis counted him out after eight one-sided rounds.[9] Willard's final career record was twenty-two, five, one, with twenty knockouts to his credit. Three of Willard's five losses came by way of knockout.

Willard's major flaw, although no fault of his own, was that he never captured the public's imagination the way Dempsey did. Then again, no athlete, except Muhammad Ali, captured the attention of the public like Dempsey. Dempsey and baseball's Babe Ruth were the athletic stars of the Jazz Age; however, it was Dempsey's natural charm that outshone all other athletes and celebrities of his era. And it was *his* era. In fact, Dempsey's star shone even brighter after losing two consecutive fights to Tunney. Dempsey was more popular in defeat than he had ever been as champion. This was because Dempsey offered no hackneyed excuses for losing. He accepted defeat with the grace and dignity of a world champion.

There is something uniquely American about Dempsey that still registers deeply within the American psyche. He had that never-say-die spirit, that indomitable will to succeed, coupled with an ironclad refusal to be conquered, even in defeat. Dempsey possessed the ability to compel himself forward against all obstacles in his way, including the Great Depression. He grew up in poverty yet overcame his humble beginnings by virtue of his own sweat and toil. He never showed fear or trepidation, and neither did he complain about whatever situation he found himself in. Dempsey, more than any other athlete in the first half of the twentieth century, epitomized the quintessential heart and soul of the American experience.

CHAPTER 6

JACK DEMPSEY VS. GENE TUNNEY II

Fight: Jack Dempsey vs. Gene Tunney II
Weight Class: Heavyweight
Title at Stake: Undisputed world heavyweight
Date: September 22, 1927
Location: Soldier Field, Chicago, Illinois
Outcome: Gene Tunney retains his title with a ten-round decision
Referee: Dave Barry

Background

Jack Dempsey held the undisputed world heavyweight title from 1919 to 1926, and the public's fascination for much longer. There is an eternally ineffable quality about Dempsey that continues to enthrall people in an almost mystical way. Dempsey's restless ring savagery was the engine that fuelled the Roaring Twenties and American sports. Dempsey was as ambitious and dynamic as the era that he embodied. He threw every punch in his arsenal with menacingly bad intentions. The famed and beloved Manassa Mauler dominated professional sports and the front pages of newspapers around the world during his time as champion and for almost another sixty years after his reign ended.

It has been more than one hundred years since Dempsey captured the world heavyweight title in explosive fashion from Jess Willard on July 4, 1919, yet the (sporting) public continues to be captivated by him. Later in life, his restaurant, the eponymously named Jack Dempsey's, became a landmark on Broadway and was as much of a fixture in New York State as the Statue of Liberty and the Empire State Building. Dempsey fans from all over the world made the sojourn to his popular eatery, hoping and praying to meet their beloved hero. Dempsey never let them down, happily signing autographs and posing for pictures with everyone who entered his establishment.

Dempsey became more popular after his rematch loss to Gene Tunney than he ever was as champion. Such is the fickleness of the American sporting public. The seventh round of their second fight remains to this day the most controversial moment in boxing history. To be sure, Dempsey was no stranger to controversy. He had been maliciously and unfairly maligned as a slacker during the First World War. This was because of the publication of a photo of him in a coal yard shovelling coal while wearing work overalls and patent leather shoes. Dempsey's manager, Jack "Doc" Kearns, should have caught the faux pas and replaced his shoes with work boots. Did Kearns miss this detail on purpose? Maybe. What we do know for certain is that Kearns ended up turning a public relations disaster into a financial boon for himself and Dempsey. The photographic gaffe resulted in endless bad publicity for Dempsey throughout the United States as it appeared during the First World War. This was grief Dempsey did not want or need. It seriously damaged his public image for years, and the ensuing furor regarding the ill-timed photograph took a heavy emotional toll on him.

During the First World War, Dempsey received a legitimate draft deferment because he was the sole means of support for his entire extended family. Although this was a legally documented fact, his ex-wife (sex worker Maxine Cates) and various opportunistic politicians tried to spin the deferment as nothing more than a well-orchestrated effort by Team Dempsey to avoid the draft. His ex-wife and her slimy cohorts knew the "slacker" label was patently false and went ahead with it anyway.[1] Unfortunately, when it came to choosing between the truth and the myth regarding Dempsey, the press usually printed the myth. Back then, as today, myth far outsold the truth when it came to the media, especially when it involved sporting gods like Dempsey, Babe Ruth, and Muhammad Ali.

However, there was another reason why Dempsey did not enter the American military, and this was primarily due to the machinations and financial considerations of his devious manager, the avaricious Kearns. Dempsey was Kearns's main meal ticket, his pathway to untold riches. Kearns was not about to lose boxing's number one draw and the money he generated, just because of some inconvenient war. As far as Kearns was concerned, the time to cash in on Dempsey's heavyweight prowess was now, war or no war.

The always-scheming Kearns saw the slacker scandal as a boon to their mutual coffers and never missed an opportunity to perpetuate this falsehood with the press. He turned a deaf ear to the embarrassment and psychological pain Dempsey experienced due to this manufactured scandal. Kearns cared about Kearns. Where Dempsey saw anguish, Kearns saw money. In time, Kearns's double-dealing and callous attitude would only add more fuel to the fire of their eventual acrimonious split.

The bad press stung Dempsey to the core. He gave thousands of dollars to various army and navy relief funds and appeared at countless war bond rallies; however, this did not stop the bad press, which helped the live gate of a Dempsey fight. The way Kearns figured it, whether you loved or hated Dempsey did not matter, only that you paid for the privilege of watching him fight.

Kearns received 50 percent of everything Dempsey earned, be it a title defence, a stage appearance, a speaking engagement, or a movie role. Kearns was often unconcerned when it came to Dempsey's best interests, especially when his own profligate spending habits outstripped his income. Kearns boasted years later that he had used various government contacts to en- sure that Dempsey remained out of the United States armed forces, even though his deferment was based on legitimate grounds. Was Kearns tell- ing the truth? Probably not. For Dempsey, the endless bad press started to place serious doubts in his mind as to the wisdom of retaining Kearns as his manager. Kearns was also leveraging Dempsey's name to sign other fighters to contracts (such as Mickey Walker) without giving Dempsey a percentage. There is no doubt that Kearns was instrumental in helping Dempsey capture the heavyweight title — it was Kearns, after all, who got him the title shot through his exploitation of the national media. The question that Dempsey had to answer was, was the price he paid for such help worth the grief it brought him?

Before he became champion, Dempsey married a sex worker named Maxine Cates. Cates was only interested in his money. After they divorced, she sued him for cruelty, neglect, and non-support. Worst of all, she was the one who vindictively labelled him a "slacker" and accused him of throwing a fight to Fireman Jim Flynn, which was untrue.[2] She was unable to back up any of her claims with evidence. She was financially destitute, and her specious claims were a blatant attempt to blackmail Dempsey into giving her money after their divorce.[3] It was despicable to say he was a slacker, but to impugn his pugilistic integrity by accusing him of tanking a fight was abhorrent in the extreme, as fighting was his livelihood.

Cates made her false accusations based on the terrible advice of inept lawyers.[4] None of her claims stood up in court — her spiteful actions only brought Dempsey more unwanted acclaim. Suffice it to say, by the time his unnecessary "slacker" trial ended in acquittal, Dempsey had experienced more than his fill of personal controversies. All he wanted to do was get back to the business he knew best: knocking men out. In fact, before his second bout with Tunney, Dempsey's most well-known controversy involved his title-winning match against the seemingly unbeatable aforementioned behemoth, heavyweight champion Jess Willard. It was many years after Dempsey had retired and he and Kearns were no longer friends that Kearns, desperately in need of money, began to peddle a false story regarding Dempsey's triumph over Willard in Toledo, Ohio, on July 4, 1919.[5]

The major controversy of Dempsey's legendary ring career, and widely considered the most famous controversy in boxing history, was "The Battle of the Long Count." It would not be an exaggeration to say that the seventh round of his rematch with heavyweight champion Tunney at Soldier Field in Chicago remains the single most debated and dissected round in modern boxing. Over ninety-seven years later, fight fans still strenuously argue about the length of the count and the legitimacy of referee Dave Barry's actions. It is difficult to understand the hold that the seventh round of the second Dempsey-Tunney tilt exerts on the public without first understanding the Mob-infested era in which the fight occurred.

The Dempsey-Tunney rematch took place in 1927. By then, organized crime was making hundreds of millions of dollars every year from bootlegging, prostitution, numbers running, narcotics, protection, and labour unions. They made millions more from prizefighting. Dempsey's first million-dollar gate fight, versus George Carpentier in 1921, convinced the Mob that there was a lot of money to be made in prizefighting. Organized crime was deeply and violently embedded in professional boxing by 1927. Dempsey always rebuffed Mob overtures. He did not want to disgrace himself, or the title, by doing business with organized crime. He despised them, but he also understood there was nothing he could do to remove them. This does not mean they were not involved in his fights after 1921. It just means they circumvented his obstinance by dealing with other people.

The same Americans that derided Dempsey for not serving his country during the First World War routinely lionized Tunney for serving as a marine, although he never saw action. For their original 1926 ten-round title match in Philadelphia, their military contrast was the perfect scenario for opportunistic promoter Tex Rickard. The patriotic, good guy challenger Tunney versus the unpatriotic, bad guy champion Dempsey. Of course, no contemporary scribe ever mentioned that their initial bout took place a full eight years after the end of the First World War.

All the attendant ballyhoo surrounding both of their encounters produced a record sold-out gate for their two fights. It is worth noting that the crowd was cheering for Dempsey in his rematch with Tunney. Dempsey seldom if ever heard such cheers while he was champion. The crowd's positive reaction to him in his second go-round with Tunney surprised and delighted him. But while the crowd of 104,943 rabid fight fans lifted Dempsey's spirits, they could not win the fight for him. He would have to accomplish that feat with his own two fists.

Tunney was the betting favourite going into the fight, but as fight night approached, the odds quickly turned to even money. It seemed that those

Dempsey looming over his fallen prey, Gene Tunney, in the seventh round of their second fight.

fans wanting Dempsey to regain the title were more than willing to put their money down on him. Tunney was viewed as too intellectual, too literate, and too snobby for most fight fans. He was friends with George Bernard Shaw and read Shakespeare for pleasure. It's safe to assume few if any fight fans had similar reading habits, if they had reading habits at all. Tunney was a very genial and kind man, the polar opposite of a snob. Then again, when has boxing ever let the truth get in the way of a fight's promotion?

Dempsey and Tunney had a lot more in common than most people realized. Both men grew up in abject poverty. They both came from very large families and had younger siblings who'd been murdered. Both had to fend for themselves at a young age. Jack Dempsey and his family lived in rural Manassa, Colorado, before moving to other small towns within the state all throughout his peripatetic childhood. Dempsey's father, Hyrum, was a gifted fiddle player, an occasional miner, and, usually, an unemployed drunkard. Dempsey's mother, Mary Celia Dempsey, was the breadwinner and the backbone of the Dempsey family. Celia operated a boarding house/diner for itinerant miners.[6] Dempsey's mother had a very difficult time feeding and clothing the Dempsey children, not to mention keeping them in school.

Gene Tunney was born on May 25, 1897, in Greenwich Village, New York. The Tunneys were a large Irish family and grew up in urban poverty. His father, John, and his mother, Mary, had seven children in all. Sadly, one child was murdered in 1920. Another boy worked for the New York Police Department for many years.[7] John and Mary Lydon Tunney both hailed from County Mayo in Ireland and left for the United States (around the year 1880) to escape the lasting economic effects of the potato famine that had ravaged Ireland from 1845 to 1852. They met, courted, and married in the United States. They then settled down to raise a family in their adopted country.

According to all sources, John Tunney was a boxing fanatic. He simply could never get enough of the sport he loved, whether it was watching professional or amateur boxing at smokers or reading about different fights in New York's various dailies and sporting magazines. The 1880s spawned a lot of legendary Irish fighters (including the original Jack Dempsey, "Nonpareil," then the world middleweight champion), and John Tunney saw them all. His favourite pugilist was legendary fellow Irishman and world heavyweight champion John L. Sullivan, a.k.a. "The Boston Strongboy." Everyone loved Sullivan. He was bigger than life and stronger than Hercules.

Boxing was illegal in New York State in the 1880s and early 1900s. Therefore, boxing bouts were usually held on Friday and Saturday nights, in the basements of various fraternal organizations such as the Knights of Columbus auditorium, conveniently hidden from the watchful eyes of the local police. New York's finest usually did not interfere with these low-level boxing matches — they had been paid off by promoters to look the other way.[8]

John Tunney worked as a stevedore on the rough New York docks at the turn of the nineteenth century and somehow managed to avoid the bloody and bruising battles that were an everyday occurrence on the violent New York piers. He made what was considered a good wage at that time, but it was hardly enough to keep seven children and two parents well fed and well clothed.

Gene Tunney excelled in school. He was smart as well as patient, two traits he exhibited in abundance in the ring. By contrast, Dempsey was impatient and never cared for school as he had already determined at a young age what his future would entail — he would become the heavyweight champion of the world and that was all there was to it. Unlike Dempsey, Tunney graduated from the eighth grade, which ended his formal education. He, too, had to find work to help his poor family. Tunney went about educating himself in earnest after leaving school, becoming an erudite and sophisticated gentleman.

When Dempsey first faced Tunney on September 23, 1926, at Sesquicentennial Stadium in Philadelphia, he was a universally recognized world figure. His long reign atop the heavyweight division had made him a household name throughout the world. His seven years as heavyweight champion brought some much-needed stability and clarity to the sport of boxing. It can be said that Dempsey left the sport of boxing in better shape than when he found it. Just how popular was he? His first bout with Tunney drew an audience of 120,557 delirious fight fans on a rain-soaked night and grossed an incredible two million dollars. It was Dempsey's third consecutive million-dollar gate. No one filled stadiums like Dempsey.

To his own surprise, Dempsey became more popular in defeat than he'd ever been as champion. The reason for this stemmed from the manner in which he graciously accepted his downfall at the extremely skilled hands of Tunney.

Tunney's unanimous ten-round victory over Dempsey was definitive. Tunney had done the impossible: he had usurped Dempsey's crown. Dempsey offered no excuses for losing the title. He was humble in defeat. He said he simply lost to the better man. How could one not love a fighter like that?

Tunney enlisted in the United States Marine Corps in May of 1918. He had actually made his prizefighting debut three years earlier, in July 1915, at the Sharkey Athletic Club in New York City, as a middleweight, stopping unheralded Bobby Dawson in eight rounds. Tunney continued boxing while in the Marines and entered the light-heavyweight division of the American Expeditionary Forces (AEF) boxing tournament held in France after the

First World War. He ended up becoming the light-heavyweight champion of the AEF tournament.[9] His final pro career stats were impressive. He boasted a record of sixty-seven fights with sixty-five wins, forty-eight of which came by way of knockout. His one defeat came against Harry Greb, which he avenged three times. Dempsey's final career ledger sported sixty-eight fights, with fifty-four wins (forty-four KOs), six losses, and eight draws.

Dempsey made his pro debut on November 30, 1914, at the Garrick Theater in Salt Lake City, Utah. He scored an impressive first-round knockout over the unfortunate Billy Murphy. Dempsey would become famous for his first-round knockouts, of which he scored at least nineteen. Contrary to popular belief, Dempsey was taller than Tunney by one inch, standing six foot one. It seemed Tunney was the taller man because Dempsey always fought from a crouch. Dempsey also held a one-inch reach advantage as well, seventy-seven to seventy-six. However, such small advantages were negligible at best. Tunney had fought on many of Dempsey's undercards and thus enjoyed many excellent opportunities to observe and evaluate the formidable champion in action.

For many years, Tunney took copious notes on Dempsey's strengths and weaknesses while studying the champion from ringside. Tunney also became familiar with Dempsey's tell signs, those small things a fighter always does just before throwing certain punches. Tunney was a master student of the game, and his study of Dempsey in action was his doctoral thesis. By the time he first fought Dempsey, Tunney knew exactly what Dempsey would do in the ring, even before Dempsey himself was aware.

Most fighters, especially heavyweights, have difficulty fighting while backing up. Tunney learned his unique backpedalling style while still in the Marines. This is where Tunney mastered the fine art of circling away from and turning his opponents, forcing them to lunge with their punches. Tunney's strict adherence to this fighting style eventually became the prototypical counterpunching ring style. Since Tunney was comfortable backpedalling inside the ropes, Dempsey's patented bull-like rushes did not faze him. Tunney's pro career was guided by the incredibly astute Billy Gibson, who also piloted the immortal Benny Leonard to the world lightweight title. Leonard worked extensively with Tunney prior to his first fight with Dempsey. Leonard stressed that by consistently circling Dempsey and counterpunching, he could effectively blunt Dempsey's aggressive forays.

Leonard told Tunney that his brain was his most potent ring weapon. Tunney never forgot that advice. Ironically, in their famous rematch, Tunney discarded his backpedalling style in favour of constantly attacking the older and slower Dempsey. Dempsey neither expected nor was prepared for Tunney's change in strategy. The older, slower Dempsey was not adept at fighting while backing up — he had never had to do so before in his career. Most great fighters have difficulty fighting while moving in reverse, with the exception of a select few such as Tunney, Sugar Ray Robinson, Willie Pep, Muhammad Ali, and Larry Holmes. As is clearly evident in the tape of the fight, Tunney clinched and held Dempsey far too often and should have been warned about excessive holding, but referee Dave Barry let it go.

Both Tunney and Dempsey were much more than the sum of their parts. Tunney was a gifted defensive specialist. He was also one tough hombre. His ring smarts were the envy of every fighter. He mastered the art of using his opponents' momentum against them, just like Jack Johnson before him. Tunney possessed a fight-ending straight right hand, which he deployed as a devastating counterpunch. Tunney kept his ring foes at bay with ramrod jabs and powerful right crosses. He was very well schooled and was a strong, accurate puncher. More than any other fighter from his era, Tunney learned from his ring mistakes and never repeated them.

Unbeknownst to the public, there existed an element that would dramatically affect the outcome of the second Tunney-Dempsey encounter — the overt influence exerted over the bout by organized crime. The Dempsey-Tunney rematch featured a triangulated tug of war between mobsters from Philadelphia, New York, and Chicago.

It was widely reputed that Chicago's Al Capone bet heavily on Dempsey in his rematch with Tunney, although there is no way of verifying such a claim, especially since mobsters only wagered on fights that were fixed. Toward that end, Capone personally offered to help Dempsey predetermine the outcome of his rematch with Tunney by having an Outfit (Chicago Mob)–influenced referee act as the third man in their upcoming battle.

Dempsey graciously declined the offer, stating he would rather win the bout on the level than through underworld interference.[10] Capone promised to honour Dempsey's wishes. It's unlikely that Dempsey was aware that Capone immediately violated said promise by having a referee beholden to the Outfit, Dave Miller, named as the official third man in the ring for the second Dempsey-Tunney brawl. Capone wanted to ensure that his "bet" was safe.[11] Capone reportedly wagered fifty thousand dollars on Dempsey to regain the world heavyweight crown.[12] Capone genuinely believed the outcome of the fight to be a foregone conclusion, thanks to his personal choice of Miller as referee. Had Capone's referee prevailed, he very likely would have counted out Tunney during that fateful seventh round. It was also rumoured that New York Mob kingpin Arnold Rothstein sent former featherweight champion Abe Attell to offer Tunney one million dollars to tank the fight. There is no hard evidence that such a bribe attempt even occurred. Even so, it would not have been out of character for someone as perfidious as Rothstein to try and fix a major sports event, as he had done so previously, in 1919, with the Black Sox Scandal.

The naming of the official referee for the Dempsey-Tunney rematch had turned into a game of musical chairs played by professional killers. Capone's hand-picked referee, Miller, was pulled from his assignment in favour of Barry, a Chicago bootlegger who, as it turned out, numbered among his criminal friends Philadelphia mobster Max "Boo Boo" Hoff.[13] Referee Barry had borrowed a significant amount of money from Hoff and had worked off his debt to the gangster doing various odd jobs for him. On this occasion, Barry, a well-known Mob confidant and boxing referee, was chosen as the third man in the ring, supposedly by Hoff.

Hoff would not have been able to appoint the referee for the Dempsey-Tunney rematch without the full backing of Owney "The Killer" Madden in New York. Madden controlled professional boxing at that time. It wasn't until the early 1930s that Frankie Carbo and his henchman Blinky Palermo took control of boxing after Madden had been exiled to Arkansas. Mind you, Madden still received hefty envelopes full of cash from Carbo and Palermo, almost until the day he died.

Madden was a vicious killer with a pragmatic mind when it came to deal-ing with other Mob families such as the Outfit in Chicago, which was one of if not the most powerful Mob family in the United States. Madden knew that internecine warfare between Mob borgatas was bad for business. He decided to keep the peace and yet still get his way. It is believed that either Hoff or Madden, or likely both, paid Capone a hefty amount of money to have his personal choice of Miller step aside for the night. The Illinois box-ing officials claimed they installed Barry as the referee, but they would not have been able to do so without Capone's approval.

Hoff had bet heavily on Tunney to retain the title. He had also loaned the champion a large chunk of money to pay for training camp expens-es.[14] Hoff was not the only person to bet large sums on Tunney. This was considered a smart bet as Dempsey was viewed as an old fighter on old legs without much chance of defeating the younger and faster Tunney. This negative view of Dempsey's chances of regaining his title existed des-pite the fact he had knocked out Jack Sharkey in seven rounds just two months earlier.

In fact, Dempsey had been losing badly to Sharkey and was on the verge of being brutally knocked out several times during their fight. The winner of the Dempsey-Sharkey fight was promised a title shot at Tunney. Dempsey knocked Sharkey out cold in round seven, after the mercurial "Boston Gob" had stupidly stopped to complain to the ref that Dempsey had hit him low. No doubt Dempsey had indeed hit him low numerous times. Still, Sharkey foolishly ignored the first rule of boxing — protect yourself at all times! Dempsey later remarked about his knockout punch, which he threw when Sharkey stopped to complain to the referee, "What was I supposed to do? Wait for an engraved invitation?"

It was this victory that catapulted Dempsey into a rematch with Tunney, and a chance to make pugilistic history by regaining the heavyweight title. It also guaranteed super promoter Tex Rickard another million-dollar gate. It is worth mentioning that Hoff, like Capone and Madden, usually didn't bet on any games of chance. Hoff, like all mobsters, only put his money on sure things. What makes the second Tunney-Dempsey fight interesting is that Dempsey came oh so close to knocking out Tunney and regaining the title, which would have made Hoff's supposedly predetermined guarantee of a Tunney victory worthless.

Controversy

The salient controversies from the second Dempsey-Tunney match stem from two simple suppositions. Firstly, if Dempsey had gone immediately to the farthest neutral corner after having knocked down champion Tunney in the seventh round, would he have regained his beloved heavyweight title? In other words, could Tunney have risen before referee Barry had reached the timekeeper's count of ten? This is a question that has aroused the ire of boxing fans and historians for almost one hundred years. Secondly, did referee Barry deliberately ignore the timekeeper's official count to appease the underworld, many of whom had bet heavily on Tunney?

The Decision

Dempsey lost the world heavyweight title to Tunney a year earlier in Philadelphia. Tunney out-boxed the tired, worn-out champion to take his coveted title by a wide, unanimous decision. The rematch was Dempsey's shot at making boxing history, a chance to become the first man ever to regain the world heavyweight title. In that sense, it was even more important than his title-winning match with Willard. Just like in their first bout, Tunney clearly won the first six rounds of their rematch, putting Dempsey so far behind on the scorecards that he knew he had to knock Tunney out if he was going to reclaim his crown. Tunney was much faster than Dempsey. He had fresher, faster legs, quicker hands, and superb lateral movement. Dempsey was certainly in better shape than he had been for their original encounter. He was becoming more aggressive, and effectively so, from the fifth round on.

Tunney eschewed his bicycle in favour of constantly attacking Dempsey in every round, which forced the fatigued, frustrated, desperate Dempsey to focus more on his defence than his offence. Tunney caught Dempsey with a terrific counter right hand in the fourth round, which wobbled the former champion. Dempsey knew he had to move in sync with Tunney and catch him on the fly, which is a very difficult thing to accomplish, especially against a masterful ring artist.

This was only Dempsey's third fight in four years; as such his reflexes were not as sharp as they had been when he knocked out Luis Ángel Firpo in 1923.[15] Dempsey miraculously caught his second wind in round seven and almost pulled off the upset. Dempsey's attacks had been successfully stymied by Tunney up to that point in the fight due to Tunney's excessive holding. Dempsey was expending a lot of energy just trying to disengage himself from Tunney's octopus-like grasp.

During the historic seventh round, an exhausted Dempsey used his last reserves of stamina to move to his left, to cut off the ring and land a murderous straight right hand that temporarily halted the champion's momentum. Dempsey then used all of his ring savvy and punching power to take the champion down. He followed the momentarily stunned Tunney along the

Jack Dempsey hovering over Gene Tunney in the seventh round of their second fight.

far ropes and quickly landed six more savage punches in succession, all of them landing on the concussed champion's chin. Tunney went down as if he had been shot. His eyes rolled into the back of his head. He was out.

As Tunney slowly slumped to the canvas, referee Barry refused to begin the count because Dempsey lost his composure in the glory of the moment — his moment — and neglected to go to the farthest neutral corner. Both fighters were advised in their dressing rooms, prior to the fight, that if a knockdown occurred, the man who scored the knockdown must go to the farthest neutral corner. This is, contrary to comments by some fight aficionados, not the first time this rule had been used in professional boxing.

The farthest neutral corner rule was implemented to prevent a fighter from standing directly over his downed opponent and striking him repeatedly as he attempted to rise, as Dempsey had done on September 14, 1923, to Firpo. Each time Dempsey knocked Firpo down, he stood directly over him and walloped him as he tried to rise. The other rule instituted after that fight stated that if a fighter is knocked out of the ring, he must get back into the ring under his own power, with no assistance from anyone else. This rule was created because Firpo had knocked Dempsey out of the ring in round one; however, ringside reporters helped Dempsey get back into the ring. These rules came into full effect four years before the second Dempsey-Tunney bout took place. They were designed to make prizefighting more equitable, to allow downed fighters the chance to rise and regain their composure before deciding whether or not to continue. It made boxing appear less savage to the general public.

Dempsey knew he was the reason these rules had been implemented — and he was most definitely aware of these changes prior to his rematch with Tunney. It is evident when watching the fight that even after referee Barry verbally and physically directed him to the farthest neutral corner, seconds after Tunney hit the floor, Dempsey still refused to do so. We must once again return to the original question at hand: If Dempsey had obeyed Barry's commands and gone to the farthest neutral corner when Tunney first hit the canvas, could the champion have beaten the official timekeeper's count? Given the film as evidence, the answer would have to be a resounding no. Of course, in pro boxing, "ifs" do not count. We can only rely on facts, and the fact here is that Dempsey had no one to blame but himself. Or did he?

The second, seldom-discussed controversy surrounding the Dempsey-Tunney rematch is, to what effect, if any, did organized crime influence the outcome of the fight? Evidence suggests the underworld did indeed play a large role. Organized crime played a huge part in every (title) fight at the time, so why would the Dempsey-Tunney bout be any different? The answer is, it wasn't. There are a lot of ways to fix a fight, and controlling the referee is just one of them. Referee Barry was known to have been very good friends with Hoff and various other organized crime figures. Barry therefore would not have been able to refuse any favours asked of him by Hoff, Madden, or any of the other mobsters involved in professional boxing at that time. By the way, the Mob never really "asked" anyone to do them a favour. They told them what they wanted done and, if that person wanted to live a long life, they immediately obeyed. It was also not unusual for boxing officials such as Barry to be associated with organized crime. The Mafia ran boxing. You couldn't be in the sport in any capacity without being around mobsters.

As mentioned above, Hoff and Madden were rumoured to have placed a substantial amount of money on Tunney to successfully retain his world title. Hoff had in fact loaned Tunney something to the tune of $250,000 prior to his second meeting with Dempsey, to cover his training camp costs and various other sundry expenses. Mobsters do not make loans to anyone unless they expect the original loan to be paid back — with interest. Tunney, however, believed that being world heavyweight champion indemnified him from retribution if he did not repay the loan plus interest to Hoff. Silly Tunney.

Hoff was confident lending money to Tunney, and for good reason. Mind you, having the referee in your pocket does not necessarily ensure that the fighter you placed your money on will win. There is no doubt that Barry did very much affect the fight's outcome by his actions in round seven. The deciding factor in the famous "Battle of the Long Count" is not that Dempsey initially refused to go to the farthest neutral corner. The salient point here is that once Dempsey did go to the farthest neutral corner, Barry did not pick up the count from timekeeper Paul Beeler, as the rules stated he must.

According to Beeler, Tunney rose at the official count of fourteen, meaning the fight had been over for at least four seconds. But Barry deliberately ignored the timekeeper and started his count at one, which was contrary to the rules. Tunney rose at Barry's count of nine. If Barry had correctly picked up the count from timekeeper Beeler, as the rulebook dictated, at five seconds, it is very likely that Dempsey would have legitimately regained the heavyweight title. So why didn't Barry adhere to the rules of boxing?

This is a very important issue because in round eight, Tunney dropped the exhausted Dempsey to the canvas. Barry rushed forward and raised his arm to start the count, but Dempsey rose immediately, making a count unnecessary. This clearly obviated the need to direct Tunney to go to a neutral corner. This was still a mistake on the part of Barry. Once Dempsey hit the mat, Barry should have immediately directed Tunney to a neutral corner, as the rules clearly stated. Barry did not do that. Would Barry have directed Tunney to go to the farthest neutral corner had Dempsey taken a longer count? Well, we will never know the answer to that question as it did not happen. To claim that the knockdown of Dempsey in round eight was an obvious example of direct bias against Dempsey, as demonstrated by Barry on the orders of Hoff and Madden, is rather ridiculous.

Did Barry owe money to the Mob? Yes. Did Tunney owe money to the Mob? Yes. However, many people in boxing owed money to the Mob. This was not an uncommon occurrence. Tunney did business with the Mob indirectly through his manager, Billy Gibson. Gibson had been having trouble raising the necessary funds to guarantee that the Dempsey-Tunney rematch would even happen. For the rematch to occur, Gibson needed an enormous amount of money immediately and was forced to borrow from Hoff. Who else other than a mobster had that kind of disposable income and was willing to spend it on prizefighting? Hoff later sued Gibson for non-repayment of funds borrowed. This does seem odd as usually the Mob would handle such matters in their own violent fashion, without using the judicial system.

So, why did Hoff sue Gibson rather than send his thugs to collect the money? Hoff decided that by suing, he could embarrass Gibson for doing business with a mobster, thereby casting doubt on Tunney's victory in his rematch with Dempsey. Hoff succeeded on both counts. It should be noted that just because Gibson and Barry owed money to organized crime does not necessarily mean that the underworld directly affected the outcome of the fight. It is, however, something to think about.

How Gibson was not killed is still a mystery. Hoff was enraged at Gibson for stiffing him on the loan and the usurious interest. Tunney's fee for the rematch with Dempsey plus concession revenues totalled well over one million dollars. Gibson could have paid Hoff back at any time. It made no sense to take such an unnecessary risk. Some boxing historians believe there is no concrete evidence that illustrates Hoff had influenced the outcome of the Dempsey-Tunney rematch, directly or indirectly. Other historians believe Barry's actions in the ring that night belie such assertions. Barry, a compulsive gambler, was working off his debt to the Philadelphia-based mobster. It is not difficult to accept that Barry acted directly on the orders of Hoff or Madden or any Mob figure. It is Hoff's lawsuit against Gibson that unequivocally proves that the spectre of organized crime hung heavily over the Dempsey-Tunney rematch. It had become a matter of court record. Hoff's lawsuit was the smoking gun.

In the aftermath of the fight, Dempsey filed a formal complaint about the long count given to Tunney with the National Boxing Association. His claim was denied. Over time, however, the now-beloved Manassa Mauler stated that he believed that Tunney would have beaten the count even if he had immediately gone to the farthest neutral corner. And if anyone knew for certain whether Tunney could have beaten the count, it would have been Dempsey.

Irrespective of Dempsey's comments, math doesn't lie. Tunney was down for more than ten seconds, and in boxing that is considered a knockout. What is often overlooked in the debate about the count is the fact that Tunney was able to rise at all. He had absorbed seven consecutive power punches squarely on his chin and still managed to get to his feet again and survive the round. That was a truly remarkable accomplishment.

Tunney was a very savvy fighter. He wisely took the extra time afforded him by referee Barry to recover his sense and retain his title. Meanwhile Dempsey's graciousness in defeat endeared him to fight fans everywhere. One thing that remains inescapable to this day, as the fight film abundantly illustrates, is that Tunney was incapable of rising within the required ten-second period. In later years, various figures in both boxing and the criminal underworld would claim that Dempsey had told them that he was informed before entering the ring that night that he would not be allowed to win. No one has ever gone on record with such a claim.

It would not have been out of the ordinary for Dempsey, or any fighter for that matter, to be told by the Mob that they were going to lose prior to stepping into the ring. Still, there is no solid proof to back up this assertion; however, stranger things have happened, courtesy of the Mob, in professional boxing. One thing we do know for a fact is that Tunney requested a larger twenty-foot ring instead of the usual eighteen-foot ring. Hoff made sure the request was granted. Did those extra two feet play a part in Tunney's victory? To some degree they did. Dempsey was forced to travel farther than normal to cut off the ring on the ultra-mobile Tunney. He was exhausted after the seventh round ended. Those last three rounds and extra two feet he spent chasing the fleet-footed former Marine must have felt to Dempsey like his lungs were on fire.

The tape of the fight tells the truth about what happened. A dazed Tunney looked directly into referee Barry's eyes at the official count of nine. That would have given him precisely one second to rise. There can be no doubt that Tunney could not have made it to his feet in under one second. It is farcical to suggest otherwise. Dempsey deserves some of the blame for his missed opportunity as he completely lost his focus in the heat of battle and it cost him dearly. Such a chance would never come his way again, and he knew it.

Significance

This was the last major professional fight of Dempsey's legendary career. Rickard offered him a third go at Tunney, but Dempsey turned him down — he did not need the money, and physically, he was spent. He was happy to retire. Undoubtedly, his three-year ring hiatus had severely diminished his skills, not to mention his hunger for prizefighting. Dempsey took his missed opportunity and second defeat at the hands of Tunney in stride. Dempsey's innate ability to accept his defeat in a genial fashion lies in stark contrast to many of today's current champions. Tunney only defended the heavyweight title once before retiring. He stopped the outmatched New Zealander Tom Heeney in the eleventh round, after giving him a terrible beating for the first ten rounds of their affair. Tunney no longer needed boxing because of his marriage to the fabulously wealthy United States Steel heiress Polly Lauder, who encouraged Tunney to retire. The wealth of Lauder's family, combined with Tunney's ring earnings, allowed him to live comfortably for the rest of his life.

Tunney and Dempsey became close friends in retirement. Dempsey, to his dying day, always said he believed in his heart that Tunney would have beaten the count even if he had immediately gone to a neutral corner. Of course, we will never know for certain if that is true, and Dempsey never wavered from his publicly stated opinion. Should Dempsey be taken at his word, if only out of respect? Maybe. Perhaps he just wanted to move on with his life and let sleeping dogs lie; however, it is still difficult to accept that Dempsey truly believed his own comments, especially when you see the film of the fight. The real significance of this fight is that almost one hundred years after it first took place, it still has a special, reverent hold on the imagination of fight fans. Not many sporting events can make such a claim. The seventh round of the second Dempsey-Tunney fight still provides us with arguably the most exciting and enduring moment in all of boxing history. In a rather ironic sense, that seventh round did more to secure Dempsey's legacy than all of his previous fights combined.

CHAPTER 7

PRIMO CARNERA VS. ERNIE SCHAAF

Fight: Primo Carnera vs. Ernie Schaaf
Weight Class: Heavyweight
Title at Stake: No title at stake
Date: February 10, 1933
Location: Madison Square Garden, New York
Outcome: Carnera by thirteenth-round knockout
Referee: Billy Cavanaugh

Background

There have been a number of notable fights in boxing history that have ended in tragedy. Sadly, it still happens multiple times every year. What makes the Primo Carnera–Ernie Schaaf fight unique is that the death of heavyweight Ernie Schaaf was as much about how it was reported as it was about the true cause of his demise. Schaaf's death was unlikely to have been caused solely by the punishment he received in the prize ring; however, certain boxing writers and press agents still perpetuate the cruel myth that the fists of Max Baer killed Schaaf, and that Primo Carnera just finished the job.

The true cause of Schaaf's collapse and subsequent death was distorted by several boxing scribes and press flacks purely for financial gain. This pernicious fabrication ended up besmirching Schaaf, Baer, Carnera, and boxing itself. Why was this false narrative sold to the public? It was done at the behest of boxing's underworld overlords. The Mob wanted to set up a title fight between Carnera and Baer, which would bring them an enormous cash windfall. Portraying Baer and Carnera as ring killers would serve to substantially increase the live gate and radio revenues for their fight. But the truth about Schaaf's death, as we will see, was far different from the printed fairy tale sold to the public.

Whenever a fighter dies as a result of punishment absorbed in battle, his opponent suffers deep emotional fissures. The goal in boxing is to achieve victory, not cause death. A naive Carnera experienced unnecessary mental trauma after the death of Schaaf, even though he was not responsible for Schaaf's demise. Carnera genuinely believed that it was his fists that laid Schaaf low, even after he was legally and medically cleared of any wrongdoing. In a sense, Carnera was also a victim of Schaaf's death, because the media intentionally obfuscated the truth regarding the Carnera-Schaaf fight in their many articles featuring Carnera. Did Carnera kill Schaaf? In no way, shape, or form can Carnera be held remotely responsible — his punches weren't hard enough to bust a bath bubble.

There are few figures more heartbreaking in the three-hundred-year history of modern boxing than Mob-controlled heavyweight king Primo Carnera. Carnera was controlled entirely by mobsters Owney Madden, Billy Duffy, and Walter Friedman. The 1956 movie *The Harder They Fall*, starring Humphrey Bogart, was very loosely based on the life of Primo Carnera. When asked to comment about Carnera, Budd Schulberg, the author of the book *The Harder They Fall*, on which the movie was based, opined, "In the case of Primo Carnera, as we would learn in time, the fix was always in, right up to the championship of the world win from Jack Sharkey. But when the mob who owned him had made their point, the handcuffs were removed from his opponents, and he was defenseless, thrown to lions like Max Baer and Joe Louis."[1] Schulberg attended almost all of Carnera's bouts in the United States.

Former heavyweight champion Jack Sharkey denied for years that he was forced by the Mob to lose the world heavyweight title to Carnera, such was his fear of organized crime. However, several months before he died on

August 17, 1994, at the age of ninety-one, Sharkey candidly admitted that he was indeed coerced by the Mob to deliberately lose the heavyweight crown to Carnera.[2] The travesty happened on June 29, 1933, at the Madison Square Garden Bowl in Long Island City, Queens. Carnera knocked out Sharkey in round six with his right forearm, in a blatantly fixed fight, to claim top heavyweight honours. The result fooled no one and remains one of boxing's biggest disgraces.

Primo Carnera

Carnera's parents had six children in all, only three of which — Primo, Secondo, and Severino — managed to survive into adulthood.[3] High infant mortality rates were not uncommon then in northwest Italy, given the dire poverty, rampant disease, and large-scale famines. Many children were born into and lived in highly unsanitary conditions.

The village of Sequals, Italy, had virtually no sanitation system, which made it a prime breeding ground for a multitude of diseases. Vaccines for different childhood viruses were a thing of the future. It was just as well, because seeing a doctor for any illness, childhood or adult, was not a consideration given that doctors' visits required money, and money was something the Carnera brood could only dream about. Carnera's father, Sante, earned a meagre existence as a mosaic artist, which meant that the Carnera family was forced to live off the land — not an easy thing to do when famines were common. Carnera's mom stayed at home trying unsuccessfully to feed and clothe her family.

As was the case with many impoverished families living in northwest Italy, geography might have been the Carneras' worst enemy, as their village, Sequals, was hit by a series of devastating enforced famines and brutal ground fighting during the First World War. Primo was only nine years of age when the First World War touched his village. A vastly unprepared Italy felt obligated to declare war against the more powerful Austro-Hungarian Empire and Germany, in order to support its allies. Italy could not feed, clothe, house, or even care for its people, let alone outfit and equip a modern army. They were no match for the vastly superior German and Austro-Hungarian armies.[4]

Unfortunately, Sequals lies in the province of Pordenone, which placed it directly in the path of some of the First World War's most savage fighting. Pordenone eventually fell in 1917 to the powerful Austro-Hungarian and German forces; the village was of strategic importance to the German and Austro-Hungarian armies, yet they still proceeded to deliberately starve the already-downtrodden villagers into submission. This was part of their new military strategy of waging war against civilian populations as well as armies.[5]

Things weren't much better for the Carnera family after the war. Primo, who stood an astonishing six foot four by the age of fourteen (due to an overactive pituitary), left home for greener pastures sometime between the ages of twelve and fifteen. There are many rags-to-riches stories in the world of boxing and various other fields of endeavour; however, Carnera's life stands out for a vastly different reason. Perhaps the saddest tale of all, his was a harrowing story of going from poverty to being cheated by the Mob to ending up in even worse poverty. Carnera's ring career served as the prototype for how the Mob would go on to control and bamboozle fighters for years to come.

Carnera lacked the education, intelligence, and wits to fully understand the true extent to which he was being financially violated by everyone he encountered in boxing. In fact, he was even cheated financially by everyone that had employed him prior to his entry into the sordid world of prizefighting, including members of his own extended family. Because of his unsuspecting nature, Carnera proved to be an easy victim for scheming individuals wanting to financially exploit him. Even if he understood how badly he was being fleeced by organized crime, what could he really have done to remedy his disadvantageous situation? Well, truth be told, nothing. No Mob-controlled fighter ever escaped the clutches of the underworld while they were alive.

Anything Carnera might have tried in order to extricate himself from the iron-clad grasp of organized crime, or to expose the Mob's already well-known influence over prizefighting, would have resulted in him receiving an incredibly swift and terrible dose of retribution. Carnera was a victim of his own size, circumstances, and time. His gargantuan size brought him unwanted notice. His circumstances were such that because he was utterly destitute, he had no choice but to seek better paydays in the ring. Of course, Carnera entered the sport when it was wholly controlled by the Mob. The Mob brooked no dissent or disloyalty. Either you played ball or you played dead. Those were Carnera's only choices once the Mob sunk their bloody hooks into him.

Carnera and many other fighters from his era (such as Jack Sharkey, Louis Mbarick Fall ("Battling Siki"), and Bill Brennan, for instance) were easy pickings for the rogues and scoundrels they encountered every day in the sleazy underbelly of professional boxing. Carnera never had a chance. The lack of humanity that touched everyone who dealt with and preyed upon him was staggering, especially among his extended family.

Carnera worked for months for his maternal uncle, Bonaventura Mazziol, as an apprentice carpenter. Mazziol rarely fed him and never paid him the wages they had agreed upon, while at the same time making the mammoth Carnera sleep on a hard floor.[6] Carnera left his uncle's carpentry shop around 1928, and because of his large size, he was able to get a job in France as a strongman with a travelling circus, which paid him literally pennies a day. By the time he became a circus strongman, he stood six foot seven and weighed 260-plus pounds.

Carnera was viewed as a modern-day Goliath. He boxed or wrestled upwards of ten opponents a day. His sheer size and strength always ensured his victory. Carnera had an appetite to match his huge bulk and never seemed to be able to satisfy his gargantuan hunger. This is why in many of his early boxing contracts, he insisted on a guarantee stating he would be fed enough food to satisfy a man of his size. It was an odd request but an important one to Carnera. It also shows you where his mind was at. The starvation he experienced while growing up was always uppermost in his mind. Food was more important to him than money, since he never had any money to begin with, and thus never enjoyed enough food to satiate his colossal appetite.

When the circus made its way to Le Mans in the late 1920s, Carnera was spotted by the former heavyweight champion of France, Paul Journee, who pitched the idea of becoming a boxer to the illiterate, starving, muscle-bound Italian kid. Journee's pro record was dismal at best (eighteen wins, thirty-six losses, three draws). Journee had scored fourteen wins by knock-out but most tellingly had been starched himself an unseemly twenty-three times. Like so many other characters that populated professional boxing, Journee was a con man, pure and simple, and began licking his chops like the Big Bad Wolf the moment he laid his eyes upon the helpless Carnera.[7]

Journee convinced Carnera to pursue boxing full time by training at his boxing camp, located in Arcachon, France. Journee obviously saw an opportunity to cash in big time with Carnera. He believed that if Carnera could learn the rudiments of boxing, which was no simple task, and com-bine that with his phenomenal size and strength, it would be enough for the Italian giant to win many fights while earning some serious paydays. Journee probably went to sleep each night thinking of different ways to financially exploit Carnera's naïveté.

Journee was no ring genius like Angelo Dundee. Journee lacked the requisite skills and smarts to turn a novice strongman into a professional prizefighter. The question that arises then is why did Carnera accept his offer? Well, Carnera had nothing else going on in his life at that time other than working for starvation wages as a circus strongman. He decided to take a big risk to pursue a better life as a boxer under the tutelage of the unskilled Journee.

Journee had a benefactor named Léon Sée, his former manager, who was the main power in French boxing. Sée published boxing magazines, promot-ed shows, and managed fighters. Carnera signed a contract giving 35 percent of all his future gross earnings to Journee in perpetuity. Carnera obviously had no lawyer looking out for his best interests and had no idea what he was signing. Sée then became Carnera's matchmaker and manager, for which he received half of Journee's 35 percent stake in Carnera.

So, even before he set sail for the United States and before he had boxed a single round of professional boxing, Carnera owned only 65 percent of himself. He was soon to lose more than that to unscrupulous American mobsters, once he set foot on American soil. This was just the beginning of the swindling of Primo Carnera.[8] It might be said that any boxer who negotiates his own contracts has a fool for a client. Then again, Carnera knew nothing about Sée and Journee and the sordid history of pro boxing.

Also, with a gun figuratively (and often literally) pointed at his head, who would have had the guts to ask for a lawyer to peruse a contract? It's likely that the thought of hiring a lawyer to peruse the contract never even occurred to Carnera. The fact that he was illiterate only made his situation that much worse — unfortunately, illiterate boxers signing usurious contracts is also part and parcel of boxing history. One can only imagine the stunned gleefulness of the bloodthirsty mobsters dealing with Carnera in the United States once they discovered that the only thing the big man demanded was more food. They could not have robbed him any better if they had used starving wolves to clean his carcass.

In retrospect, the Europeans who first discovered Carnera were no better than the New York Mob. They were supposedly negotiating on his behalf, but in reality, they were simply adjuncts of the New York Mob's criminal empire. This brings us to a salient juncture in ring history. The oft-stated line on Carnera, incorrectly accepted by some historians, is that he was treated well in Europe, until the New York Mob, under the auspices of Madden, got ahold of him. The truth, however, tells a different story.

Carnera was horribly exploited by unscrupulous French boxing figures long before he ever sailed to America. New York gangsters first saw him in France and made a deal with French mobsters to bring Carnera to New York. The New York Mob merely expanded the extortion of Carnera by continuing to fleece him financially, as well as his opponents and the fans. In fact, the Mob never took their hands out of Carnera's pockets. Even when Carnera retired from boxing and went into wrestling (with the help of Max Baer) later in his life, the Mob still stole his money. The Mob hounded him financially almost until the day he died.

Ernie Schaaf

Carnera's opponent on that fateful night of February 10, 1933, was the talented heavyweight contender Ernie Schaaf, the fourth child and first son of Frederick and Lucy Schaaf, born on September 27, 1908, in Elizabeth, New Jersey. In all, the Schaafs would have seven children. Elizabeth was considered to be a real boxing town, with many fight gyms full of aspiring fighters. At the time of Schaaf's rise to prominence, the city had already produced former world welterweight and middleweight champion and future Hall of Famer Mickey Walker, a.k.a. "The Toy Bulldog."[9]

Schaaf's adolescence coincided with the Great Depression. His sisters all took jobs working in factories. Ernie dropped out of high school to get a factory job, too, in order to help support his family. Schaaf came from a working-class family of German descent, and everyone felt it was their job to contribute to the family's resources. This was a sentiment shared by all Americans during the Great Depression. Schaaf's father, Frederick, delivered booze for the local brewery, a steady if mundane job.

Unfortunately for Ernie, jobs were very difficult to come by in those terrible years during the Great Depression. So, Schaaf did what many young boys did back then; he joined the U.S. Navy in 1923. He was just fifteen years of age and needed his parents' consent to enlist. The Navy taught Schaaf discipline and focus and imbued him with a strong work ethic.[10] Schaaf took up boxing while in the U.S. Navy, as had former United States Marine Corps member Gene Tunney before him. Schaaf was not the most gifted boxer in the Navy, but what he lacked in technique, he more than made up for with boundless courage and a willingness to mix it up.

Schaaf was lucky in another sense. He was stationed on the same ship as future world heavyweight champion Jack Sharkey. They became fast friends and would often spar together. Sharkey usually got the better of Schaaf in their sparring sessions; however, this never dissuaded Schaaf, as he was keen on learning and honing his craft. In Schaaf's mind, there was no one better to teach him the ins and outs of pugilism than the gifted Sharkey. Sharkey patiently schooled his young protege in the finer points of the Sweet Science.

Sharkey's influence on Schaaf was immeasurable. Sharkey improved Schaaf's ring balance, which helped Schaaf become a much more effective puncher. Sharkey schooled Schaaf on how to throw hooks off of his jab while at the same time punching in combination. Schaaf absorbed all of Sharkey's lessons well and eagerly incorporated them into his expanding fistic arsenal. It wasn't long before his improvement as a prizefighter was noticeable in the ring. In time, under Sharkey's tutelage, Schaaf became a good, skilled professional heavyweight fighter. On March 11, 1927, Schaaf (nicknamed

"The Tiger of the Sea," because of his Navy affiliation) made his pro debut by knocking out Jack Darnell at the Armory in Elizabeth in the second round.[11] Schaaf's career was off to a good start.

What made the Carnera-Schaaf fight significant is that the winner was promised a shot at the heavyweight title then held by Sharkey. Sharkey, along with Mob-associated manager Johnny Buckley, was Schaaf's manager. The two were very close friends, so had Schaaf beaten Carnera, it would have provided an interesting predicament for both men. Sharkey was considered by the boxing cognoscenti to be on the downside of his career at that point in time. It was even rumoured that Schaaf was considering not renewing his contract with Sharkey and Buckley if he beat Carnera, in order to assure himself a shot at the heavyweight crown. Unfortunately, fate cruelly intervened.

Schaaf was well thought of by the media and fans alike, and the odds-makers had installed him as a solid seven-to-five favourite over Carnera. This was because Schaaf had fought and defeated a much better class of opponents than Carnera, and unlike Carnera's fights, Schaaf's were on the level.[12] Schaaf had beaten such top fighters as Tony Galento, Stanley Poreda, Max Baer, Tommy Loughran, Paulino Uzcudun, William Lawrence "Young" Stribling Jr., and Jimmy Braddock. Carnera, prior to facing Schaaf, had defeated fighters such as King Levinsky, Art Lasky, Brit Don McCorkindale, and Canadian Bud Gorman. These were not bad fighters, but they were not in the same class as Loughran and Baer.

The Mob likely had something to do with the odds being in Schaaf's favour. If the odds had been in Carnera's favour, the Mob would have stood to make no money out of the bout. The Mob was certainly aware that Schaaf was seriously physically ill going into the Carnera brawl. Had Schaaf been in good health, the fight would never have been allowed to happen on the level.

Even prior to his bout with Schaaf, Carnera was not well respected by the boxing media, except for those scribes on the Mob payroll. The boxing writers from that era knew he was a Mob patsy and that his fights were rigged. Even so, the Mob had hired influential writers such as Grantland Rice and Jimmy Cannon to promote Carnera by convincing the public that he was the real deal. Carnera was by no definition an elite-level fighter. He wasn't even a good club fighter. At best, he was a middling club fighter.

However, through repetition and continuous effort he somehow managed to develop a small modicum of boxing skills.

Carnera's enormous size and clumsiness both helped and hindered his ring performances. He would often step on his opponent's feet (through sheer ineptitude), breaking their toes. His massive size (267 lbs.) worked to his advantage as he would lean on his opponents, gradually exhausting them over the course of a fight. Without the power of organized crime behind him, Carnera would have been just another unsuccessful pug. Almost all of Carnera's pro fights were fixed by mobster Owney "The Killer" Madden. Madden was the underworld czar of boxing at that time and he knew Carnera had a chin that could not withstand a stiff breeze, let alone a good punch from an average heavyweight. Carnera's fights were fixed, mostly through payoffs, intimidation, and his opponents' managers, who were also on the Mob's payroll.

Carnera scored 89 knockouts in 103 professional fights, and there is a high likelihood that most, if not all, of those victories were set-ups. There is a rather common misconception among fight fans regarding fixed fights from that era that still somehow persists to this day. It's always been written that the Mob fixed Carnera's fights in order to make huge cash earnings by betting on him to win.

As mentioned in another chapter, there was no betting per se on fights fixed by the Mob. Betting implies the element of risk; the Mob only put their money on fights that were already in the bag. The money placed by the Mob on Carnera's fights was part of an elaborate fraud perpetrated on the public by organized crime and the media members in their employ. For the Mob, it was business as usual.

Aside from their betting coups, the Mob made their money off of Carnera by stealing his fight purses and skimming off the gross gate as well as from the exhibition of the fight films. What differentiated the Mob's control of Carnera from its control of many other boxers is that, incredibly, Carnera genuinely thought that he was actually winning his fights based on his boxing skill and physical acumen. This gives us an idea as to how thoroughly clued out the big man was regarding his own successes. He refused to believe that his fights were not on the level.

Of course, later on, when defending the heavyweight title against Baer, Carnera was quickly and brutally disabused of his mistaken beliefs. On June 11, 1934, at Madison Square Garden Bowl in Long Island City, Carnera hit the canvas multiple times and was viciously stopped at the 2:16 mark of round eleven. The Associated Press said Carnera was knocked down eleven times, while *Ring* magazine founder and editor Nat Fleischer said Carnera tasted the canvas twelve times. Either way, it was a very rude welcome to the land of legitimate fights for the Italian giant. The fight was on the level because the Mob owned a large percentage of Baer. Baer didn't like forking over a hefty piece of his title purse to the Mob, but, like Carnera, there was nothing he could do about it. If Baer had refused to allow the Mob to manage him, he never would have got the title shot against Carnera. Baer and his manager, Ancil Hoffman, knew this was the price of doing business in boxing in the 1930s.

Like all Mob bosses, Madden could not have cared less about the physical or financial welfare of Carnera, or any fighter for that matter. He just wanted his money off the top from the gate gross, the fighters' purses, and the Mob bookies who laid his bets through underworld intermediaries. That's how the mobsters made their dough. For Madden and his cohorts, Carnera was just a means to an end, a bank account to be emptied. Madden took 25 percent of Carnera's gross earnings once the big Italian arrived in America. Carnera's de facto American trainer, mobster Bill Duffy, took another 25 percent of Carnera's gross earnings. Along with the 35 percent he had previously sold to Journee before he travelled to the United States, Carnera now owned less than 15 percent of every dollar he made.

It would only get worse for Carnera. Along with the smaller percentages that were sold to Luigi Soresi and a Madden sidekick, mobster Walter Friedman, Carnera had been coerced into selling more than 100 percent of himself. He must have felt like he had taken a bath in a tub full of piranhas. In effect, Carnera was losing gobs of money every time he entered the ring to do battle. This could only happen in professional boxing.

Carnera's opponent and the betting favourite in their fight, Ernie Schaaf, was infinitely luckier than Carnera when it came to career management. Schaaf did not have to worry about being cheated out of his ring purses — Sharkey and Buckley financially protected Schaaf from the Mob. They paid the Mob off from their interest in Schaff's purse. This allowed Schaaf to concentrate solely on prizefighting rather than Mob thievery. If ever a man was physically built to be a prizefighter, it was Ernie Schaaf. The man stood an impressive six foot two and sported a chiselled, much admired physique. Various popular American health magazines claimed that Schaaf possessed the perfect male body.

Schaaf was a terrific two-fisted puncher, as was evidenced by his many significant ring victories. As mentioned above, by the time he squared off against Carnera, Schaaf had bested the top tier of the heavyweight division, which included Al Ettore, Tony Galento, Young Stribling, Tuffy Griffiths, Paulino Uzcudun, Stanley Poreda, Tommy Loughran, Jim Braddock, and even Max Baer, in their first go-around. This was indeed an impressive list of victories for Schaaf or any other heavyweight. But there was trouble lurking on the horizon. Schaaf was undoubtedly fighting much too often for his own good. He fought from 1927 until his death in 1933. In that short six-year time span, he squeezed in seventy-five professional bouts. That averages out to 12.5 bouts a year for each year he fought, which is just too much sustained punishment for any fighter to physically endure regardless of their ability.

Schaaf faced the former undisputed light-heavyweight world champion and defensive wizard Tommy Loughran. Loughran is still considered by many boxing historians as perhaps the greatest technical boxer of all time. He rarely if ever lost, and when he did, it was usually because he'd been stiffed deliberately or was fighting as a heavyweight. Schaaf lost his first match with the vastly more experienced Loughran and then defeated him in back-to-back fights in April and June of 1930. For Schaaf to beat Loughran in consecutive fights was certainly a feather in his cap and a career highlight. Carnera also beat Loughran later on in his career, although he held an astronomical advantage in weight and height, and clumsily kept stepping on Loughran's feet. By 1933, Schaaf was legitimately viewed as a rising heavyweight talent who was coming into his own as a genuine title threat.

At the time Schaaf fought Carnera, he was not in good physical condition. His poor health had little if anything to do with boxing. Schaaf entered the ring that night against Carnera dehydrated and with a very high temperature. He belonged in the intensive care unit of a hospital and not in the squared circle under hot klieg lights. Schaaf had been suffering from severe influenza for several weeks. The influenza had since developed into a much deadlier contagion, spinal meningitis. Schaaf's severe illness put his life at extreme risk.

This is vital information because Schaaf entered the ring that night as a prohibitive betting favourite. Defeating Carnera was considered a formality for Schaaf. The truth is, if Schaaf had been completely healthy and at the top of his game, it is unlikely he would have been allowed by the Mob to face Carnera, unless he had agreed to lose deliberately. His health that night was in such critically bad shape that the Mob had to know he would not last the full fifteen rounds.

It is simply not believable that those intimately involved in prizefighting did not know that something was terribly amiss with Schaaf when he entered the squared circle that night. Schaaf was given a full professional medical examination by Dr. William Walker of the New York State Athletic Commission (NYSAC), who missed something he was unable to detect in the first place. In other words, Dr. Walker was in no way medically responsible for the death of Schaaf. At that time, spinal meningitis was only detectable during an autopsy.

Carnera was twenty-six years old, whereas Schaaf was only twenty-four. Carnera stood six foot seven with a reach of eighty-five inches and weighed in at 264 pounds. Schaaf stood six foot two with a reach of seventy-five inches and weighed in at 207 pounds. By the standards of the day, Schaaf was a big man; Carnera, however, was a much bigger man.[13]

In prizefighting, physical advantages mean nothing unless you know what to do with them. Other than using his added weight to lean on his opponents, Carnera was deficient in technical boxing skills. His padded pro record up to that point stood at seventy-four wins and six losses with sixty knockouts. Schaaf had a very respectable record of fifty-three victories against twelve defeats and two draws, with twenty-three of his wins coming via KO. The important difference in their records was that all of Schaaf's fights were on the level and had been against superbly talented opponents.

The Carnera-Schaff melee was timid and boring. Schaaf threw very few shots — he was too weak to even maintain his balance and could barely raise his hands up to protect himself. His body was not the body of a taut, physically fit prizefighter. Given the severity of his illness, he had been unable to train for the bout. Carnera, meanwhile, threw his typical feather-fisted jabs, which mostly missed their target or landed with little to no impact.

Aside from being Schaaf's manager, Sharkey was also his best friend and confidant. This was not uncommon in some instances, but this particular situation was indeed unique. Both men were considered the leading heavyweights of their day, so for Schaaf to be chasing a title fight with champion Sharkey while also being co-managed by Sharkey was certainly a boxing oddity for the time. So why did Sharkey and his mobbed-up partner, Johnny Buckley, end up managing Schaaf?

Sharkey liked Schaaf and wanted to help him avoid some of the pitfalls of the game. Unfortunately for both men, the Mob was not a pitfall but rather a structural fault intricately woven into the very fabric of prizefighting. You either did business with the Mob or you didn't fight. You had to pay them what they wanted in order to keep getting fights. Not only did you have to pay them to play, you had to play in the manner in which they dictated.

Schaaf was not your typical prizefighter with typical post-career ambitions. After each of his victories, he would send his mother bouquets of roses and carnations. He attended church on a regular basis and told his mom that he would like to become a priest after his boxing career ended. There existed no anger or hatred in his heart for any man, in the ring or outside of it. Boxing was just a day job for him. It was a way to help support his family during a very rough time.

Schaaf was a mama's boy and proud of it. He often escorted his mom whenever she went out, and he regularly practised Christian kindness. He was innocent as a lamb, participating in a sport that was exclusively run by wolves. Needless to say, whenever lambs and wolves mix, the lambs never come out on top. Just after turning pro, Schaaf's original manager, Phil Schlossberg, sold Schaaf's contract to Sharkey and Buckley. Buckley and Sharkey were better connected in boxing circles than Schlossberg and were

Primo Carnera lands a light jab that knocks out Schaaf in the thirteenth round.

able to fast-track Schaaf's career, getting him important fights with ranked contenders. This helped Schaaf rise quickly through the heavyweight ranks.

Prior to fighting Carnera, Schaaf had complained to his trainer, Jerry Buckley (Johnny's brother), that he had been experiencing very severe headaches and an excruciatingly painful stiff neck for some time. Buckley chalked it up to pre-fight jitters. Is it possible, had Schaaf's claims been investigated by a medical specialist such as a neurosurgeon, that he might have been prevented from stepping into the ring against Carnera? That's not really a fair question to ask, because his affliction was not able to be diagnosed while he was still alive. Schaaf was, through no one's fault, a dead man walking.

Controversy

The outcome of this fight remains controversial over ninety years later. Did Ernie Schaaf die from blows he received from Primo Carnera? Or, did

Schaaf expire from the murderous punches he'd absorbed in a previous fight with Baer? If Carnera's punches caused Schaaf's catastrophic brain damage, how the heck did he last twelve rounds before succumbing in the thirteenth from a seemingly harmless jab? Why did Schaaf not enter a hospital after experiencing unrelenting head and neck pain prior to his battle with Carnera?

The Decision

Boxers at the time often fought while suffering from a cold, the flu, or even without sight in one eye, such as Harry Greb, Tiger Flowers, John Henry Lewis, and Art Lasky. Times were tough. This all happened during the Great Depression — fighters with fevers and injuries still had to make a living. Also, many pre-fight physicals were just perfunctory examinations. However, it's important to note that this was decidedly not the case with Schaaf. In Schaaf's situation, NYSAC physician Dr. William Walker gave Schaaf a thorough examination and pronounced him ready to fight. The doctor did his job and did it professionally.

The only problem with the theory that Schaaf died as a result of blows he received in his previous fight with Baer is that his previous fight was not with Baer. His previous fight was in fact a victory over Stanley Poreda, just one month prior to facing Carnera. It is absurd to claim that Schaaf incurred catastrophic brain damage in his rematch with Baer, yet fought three more times with no repercussions until he faced Carnera.

Schaaf fought Baer twice. In their first encounter, on December 19, 1930, at Madison Square Garden in New York, Schaaf emerged victorious. This was Baer's first fight after the death of Frankie Campbell and Baer was unprepared emotionally to be in the ring again so soon. Schaaf jumped on Baer immediately and crowded and pounded him for the full ten rounds, winning a unanimous decision. The Schaaf-Baer rematch took place two years later, on August 31, 1932, at Chicago Stadium. Baer scored a majority decision win over Schaaf but gave the New Jersey fighter a terrible beating. Baer knocked Schaaf out with just two seconds to go in the final round. Schaaf was saved by the bell but lost the fight by decision.

Rarely mentioned about Schaaf's bout with Carnera is that it was Schaaf's fifteenth fight in twelve months. It is likely he had incurred several brain bleeds in that time that went unnoticed. After he collapsed against Carnera, angry fans shamefully pelted the inert Schaaf with debris as he was being carried out of the ring in a comatose state on a stretcher. They thought Schaaf had taken a dive. Obviously, if he had planned on tanking the fight, he would not have waited twelve rounds to do so. It is hard to gauge whether the seven-to-five odds in Schaaf's favour that night were a true reflection of how sure the boxing public felt about a Schaaf victory, or a manipulation by the Mob to increase their winnings by placing significant money on the underdog Carnera.

The rumour floating around Madison Square Garden that night was that the winner of the fight would get a shot at the world heavyweight title, then held by Sharkey. Schaaf and Carnera exhibited distinctly different ring styles. Schaaf preferred to engage his foes at close range in telephone-booth warfare. Carnera liked to fight from a distance, utilizing his ponderous jab. Also, Carnera had a fragile chin, so fighting at close range was verboten. Schaaf was widely expected to knock out Carnera early in the fight. Joe Humphreys, the Madison Square Garden ring announcer, exclaimed that the fight was scheduled for "Fifteen rounds ... possibly."[14]

The fight drew eighteen thousand fans to Madison Square Garden, which was a good gate for the Great Depression. The fight between Carnera and Schaaf was a boring, lacklustre affair with very little action. To those observers at ringside, it appeared as if Schaaf was just going through the motions, deliberately throwing the fight.

Most ringsiders agreed that Carnera won the first twelve rounds of the bout rather handily. In the fatal thirteenth round, Carnera hit Schaaf with a powder puff of a left jab, snapping Schaaf's head back and sending him reeling backwards. He fell to the canvas awkwardly on his left side, coming to rest ever so briefly on his left elbow. Referee Billy Cavanaugh began his count. At the count of four, Schaaf rolled over onto his front. Cavanaugh counted five and then immediately waved the fight off. The time was fifty-one seconds into the thirteenth round.

The fans booed loudly while Schaaf was rushed to the Polyclinic Hospital where neurosurgeon Dr. Byron Stookey performed a craniotomy to relieve the mounting pressure on Schaaf's swollen brain. The common belief in boxing has always been that when a fighter dies after a bout, the real damage occurred in his previous bout. This assumption is often correct. However, we now know that fatal boxing injuries are cumulative and acquired from too many tough fights in an abbreviated time span. The boxing community and the media stated it was the hellacious beating Baer had given him four fights earlier that had caused Schaaf's death. Such a supposition must have sounded implausible even back then.

The Baer theory falls short when you peruse the full coroner's report by New York City's chief medical examiner, Dr. Charles Norris. The coroner's report was available to the media, as was Dr. Norris himself. In fact, Dr. Stookey, who had performed the procedure, agreed with Dr. Norris's autopsy conclusions, which stated that Schaaf died from the effects of spinal meningitis.

How then did Schaaf manage to make it to the thirteenth round? That's how long it took for his brain to swell just enough to cut off the oxygen supply to his cranium. The boxing media ignored the autopsy report in its entirety and persisted in propagating the myth that it was the fists of Baer and Carnera that did him in. Those boxing scribes knew that claim to have no validity and yet pushed that narrative for many years. Also, had Schaaf suffered a previous traumatic brain injury, it is highly unlikely that he would have lasted twelve rounds against Carnera before finally succumbing in round thirteen. According to neurosurgeons Norris, Stookey, and assistant New York medical examiner Dr. Benjamin Morgan Vance, all of whom examined Schaaf's brain after the fight, Schaaf was a very ill man and would have very likely collapsed and died that night even if he had not entered a prize ring to do battle. This is a very significant point that boxing writers from that era chose to ignore.

The loss to Carnera was the first knockout loss of Schaaf's career. Carnera was as much of a knockout puncher as the aptly named "Two Ton" Tony Galento was a ballet dancer. It was inconceivable to the tight-knit boxing community that Carnera had punched hard enough to critically injure Schaaf. Carnera did not hit hard enough to critically injure a marshmallow. Schaaf is unique in boxing history as he did not die specifically as a result of ring injuries. After the fight, referee Cavanaugh remarked that Schaaf seemed to have been fighting in slow motion.

While the causes of Schaaf's death were contained in the autopsy report, unfortunately, boxing people don't usually read such reports. Dr. Norris specifically stated that Schaaf was suffering from "recent signs of Spinal Meningitis." This meant that Schaaf was extremely dehydrated, very weak, disoriented, and suffering a high fever. The spinal meningitis along with the influenza and accumulated light punches he'd absorbed throughout the Carnera fight caused his brain to swell significantly. [15]

The fiction that Baer caused Schaaf's death was repeated so often that it eventually became the accepted version of events. Such stories only served to create an even bigger gate for the Carnera-Sharkey title match and the subsequent Carnera-Baer title bout. In boxing, truth has never been permitted to interfere with a strong promotion. Dr. Norris was rather chagrined about such circulating falsehoods. In fact, he reiterated his findings on February 18, 1933, in the Saturday edition of the *New York Times*. In that article, he restated that Schaaf's death was not caused by punches he received while fighting Carnera. At that point, Schaaf's brain had yet to fully be examined, but preliminary findings showed that his death was not caused by boxing.[16]

On Monday, February 20, 1933, the *New York Times* printed a much more in-depth article featuring Dr. Norris's specific findings. Parts of the autopsy findings were published as well. The article was titled "Schaaf Suffered from Brain Inflammation; Ill When He Entered Ring, Tests Show." The article went on to state, "Ernie Schaaf, the heavyweight boxer who died in Polyclinic Hospital last Tuesday, four days after being knocked out by Primo Carnera, the giant Italian, at Madison Square Garden, was suffering from an inflammation of the brain before he entered the ring, according to a report made public yesterday by Dr. Charles Norris, Chief Medical Examiner, and Dr. Benjamin Morgan Vance, Assistant Medical Examiner."

Their report was based upon a microscopic examination of Schaaf's brain. According to the report, Schaaf's condition was aggravated by blows not in themselves dangerous, and his condition made him less able to avoid further blows. He'd entered the ring that night with several small brain edemas. Together with the effects of the spinal meningitis, it was enough to end his life.

What we do know is that Schaaf caught influenza right before his fight with Carnera. In fact, Schaaf was so desperate to rid himself of the flu that he went on a religious retreat prior to the Carnera fight rather than going to a hospital. The religious retreat obviously did nothing to alleviate his illness.

There is one other factor here that has rarely been mentioned. Specifically, Schaaf had no other way of earning a wage. Regardless of how he felt beforehand, Schaaf genuinely wanted to fight that night. Also, given the terrible financial downturn plaguing the United States and the rest of the world at that time, Schaaf likely felt compelled to fight, regardless of his dire physical condition. He and his family needed the money, and he could ill afford to miss any fight, especially when an impressive win over Carnera could have gotten him a shot at the heavyweight crown. Fighters have fought with broken hands and busted jaws. Fighters like to fight, and above all else, Schaaf was a fighter.

It is safe to say that Jack Sharkey, who was in Schaaf's corner that fateful night, did not recognize that Schaaf was critically ill, although he knew Schaaf had been suffering from a terrible case of the flu. Often, when a fighter loses his life as a result of a prizefight, it is because of a catastrophic system failure occurring in the boxing safety net. This was not the case in Schaaf's death. No one was at fault in his death.

Significance

Schaaf died four days after the fight, on February 14, 1933, at 4:20 in the morning. Carnera was arrested on a technical charge of manslaughter but was cleared of any wrongdoing after the official autopsy was released. Sportswriters were perplexed as to what to write about the passing of the young pugilist. The press and boxing insiders knew that Carnera was entirely innocent of causing Schaaf's death. The self-anointed wizards of the typewriters implicitly understood that Baer was equally innocent. Even so, they shamelessly blamed Baer and, to a lesser extent, Carnera for Schaaf's death. Sadly, the public believed their stories as Baer's fists had already unintentionally taken the life of a fighter in a previous bout.

Unfortunately for Baer, the inevitable passage of time helped disguise the truth surrounding Schaaf's death. This gross distortion lasted for many years, causing Baer untold grief. The truth was always right there in the coroner's report, which was ignored by many of the boxing media. Boxing press agents felt giving Carnera credit for Schaaf's death would help secure the big Italian a title shot against Sharkey. It did.

The Mob felt that crediting Carnera with a ring death would help to substantially build up the gate for a Carnera-Sharkey title match. It was always about money with the Mob. They cared about nothing else. Schaaf's body was not even cold when the Mob started deliberating about how best to use his death to help further promote Carnera. To give Baer or Carnera so-called credit for the death of Schaaf was not only distasteful, it was extremely insulting to all three men.

In the end, Carnera did win the world heavyweight title by stopping Schaaf's best friend and manager Sharkey in a fixed bout. Schaaf never saw his best friend lose the world heavyweight title, nor did Schaaf ever challenge for the world heavyweight title. In perhaps the cruellest of all ironies, Schaaf was already dead when he entered the ring to take on Carnera. He just didn't know it.

CHAPTER 8

EMILE GRIFFITH VS. BENNY "KID" PARET III

Fight: Emile Griffith vs. Benny "Kid" Paret III (*Muerte en el Ring*, "Death in the Ring")
Weight Class: Welterweight
Title at Stake: Undisputed world welterweight
Date: March 24, 1962
Location: Madison Square Garden, New York
Outcome: Griffith by twelfth-round KO (Paret died ten days later from his injuries)
Referee: Ruby Goldstein

Background

The third Emile Griffith-Benny "Kid" Paret fight was a classic blood feud. These two combatants clearly did not like each other. Their rubber bout was the most renowned of their three torrid battles because of the catastrophic manner in which it ended. All three of their encounters were bruising, savage affairs. Their third fight was by far the most vicious of their trilogy, due in large part to the intense dislike each man held for the other. The two adversaries squared off in that bastion of honesty, the prize ring, at Madison Square Garden. It turned out to be Paret's last fight ever.

The death of Paret caused a deep emotional chasm within Griffith. He never got over it — a large piece of his own soul perished alongside Paret that night. It was obvious to all who knew Griffith that he was never again the same.

Paret's death touched something deep and terrible within the collective American consciousness. Sure, fans had seen boxers get knocked down and even knocked out, but they always got up and continued fighting, if not that night then in their next fight. Not this time. Paret's demise did not follow that time-honoured script. There would be no heroic Hollywood comeback for him. Paret was stretchered unconscious out of the ring, a limp figure on a plywood board, ferried by indifferent strangers to a waiting ambulance. The country would never look at boxing the same way again.

There exists a sizeable, visceral difference between viewing boxing in person and seeing it on television. You don't hear the booming echo of the punches, or the hurt they inflict, when sitting in your living room in front of your television set. Only those fans who have experienced boxing in person fully understand the cruel paradox that is prizefighting: the closer a fighter comes to being knocked out, the more the fans come alive. It is this contradiction that animates prizefighting and its patrons. Nothing brings fans to their feet like the sight of an injured man about to be vanquished. Nowhere is this better illustrated than in the third Griffith-Paret fight.

Emile Griffith and Benny "Kid" Paret were two experienced, highly skilled world champions, and still Paret died. The prospect of a stunning knockout is what drew fans to all three Griffith-Paret fights. It is what draws fans to every fight, along with the real possibility that a fighter may die in the ring — though few fans will admit to this. The fact that both Paret and Griffith openly despised each other was just an added bonus in this instance. Both combatants eagerly entered the ring at the sold-out Madison Square Garden that awful night of March 24, 1962, wanting to score a spectacular knockout victory. The fans both in attendance and at home were mostly unaware of the intense dislike that existed between the two warriors.

The Kid

The popular two-time world welterweight king Benny "Kid" Paret was born in Santa Clara, Cuba, on March 14, 1937, to Alberto and Maxima Crespo. He was named Bernardo Paret y Valdes and spent his early years in the hot Cuban sun, working in sugarcane fields. Paret never had any formal schooling to speak of, which left him at the mercy of those unscrupulous lowlifes who seemed drawn to prizefighting like so many wolves to a freshly killed caribou. From a young age, Paret displayed a real passion for fighting. Most kids only fight when they are cornered and have no other option. Paret actively sought out fights. He entered the amateur boxing ranks at the age of thirteen, and he excelled. His all-action style made him a big fan favourite.[1]

Paret's idol growing up was the charismatic Cuban world welterweight champion Kid Gavilán. Gavilán, also known as the "Cuban Hawk," could always be depended upon to put on a great show. The flash and flare that Gavilán displayed, along with his exquisite fistic skills, appealed to ardent fans of prizefighting. To an aspiring young Cuban fighter like Paret, Gavilán must have seemed like a superhero. Gavilán's ring victories and lifestyle clearly showed Paret that there was a good life far beyond the sugarcane fields of Cuba.

The colourful Gavilán's influence on Paret extended beyond their shared nickname. Like his hero, Paret was exceedingly tough, and gifted with fast hands and feet. Like Gavilán, Paret also enjoyed giving fight fans a show to remember. His refusal to take even a single backwards step in the prize ring endeared him to fight fans everywhere. His exciting, no-nonsense style helped him move quickly to the top of the welterweight division and practically assured him a shot at the world title.

There was, however, one major stylistic difference between Paret and Gavilán that set them apart as top-level fighters. Gavilán was as superb a defensive fighter as he was an offensive machine. Paret, on the other hand, was an offensive powerhouse, a prototypical face-first, walk-in slugger with little defence to speak of. Punchers like Paret typically have exciting careers. But what they don't have are lengthy careers. Early on in his career, Paret showed a frightening willingness to absorb multiple power shots to his head, just to land a few of his own blows. His facility for taking punishment would prove to be his ultimate undoing.

Wealthy Cuban restaurateur Manuel Alfaro saw boxing as an easy way to make a quick buck. On the advice of one of his other boxers, Alfaro went to Santa Clara and saw the teenage Paret fight many times as an amateur. Alfaro became Paret's manager when the young slugger turned professional. Paret fought twenty-four of his first twenty-five professional fights in Cuba. He won twenty-one of those encounters.[2]

Emile Griffith Jr.

Emile Griffith Jr. was born in St. Thomas, in the U.S. Virgin Islands, on February 3, 1938. He was eleven months younger than Paret. Emile was the eldest of five children born to Emelda and Emile Griffith. Next came Gloria, Franklin, Elenore, and Joyce. Griffith remained very close to his siblings and his mother throughout his life. From a young age, Griffith was a very sensitive person, extremely emotional at times and deeply attuned to the feelings of others.[3] He had a rather unusual mental makeup for a professional fighter. He actually did not like to fight. His siblings defended him whenever he was attacked by bullies as a kid.

As a teenager, Emile eventually made his way to New York City (like his father before him) looking for greener pastures. He found a job in a woman's hat shop owned by Howie Albert, Gil Clancy's boxing business partner. This was rather fortuitous as it's safe to assume that not many world boxing champions started out in the millinery business. Clancy trained fighters, and Albert managed them. Griffith's first love was actually baseball, but he fell into boxing by accident and never looked back.[4] Needless to say, Griffith was always in superb physical condition during his boxing career. He enjoyed a brief but successful amateur boxing career. Clancy was a brilliant trainer and a gentleman — Griffith was lucky to have such a wonderful man in his corner.

Paret's American debut came in his twenty-fifth professional bout, on May 15, 1958, against the unheralded Bobby Shell, who entered the ring at New York's famed St. Nicholas Arena with an underwhelming pro record of six wins, seven losses. The six-round fight ended in a draw. Paret was less than scintillating. For his part, Shell remained unheralded. In Paret's defence, he was still getting acclimated to his surroundings in a strange new country.[5]

There were great things ahead for the expat Cuban. Through his next fifteen fights, Paret sported a record of nine wins, four losses, one draw while displaying a crowd-pleasing style. Two of his losses were to Luis Rodriguez (who would eventually win the world welterweight title from Griffith) and Gaspar Ortega. There is no shame involved when you lose to fighters of that calibre. Three of Paret's four professional losses were by split decision, while the other loss was by majority decision, to future light-heavyweight champion José Torres. In other words, even though the split decisions went against him, they were very close fights. Fans knew when they came to see the Kid, they would always enjoy a bruising, fast-paced battle. When Paret was in the ring, retreat was never on the menu. The turning point for him occurred when he faced the highly touted Charley Scott at Madison Square Garden twice within five weeks. He first beat Scott on December 18, 1959, by unanimous decision and then again on January 29, 1960, by split decision. These two victories helped launch Paret into the upper echelon of the welterweight division.

Paret was now beginning to get a taste of the big money. In his very next bout, he fought to a close draw with the ultra-tough Argentinean welterweight Luis Federico Thompson. It was Paret's unwillingness to give ground against a stronger, power-punching veteran that earned him a crack at the world welterweight title.[6]

Paret reached the pinnacle of the boxing world by defeating welterweight champion Don Jordan by a unanimous fifteen-round decision on May 27, 1960, at the Las Vegas Convention Center.[7] Paret fought all out from the first bell to the final. He knew of no other way to fight. Paret's annexation of the welterweight title was quite an achievement because at the beginning of the 1960s, there were only eight weight divisions in pro boxing and thus, only eight world titles. There weren't four world titles for every weight division, as there are today. Winning one of those highly sought-after belts signified that you really were the best fighter in the world in your weight class.

It also guaranteed that your future fight earnings would increase substantially, which is why many world champions defended their titles so frequently.

Although winning a title belt was no easy task back then, retaining it was even more difficult. The welterweight division in boxing during the 1960s was loaded with tremendous talent that could, on any given night, win the title. Paret loved being champion and, like any titlist, enjoyed the cash and perks that came with it. According to Paret's family, he never saw all of the money promised to him for each of his fights. His manager, the Mob-connected Alfaro, often shortchanged him on his ring earnings. What makes Alfaro's actions even more galling is that he owned a piece of the Mob-run Tropicana Latin Club in the Bronx (along with his brother, Tony) and did not need the money he stole from Paret.[8]

Paret's first fight against Griffith occurred over one month after Paret had lost a non-title ten-round decision to Ortega, on Saturday, February 25, 1961. A familiar but unfortunate career pattern was emerging — Paret was back in the ring before his body had had sufficient time to recover from his loss to Ortega. He persevered as always, afraid of disappointing his family, his manager, and the people of Cuba. Fear is a great motivator for a prizefighter.

When a fighter is young and in outstanding physical condition, he can sometimes fight at one- or two-month intervals, as Muhammad Ali often did at the beginning of his career. Paret fought often because he needed the money. The human body's ability to absorb brutal punishment and still perform at a high level is not infinite, though. This is why a champion has to make as much money as he can, while he is physically able to do so. Even for a tough guy such as Paret, the window of opportunity is always closing. The first fight between Griffith and Paret, on April 1, 1961, was a savage, gruelling war fought at close quarters, at the Miami Beach Convention Hall. Griffith knocked out Paret at 1:11 of the thirteenth round to capture the world welterweight title, in a bout promoted by International Boxing Hall of Fame promoter Chris Dundee.[9] Interestingly enough, Griffith had been losing the fight but staged a late rally to capture the welter crown.

At the time of their first encounter, Griffith and Paret were casual friends. They both lived in New York, not far from each other. They sometimes played basketball together. However, any chance of a substantive friendship between them evaporated quickly prior to their rematch, only six months later. Paret and his team publicly used vile homophobic slurs about Griffith during the weigh-in ceremonies ahead of their second fight. Paret wanted to throw the emotionally sensitive Griffith off of his game. Team Griffith was outraged but said nothing.

One of the most well-known secrets in boxing was that Emile Griffith was bisexual. The press never mentioned or even hinted at it in their articles. The assembled boxing media, which was not liberal in any sense, chose to ignore Griffith's sexual orientation as it was not in any way germane to his boxing career. Griffith's sexuality, just like President Kennedy's sexual indiscretions, were topics that the media simply did not discuss during that era. There is no doubt that some of the older reporters, who had covered Joe Louis, did not approve of Griffith's bisexuality, but they ignored the issue entirely as they knew their respective newspapers would never run such a story. During the 1920s, it was known that world bantamweight champion "Panama" Al Brown was gay. It was never mentioned in the media, nor was it discussed publicly in any forum until recently. Even forty years later, in the early 1960s, nothing had changed in that regard as far as the media was concerned. Incredibly, in 1962, homosexuality was considered a crime in every American state except Illinois, and as a mental defect by the American Medical Association.

No one believed at that time (as silly as it sounds today) that a gay or bisexual man could succeed in a sport like boxing (even though there had no doubt been gay boxing champions before Brown). The Mob controlled boxing then, and they were not very enlightened when it came to human rights. The Mob believed that such a revelation could do untold damage to both Griffith's ring career and to professional boxing as a whole. Paret's egregious remarks seem to have thrown Griffith off of his game — in their second go-round, Griffith again fell asleep at the wheel during the middle rounds, and it cost him the title. Even great fighters sometimes lose focus during a bout. For Griffith, it could not have come at a worse time.

Many of those present firmly believed that Griffith was the better man that night. They were raucously displeased with the outcome. Paret suffered two swollen eyes and a cut under his left eye while Griffith remained totally unmarked. Griffith certainly looked like the winner at the fight's conclusion. Their first two punch-ups followed a similar pattern. Griffith dominated Paret for long stretches in the early rounds. Then Griffith lost his concentration during the middle rounds, before staging furious rallies in the championship rounds. According to the judges, Griffith had not done enough, and Paret regained his cherished welterweight title in a disputed split decision. Why did Griffith lose his concentration in the middle of such an important fight? The answer to that question might lie in what took place at the weigh-in just prior to their second brawl.

The Slur

Throughout boxing history there have always been certain unwritten rules as to how far a fighter can go when engaging in trash talk. The rule of thumb has always been to never make it personal. This may be only a tacit rule, but as Angelo Dundee once told me, "Why give your opponent extra motivation to beat you?"

Both fighters had behaved respectfully toward each other before their original encounter. Unfortunately, Paret, in an affront to the dignity of everyone present — including himself — made disparaging personal comments about Griffith's sexual orientation at the public weigh-in ahead of their second fight. Paret repeatedly called Griffith a *maricón*, which translates from Spanish as "faggot." Whether Paret deliberately did this or was told to by his manager, Alfaro, is unknown. What we do know is that an enraged Griffith had to be physically restrained by his trainer, Clancy.

Paret exacerbated the enmity that already existed between the two proud warriors by continuing his public attacks on Griffith's sexual orientation at the weigh-in prior to their third bout. Paret knew he had touched a nerve — he and his handlers repeatedly called Griffith a *maricón* in front of the assembled media. Even worse, Paret was laughing and sneering each time he repeated the abhorrent, homophobic slur. Griffith's terse response to being called a *maricón* spoke to the rising tide of anger inside him: "I ain't nobody's faggot!"[10] Now their third battle took on a new urgency. This fight will be remembered forever, but for all the wrong reasons.

The veteran members of the press flinched upon hearing Paret's words. They thought, *Is Paret out of his mind?* Griffith was a truly great fighter, and to insult him in such a demeaning and public manner was not conducive to a successful title defence. Regrettably, the hard feelings between the two fighters were now etched in stone. Griffith was seething with incandescent rage over Paret's conduct. Their third bout could not happen soon enough for Griffith.

Paret had used the sexual slang of a nine-year-old to insult Griffith. However, this was professional boxing and not some schoolyard dust-up. It's inconceivable that Paret was not aware that he was playing with fire by openly challenging Griffith's masculinity in public, a tactic that served no useful purpose. As a boxer, he should have known that it is always dangerous to take such liberties. Their third brawl had morphed into a battle during which both contestants would fight to decide not only who was the better man but also who was more of a man.

Griffith-Paret III almost took place at the weigh-in. In a move that's unfathomable even today, Paret, unbelievably and to the sheer astonishment of everyone present, upped the ante to a new high (or low, as it were) when both fighters were told to strip down to their underwear to be weighed. Gary Smith noted in *Sports Illustrated* what happened next: "Emile steps on the scales. 'Watch out,' hisses Clancy. Too late: Benny's already slipped behind him, wriggling his body, thrusting his pelvis, grabbing Emile's ass. 'Hey, *maricón*,' Paret coos, 'I'm going to get you *and* your husband.'"[11] It was a brazenly shocking display of homophobia. Incredibly, Paret did not seem to care in the least that he had just offended Griffith and everyone else present. No one present that day would ever forget how quickly the emotion drained from Griffith's face. If looks could kill, Griffith's malevolent scowl would have dealt Paret a fatal blow right then and there.

It is hard to believe that the NYSAC didn't make them weigh in at separate venues, given that nearly the same thing had transpired just prior to their second bout, only six months earlier. Before anyone could fully digest what had transpired, Griffith whirled around and told Paret that he would take his life in the ring that night. Griffith's threat was not genuine. He was reacting emotionally and his temper got the better of him. Still, Griffith's words were chilling.

Clancy calmed Griffith down and reminded him that he should confine his fighting to the ring for money, rather than giving it away for free at the weigh-in. Griffith took several deep breaths and then departed the scene. After the incident, Griffith was asked to pose for photos with Paret. Griffith tersely replied, "I'd better not. I'm liable to swing right now."[12] There was a real sense of foreboding in Madison Square Garden that evening. Many people from the boxing community felt that the bad blood between Griffith and Paret would be resolved permanently.

Both men bristled with kinetic energy in their respective dressing rooms, bouncing up and down on their toes while shadowboxing, waiting to make the long walk to the ring. Griffith always had a warm handshake and a ready smile for his ring opponents. On this night, his gleaming smile was noticeably absent, replaced by a menacing scowl when he came face to face with Paret in ring centre. Such rage can consume a fighter. It needs an outlet.

Both men came out for round one swinging for the fences, looking to score an early knockout. Soon, they fell into a familiar rhythm of mutually agreed destruction.

Boxing matches offer us rare insights into the human condition. At some point in our lives, we will experience intense hatred toward another individual. Hatred is an unbridled emotion, whereas boxing is a sport of controlled fury. Angry boxers rarely perform well. Anger clouds a fighter's ability to concentrate and prevents him from performing well. The truth is that boxing is rarely if ever personal. It is just business. Hatred rarely enters the equation. Paret knew this when he insulted Griffith.

The Third Fight

The first six rounds of the third Griffith-Paret fight, not surprisingly, followed a pattern similar to their first two bouts. The early momentum belonged to Paret, who landed more often and with heavier blows. By round six, Griffith's concentration had once again evaporated. The turning point came when Paret caught Griffith with a huge counter left hook, dropping him in his own corner near the end of the round. Griffith was clearly hurt and his chances of victory were fading as rapidly as his focus. Had the round continued, Paret might have had time to finish him. However, the round ended almost immediately. It was the last round of professional boxing Paret would ever win.

During the one-minute rest period, Clancy didn't mince words. He leaned in close to Griffith's face and told him to pick up the pace, cut off the ring, and let his hands go. Clancy let Griffith know that if he could not refocus himself immediately, he could say goodbye to regaining his title. Clancy's words galvanized Griffith, who came out for round seven with renewed vigour and focus. Griffith became a different fighter. The momentum now began to swing heavily in his favour.

Paret had six rounds to live.

Griffith launched ferocious combinations at Paret's body, finishing each salvo with a booming left hook to the liver — the most debilitating punch in any boxer's toolbox. Griffith's body work paid huge dividends over the next several rounds, as Paret's last reserves of energy faded. Paret's ring sharpness began to wither noticeably in the championship rounds as Griffith's punch rate rose dramatically. It also did not help Paret that both men were using six-ounce gloves, which made Griffith's blows much more destructive. Paret was now fighting on muscle reflex alone. His legs were gone and his punches had no sting. He looked like a man slowly drowning. Paret retreated to the ropes each time Griffith attacked. The latter's quick combinations were coming in from all angles, like a swarm of attacking bees. Paret's head was being snapped back with sickening regularity.

Paret's body was simply no longer obeying his brain's commands. When a walk-in slugger's ring style catches up with him, it usually happens in one fight. For the unlucky Paret, this was that one fight. As the bout ran into the later rounds, Paret was seen gasping for air. He faced a terrible conundrum: If he protected his body to conserve energy, he would then be exposing his head to Griffith's punishing left hooks and straight right hands. Paret's legs were lifeless, forcing him to square up against Griffith, which was an unwise strategy so late in the fight. Paret was in full survival mode.

Just three months earlier, a similar scenario had played out when Paret unsuccessfully challenged Gene Fullmer for the middleweight crown. Paret fought parts of that fight with his back against the ropes, trading huge blows with the much bigger and stronger Fullmer. The champion had pummelled Paret with viciously hard shots, dropping him three times in the tenth round. Paret was counted out by referee Harry Krause after the third knockdown. The fight with Fullmer was Paret's tenth fight within less than two years. Whatever remained of Paret's fighting ability had been pounded into jelly by Fullmer's sledgehammer shots. Paret's career as a viable prizefighter was over. He required an extended layoff to recover his health. He never got it. Retirement would have been a better course of action.

Paret was not in proper fighting trim, physically or mentally, to face Griffith a mere fifteen weeks after being annihilated by Fullmer. After the Fullmer defeat, Paret was a prizefighter in name only. This is one of the eternally cruel ironies of the fight game. Paret, a young man, was now an old fighter. His reflexes were nowhere close to what they had been even one year earlier. This is why in his third and final fight with Griffith, from round seven on, Paret took such a hideous beating. His heart was still willing to fight, but his body had nothing left to offer. All he had left was his machismo, and that was being beaten out of him.

The fight should have been stopped well before the twelfth round. The only question that remained after round ten was how much more punishment Paret could take before his heart gave out or, mercifully, the referee or his corner stopped the carnage. Paret finally reached his breaking point at the 2:09 mark of round twelve.

Every television station in North America repeatedly played the last few gut-wrenching seconds of round twelve, showing Griffith landing twenty-seven consecutive shots to the head of a defenceless Paret, whose arms hung limply by his side. What on earth was referee Ruby Goldstein waiting for? After Goldstein finally jumped in between them, the unconscious Cuban slowly slid down, disappearing into his final repose, the canvas acting as his de facto coffin. Such horrifying images only magnified Paret's graphic downfall. This was one boxing tragedy that could not be even slightly mitigated by words, although, God knows, many writers tried.

Paret's death, by the very nature of television, was intimate and up close. Words weren't necessary because the images told the story. No one who witnessed the fight would ever forget how long it took Goldstein to halt the slaughter. The ghastly image of the battered Paret, his right arm eerily draped over the ropes as he slithered slowly to the canvas, seemed to hang suspended forever in time. Paret was not the first well-known boxer to die from cumulative punishment received in too many ring wars. In fact, between 1900 and 1962, 450 fighters had expired as a result of ring injuries.[13] Why then did the death of Paret have such a cataclysmic effect on boxing? Paret's death was so impactful because it was the very first ring death ever to be broadcast live on American television. The tragedy had unfolded in real time — all who watched became inadvertent material witnesses to the horror of Paret's demise. Television had turned his death into mass entertainment. It seemed to be all anyone in the United States would talk about in the days to come. This was something new and awful, and so far removed from a fan's normal boxing experience.

Emile Griffith was not equipped emotionally to deal with the death of Paret. Who would be? It was not supposed to happen. Such a tragic loss had never presented itself to Griffith as a possible outcome in any of his previous matches. Both Griffith and Paret had achieved the American dream, but at a terrible price. No one who saw Paret perish was ever the same again either.

For some strange reason, Griffith seemed to be cursed when it came to ring deaths. On March 23, 1963, exactly one year after the death of Paret, Griffith fought in California, losing his welterweight title to Luis Rodriguez.[14] That night Griffith shared a dressing room with world featherweight champion Davey "The Springfield Rifle" Moore. Moore lost his title that night to Sugar Ramos and later fell into a coma and died from injuries suffered in the ring.[15] Moore's death no doubt brought back horrible memories for Griffith.

Paret's third fight with Griffith was one fight too many for the faded Cuban slugger. It took place much too soon after Paret's loss to Fullmer. The passing of Paret might have been prevented if the NYSAC and his manager, Alfaro, had acted more aggressively, to protect Paret's well-being after his debilitating loss to Fullmer. Consider this fact: Fullmer demolished Paret and yet did not fight again for ten months, and never won another pro fight. Paret, who was kayoed, fought a mere three and a half months later against a prime Griffith.

The boxing community believed Paret should have retired as world welterweight champion after his loss to Fullmer; however, Paret had never considered retiring from the ring. In the documentary *Ring of Fire*, Paret's widow, Lucy, said that after the loss to Fullmer, what else was Paret going to do with his life? He was illiterate. He had fought too often because his manager wanted it that way — Paret's fights provided Alfaro with a steady stream of income. Alfaro had taken Paret from fighting in smoky clubs in Cuba to the world welterweight title. He accomplished this feat in record time due to his Mob connections. Paret did not know how much money he was earning or even what percentage of commissions from his fights went to Alfaro. He was at Alfaro's mercy.

The record shows that Paret lost five of his last seven fights, with three of those losses coming by way of knockout. His career was definitely on the downslope. Paret's kamikaze fighting style was antithetical to a long ring career. Even more disturbing is that Paret's widow said that had Paret some-how miraculously survived his third fight with Griffith, he likely would have fought again. Boxing was all he knew.[16] The doctors that tended to Paret in the ring post-fight tried to revive him. Failing to do so, they rushed him by ambulance to what was then Roosevelt Hospital, according to the *Oakland Tribune* on Sunday, March 25, 1962:

> Paret was removed unconscious from the Garden to Roosevelt Hospital after he was administered oxygen and examined by three doctors of the New York State Athletic Commission.
>
> After about a two-and-a half hour probing operation Paret was removed from the operating room with his con-dition still unchanged. A spokesman for the hospital said surgeons had found two blood clots, one on each side of the injured boxer's brain. He was removed to the hospital's special service unit for further care and observation.
>
> Paret, who had been unconscious ever since the sched-uled 15-round bout was stopped at 2:09 of the 12th round, went on the operating table at approximately 1 a.m. E.S.T.

A priest administered the last rites of the Roman Catholic Church before Paret left the Garden. Dr. Alexander Schiff of the New York State Athletic Commission performed the operation at Roosevelt Hospital.

Dr. Lawrence Schick, a brain surgeon at the hospital, said the 25-year-old Paret had suffered a cerebral laceration and that four holes would be made in his skull to remove pressure on the brain.[17]

This was common medical practice back then, and the quickest way to reduce the swelling of his brain. Sixty years ago, the current scanning technologies now in use, such as MRIs or CT scans, did not exist. A visit to a medical specialist like a neurosurgeon (along with X-rays) prior to the fight might well have prompted calls for the cancellation of his rubber match with Griffith, and with it, a demand for Paret's immediate retirement. For Alfaro, that was out of the question. He would not allow Paret to pass up such a large purse. Most fight managers back then would have done the same thing.

--- **Controversy** ---

During the pre-fight weigh-in, Paret called Griffith a *maricón* and then stepped on the scales to simulate sodomizing his foe in full view of the press and public. Why did he do this?

And why did Paret fight Griffith so soon after his brutal loss to Fullmer? Wasn't he entitled to some time off? Why did Alfaro deliberately ignore Paret's physical complaints? Was the NYSAC even aware of them? Had anyone from the NYSAC seen the Fullmer fight that took place at the Las Vegas Convention Center on December 9, 1961? Why didn't the NYSAC step in and order Paret to undergo a neurological examination after the Fullmer fight?

Paret was receiving forty thousand to fifty thousand dollars per fight once he hit the championship level. Why then, at the time of his death, was he financially insolvent?

The doctors who examined Paret post-fight believed the physical abuse he'd received in the Fullmer fight did not exacerbate his demise. How did they come to such a determination, and were they correct?

Why did referee Goldstein wait so long to stop the fight? Who was responsible for Paret's death?

The Decision

Paret had complained to his wife and manager numerous times following the Fullmer fight, citing terrible headaches, nose and ear bleeds, and neck pain. These symptoms became more acute the night immediately before his third bout with Griffith. These were definite red flags that he was in no shape to continue boxing. These symptoms were ignored by Alfaro and the NYSAC. It should have been glaringly obvious to the NYSAC doctors that Paret was in no shape to fight again a mere seventy-seven days after losing to Fullmer.

Such complaints would seem to indicate that he was suffering from an undetected brain injury. Often, when a fighter dies as a result of a beating or beatings he took in the ring, reporters and the boxing community remark that although the outcome is indeed tragic, it is just one of those things that sometimes occurs. Deaths in boxing are rare but statistically, they are more common than you think. Boxing has a built-in safety net that works 99 percent of the time. When it fails, and in Paret's case it failed spectacularly, boxers die. It's difficult to affix the blame for Paret's demise to any one party (with the exception of his manager, Alfaro) because his death was the result of an unlikely confluence of disparate events.

The most famous controversy surrounding this bout involved the homophobic slurs uttered by Paret. He insisted on calling Griffith a *maricón* hundreds of times. And while his comments about Griffith's sexuality, insensitive though they were, did not directly lead to the champion's death, they are part of the overall story. While there is no excuse for Paret's actions or comments, the reason for them might have had something to do with his upbringing. While growing up in Cuba, Paret was reared in the Spanish ethos of machismo, which stresses an exaggerated and aggressive masculinity. This Latin life view arose during the 1930s and 1940s, when Paret was coming of age in Cuba.

The machismo ethic played into Paret's take-no-prisoners boxing style. As an adult, it informed Paret's world view. Homosexuality was viewed as the polar opposite of machismo at that time. The boxing world has never been a progressive environment. It likely never occurred to the boxing community that a man could be gay and macho at the same time, although, as the law of averages dictates, some fighters were undoubtedly tough and gay.

As a world champion prizefighter, Paret viewed himself as the personification of machismo. Is it possible that Paret's skewed interpretation of the principles of machismo allowed him to view Griffith as beneath him because he was gay or bisexual? Perhaps. We also have to consider the possibility that the substantial brain trauma Paret had incurred up to that point in his career may have also played a factor regarding his demeaning of Griffith's masculinity. To salaciously degrade an opponent's masculinity was not uncommon then or now in professional boxing circles. Whatever the reason for his actions, Paret assumed he could openly cast aspersions on Griffith's sexual orientation without suffering any repercussions. He thought wrong. Paret's insults made Griffith fight that much harder. It never dawned on Paret or his team that they were the only ones amused by his actions. No one else at the weigh-in was laughing. Paret and his handlers kept up their stream of noxious abuse right up to the opening bell.

Undoubtedly, Paret was fighting Griffith much too soon after his loss to Fullmer. Even Fullmer believed that Paret had engaged Griffith in their rubber bout too quickly. Fullmer summed up his dismantling of Paret as follows:

> Paret was one of the toughest guys I'd ever fought as far as actual tough. I never hit anybody more punches harder than I hit Paret. I beat Paret like I never beat anybody in my life. And he fought way too early again in his next fight and, of course, he died. A lot of people say that I killed Paret, which I'm not taking credit for killing him because this is not something a guy wants to take credit for, but I know I beat him so bad he should have never fought that

early again. It was the commission's fault for allowing that fight to go on because he took a terrible beating, because I didn't feel like fighting again in six months and I'd won! And I didn't take nothing compared to what he took. So, I know that they rushed him way too fast into this fight [with Emile Griffith] and it consequently killed him. The blame was the commission. It had to be the commission's fault after a beating that was unbelievable, being punched so hard even when he wasn't down. He was hurt.

Fullmer's comments were not only poignant but true. Fullmer cannot be held responsible for Paret's death. He did not force Paret to fight again three months later. After Paret's loss to Fullmer, trainer Angelo Dundee told Alfaro that Paret was a shot fighter and that another fight could be fatal. Alfaro's response to Dundee spoke volumes about where his real interests lay: "If something bad happens, I will have to go back to Cuba and find me another boy."[18] Such callousness permeates boxing to the core. Why did Paret go through with the Griffith fight if he was not feeling up to par? He was, like so many other great fighters, too stubborn for his own good. The night before the fatal fight with Griffith, Paret spoke to his wife over the phone. He said he did not feel good and that he felt something was seriously wrong with his head. Paret's brain was likely still swollen from the Fullmer fight and probably bleeding. Paret can be seen blinking during both the Fullmer and Griffith fights, which is a clear sign of catastrophic brain trauma. When his wife suggested he pull out of the fight, Paret said that Alfaro would not let him do so because too much money was at stake and contracts had to be honoured. Paret's sense of fealty to his manager was sadly never reciprocated.

Interestingly, Paret's forty-thousand-dollar purse for his final scrap with Griffith went missing after the bout. Paret's widow, Lucy, thought that Alfaro may have absconded with it although there is no evidence to substantiate such a claim.[19] Alfaro, and likely Paret himself, thought he had one more good fight left in him. All fighters believe that, otherwise how could they ever go into battle? Doubt is a luxury that fighters cannot afford.

Did the NYSAC doctors miss Paret's physical complaints during their pre-fight examination of him? Well, unfortunately, we have no way of knowing this because it is likely that Paret never mentioned any of his symptoms to the commission's doctors. With the fight so close, Paret probably did not want to risk losing a big payday and seriously upsetting his Mob-controlled manager. The NYSAC could have forced Paret to undergo a full medical examination before he entered the ring, which would have been the wise thing to do given the severity of his previous defeat. This would have allowed the NYSAC to publicly indemnify themselves in case something adverse happened in the third Griffith fight. The NYSAC chose not to do so.

Why didn't Paret's manager send him to a doctor after his loss to Fullmer? Alfaro and Paret were probably equally terrified that a visit to a medical specialist would leak out to the press, jeopardizing their future ring earnings. Keeping a fighter's injuries or physical complaints quiet was not considered abnormal behaviour at that time. Boxers were expected to "suck it up" and fight while injured. Such dismissive attitudes are still very much a part of the ethos of boxing today.

Venerable referee Goldstein received a lot of blame over Paret's death. He was accused of waiting too long to stop the fight. Goldstein's inaction haunted him for decades. There is no doubt that Goldstein was one of the most skilled referees that boxing has ever produced. On this night, however, he fell short. It was crystal clear that Paret was unconscious and therefore defenceless after Griffith landed his initial flurry of power shots. Goldstein said afterward, "I never thought there was a possibility of Paret being hurt when I looked at him. He had been known as a courageous fighter, one who could lose a round and come back and win the next. I had only seconds to act. I still believe I did the right thing."[20]

In deference to Goldstein, there were many people in boxing who believed that he acted appropriately. I am sure, had he lived, Paret might have offered a dissenting opinion. In the film of the fight, we see Griffith land almost thirty consecutive shots to Paret's unprotected head before Goldstein jumped in and stopped the carnage. After watching this, it is hard to believe that Goldstein did not freeze. Goldstein thought, as did most referees back then, that since Paret was a world champion, he deserved a chance to recover from Griffith's initial onslaught. Perhaps he was playing possum; however, a veteran referee like Goldstein should have been able to tell the difference between a thoroughly beaten fighter and one playing possum.

Goldstein never refereed another prizefight. The salient question here is, if Goldstein had stopped the fight sooner, would it have made any difference to Paret's eventual outcome? Probably not. It was Griffith's first flurry of power shots that caused the fatal damage, and you can't blame Goldstein for that.

The Medical Viewpoint

We know that boxers and football players incur cumulative brain injuries over the course of their careers. More than likely Paret died from a career's worth of head trauma. We can never know for sure because no X-rays of Paret's brain were ever taken prior to his third bout with Griffith.

Sometimes it takes just one bad beating at the hands of an opponent to expose the extent of brain trauma a fighter has experienced. That said, Paret's autopsy made clear that his previous fights did not factor into his death. The April 4, 1962, edition of the *Fresno Bee* published the following story:

> NEW YORK — An autopsy report on Benny (Kid) Paret says he died of brain battering suffered in the Madison Square Garden ring March 24th — and there was "no gross evidence of old brain injury." Before the autopsy, there had been speculation that Paret's knockout last December by Gene Fullmer, the National Boxing Association's middle-weight champion, might have contributed to Paret's death.
>
> New York City's chief medical examiner, Dr. Milton Helpern, reported death was caused by complications of brain injuries sustained as a result of the boxing "bout" March 24th. Dr. Helpern performed a four and one half hour autopsy in Bellevue Hospital a few hours after the 25 year old Paret died in Roosevelt Hospital. The report described hemorrhages in the brain caused by blows, and

concussion. It also mentioned the pneumonia that developed the day before Paret died. He had been in a coma since he was carried out of the ring. Paret died of pneumonia ten days after collapsing in the ring against Griffith.[21]

So, according to medical science, the commonly accepted boxing wisdom about the "fight before" the fatal fight causing a fighter's death was, on the surface, erroneous. Or was it? The beating he absorbed from Fullmer might not have caused the most recent edemas in Paret's brain, but they certainly exacerbated brain bleeds that were already present. How could they not? We know for a fact that Paret had experienced nose and ear bleeds, neck stiffness, and severe headaches prior to his third match with Griffith, but that is never mentioned in the autopsy report. It is unlikely that Dr. Helpern was aware of these pre-fight symptoms. Could something other than boxing have caused such symptoms? Yes, but that is unlikely in Paret's case.

NEW YORK DAILY NEWS
Wednesday, April 4th, 1962
By Jim McCulley
Dr. Charles P. Larson, Tacoma, Wash., pathologist and president of the National Boxing Association, came to the defense of the sport.

At Tacoma, Dr. Larson, head of the NBA, told reporters: "At the risk of incurring the ire of second guessers, I must defend boxing. Fatalities are common in other sports, but I hear no hue and cry to abolish them." Larson asked that boxing be judged without malice. "Are we," he asked, "because of this incident going to destroy boxing programs which have as their objective the making of a lad into a physically fit man?"[22]

Of course, Dr. Larson conveniently omitted the fact that boxers suffering injuries during fights is not an anomaly but rather a common occurrence. Yes, he was correct in noting that athletes are injured (sometimes fatally) in all contact sports; however, unlike with other sports, in boxing, the intent of a boxer is to achieve victory by causing injury to his opponent. Dr. Helpern responded to Dr. Larson's ludicrous statement in the same *New York Daily News* article of Wednesday, April 4, 1962, as reported by Jim McCulley. Dr. Helpern issued a more comprehensive statement than the one quoted above, after performing the autopsy on the body of Paret, who died at 1:55 a.m. Wednesday:

> Death was caused by complications of brain injuries sustained as a result of the boxing bout. These injuries consisted of scattered small traumatic hemorrhages in the brain substance and were associated with cerebral concussion. There were also small subdural (under the outermost covering of the brain) hemorrhages that resulted from tearing of small veins extending from the surface of the brain. As a result of the injuries, edema or swelling, of the brain occurred which, despite surgical evacuation of the subdural hemorrhages, continued to produce additional irreversible damage to the brain structure ... there was a terminal severe bilateral broncho-pneumonia which developed during the prolonged comatose state. The autopsy did not reveal any gross evidence of old brain injury.[23]

By stating that there was no gross evidence of an old brain injury, Dr. Helpern was implying that the beating Paret suffered in his losing bout with Fullmer did not contribute to his death. Why did Dr. Helpern make such a comment? Primarily because he was effectively prevented from determining if Paret's brain had suffered trauma in earlier fights because Paret's brain was simply too swollen to see any previous injuries that might have been present. Dr. Helpern could only report what he actually saw. It isn't that such injuries were not there but more so that they could not be detected at that specific time. In addition, Paret developed pneumonia while in a coma following his third bout with Griffith. This contributed to his demise.

Paret's manager, Alfaro, claimed post-fight that he was about to throw in the towel. Really? What took him so long? He should have thrown in the towel one fight earlier. Alfaro also declared, "I screamed for Goldstein to stop it, but apparently he didn't hear me."[24] Excuses are always easy to come by after the fact. Had Alfaro really wanted to protect Paret, he could have stepped into the ring, immediately disqualifying Paret but forcing Goldstein to stop the fight. Why did the NYSAC doctors pronounce Paret fit to fight? Well, back then, most pre-fight medical examinations were superficial. On the surface, Paret probably appeared fit and healthy and ready to wage war. The damage that proved to be his undoing was internal, not external, something only a highly trained specialist would have caught.

Without being apprised of his pre-fight symptoms, the NYSAC doctors had no way of knowing that Paret had likely suffered severe brain trauma in his bout with Fullmer. According to the Tuesday, April 3, 1962, edition of the *Lima Citizen*, "Commission doctors who examined Paret before Saturday night's bout pronounced him in excellent condition."[25] Paret had engaged in six extremely tough fights from December 10, 1960, until his final fight on March 24, 1962. No brain can survive that kind of punishment. Ultimately, it was Paret's almost biblical eye-for-an-eye style of fighting that cost him his life.

Paret was critically injured during the Fullmer fight, and Griffith's punches just finished the job. Could Paret's death have been prevented? Probably not. Fighters fight and boxing was part of Paret's soul. Would he have lived if he had taken six months or a year off after the Fullmer fight? There's simply no way of knowing.

Significance

The third bout between Paret and Griffith is significant because it was the first time a fighter's death was broadcast live across America. The immediate significance of Paret's death was that ABC dropped boxing from its schedule. It would be almost a decade before live boxing events appeared again on the ABC network. No significant changes occurred in pro boxing after Paret's death. Boxing has always maintained the fiction that ring deaths are anomalies, when in fact they are the norm. After Paret's death, there were the usual calls for banning boxing. These protests have rarely, if ever, led to any significant changes in the sport.

No fighter gets out of boxing unscathed. Even those who appear to retire undamaged eventually fall prey to dementia. Did Griffith change his style after Paret's death? Well, he fought on for another fifteen years and eighty-one fights, scoring just eleven knockouts. He was mostly content to win the majority of his fights by decision. He lived in constant fear that history might repeat itself in the ring. His "killer instinct" had been greatly diminished. Sadly, Griffith suffered from dementia pugilistica near the end of his life. Ultimately, the true culprits in Paret's death were the NYSAC and Manuel Alfaro. Paret should have been suspended indefinitely or forced to retire after losing to Fullmer. That would have been the prudent thing to do. Of course, throughout boxing history, prizefighting and prudency have seldom, if ever, crossed paths.

CHAPTER 9

MUHAMMAD ALI VS. SONNY LISTON II

Fight: Muhammad Ali vs. Sonny Liston II
Weight Class: Heavyweight
Title at Stake: World heavyweight
Date: May 25, 1965
Location: Central Maine Civic Center, Lewiston, Maine
Outcome: Ali by first-round knockout
Referee: Jersey Joe Walcott

Background

Along with the second Dempsey-Tunney fight, the rematch between the newly named world heavyweight champion Muhammad Ali and challenger Charles "Sonny" Liston is considered the most controversial heavyweight title bout in modern boxing history. The outcome of Ali-Liston II still remains shrouded in mystery and unproven conspiracy theories, which fight fans debate even today.

There is no doubt that the fleet-footed Ali caught an off-balance Liston coming in with a legitimate, hard, straight counter right hand (over Liston's lazy left jab), which froze the challenger for a split second before depositing him on the canvas. In fact, anyone who has seen the film of the fight will notice that at the opening bell, Liston immediately came out and threw a ponderous left jab at Ali, which the champion easily slipped and then countered with a lightning quick hard right hand to the head. This was the exact same combination of moves with which he knocked out Liston over a minute later, in the same round. The only difference was that Ali was flat-footed when he threw the second right hand.

Everything happened so quickly that many of those in attendance actually missed Ali's lightning-fast counter right hand, which dropped Liston to the mat. The bedlam that ensued in the ring after the knockdown didn't exactly help clarify the already-existing confusion. Ali himself was surprised, which is why he stood over the fallen Liston screaming at him to rise. That image of Ali (photographed by the brilliant photographer Neil Leifer), in all his ascendant glory, is the single most famous photograph in sports history.

Up until the knockdown, Liston was simply chasing Ali rather than smartly cutting off the ring and cornering the new champion. Liston was slow, plodding, and throwing only half-hearted jabs and right hands to Ali's body and head, which were woefully short of the mark. The former champion managed to land several mediocre, light shots to Ali's body. Liston's timing was off and his punching accuracy was non-existent. Liston seemed to be listless, almost uninterested in fighting. He appeared to just be going through the motions of boxing. There was no urgency to his actions, as there must be when fighting for a world title.

Everything that happened in the ring after Liston hit the canvas has been the source of many bar arguments, wild conjecture, and unproven armchair opinions for six decades. No one in attendance that night could agree on precisely what transpired on that bizarre evening in Lewiston, Maine.

Liston never saw the shot that dropped him. As Angelo Dundee accurately pointed out after, "He hit him with a shot Liston didn't see. They're the ones that knock you out."[1] Liston himself said years later that he simply got caught with a good shot to the temple, which disoriented and dropped him. Liston originally said he stayed down to protect himself, because Ali refused to go to a neutral corner and was prancing around the ring like a madman. The film of the fight proves that Liston was telling the truth. Ali only stopped long enough to scream at Liston, "Get up, you big bum!"

Liston rose to one knee after the knockdown. It is evident only when Ali ran by him, celebrating wildly, that Liston went down again in what looked like a swan dive. Perhaps Liston was still disoriented. Liston was concerned, or so he later claimed, that Ali might bump or hit him while he was in the process of getting up. That was not an unreasonable concern. In retrospect, it is rather remarkable that Ali didn't collide with Liston while running around the ring like a lunatic with a hotfoot.

It is abundantly clear that the moment Liston hit the canvas, the fight descended into chaos. That's the only point everybody agrees on. Referee Jersey Joe Walcott futilely tried to physically guide Ali to a neutral corner several times but to no avail. Ali simply ignored him and continued running around the ring. Walcott supposedly never heard or even visually picked up timekeeper Francis McDonough's knockdown count. Once Liston got to his feet, Ali, only a few feet away, was chomping at the bit to attack him again. Walcott, who was standing between both warriors, unbelievably just walked away to the far side of the ring without calling time and sending the fighters back to their respective corners. Walcott had gone to confer with *Ring* magazine founder Nat Fleischer. This only added to the confusion.

With Walcott temporarily out of the picture, Ali jumped on Liston with a fierce barrage of punches, only some of which landed. Walcott then reappeared, and just as suddenly as the fight began, it was over, stopped by Walcott, per Fleischer's instructions, because Liston had been on the canvas for more than ten seconds. Estimates differ, but Liston was reputedly on the canvas for between 16.25 and 16.73 seconds. This was the moment when chants of "Fix!" began to emanate from the crowd. No one experienced more disbelief regarding the fight's sudden stoppage than Ali and Liston.

Sadly, for both fighters, the moment Liston hit the canvas, all hell broke loose and proper decorum in the ring was never restored. The fault for the pandemonium that immediately ensued, after Liston was dropped, lies with three individuals. To a large extent, Walcott fumbled the ball by losing control of the fight. Fleischer improperly interfered with the outcome by imposing himself on the proceedings. Ali knew the rules and should have immediately gone to the farthest neutral corner and stayed there. It is more than likely that an experienced, veteran referee, such as Barney Felix or George Latka, would have exercised proper control over the situation. Unfortunately, we'll never know.

Walcott should have ignored Fleischer entirely as he was there covering the match for *Ring* magazine and not present in any official capacity. Walcott should only have spoken with knockdown timekeeper McDonough. He didn't. After conferring with just Fleischer, Walcott walked back to centre ring and declared the fight over. This was how the "fix" controversy, which persists (unfounded) to this day, began.

Walcott neglected to call time for three reasons: he was not an experienced, veteran referee; Fleischer had distracted him, disrupting his thought process; and more importantly, Ali was ignoring Walcott's explicit instructions and cavorting around the ring as if he was getting ready to take flight. To be frank, Walcott was in over his head. McDonough has been unfairly criticized over the years for not hitting the canvas with his hand to indicate the count, and for not using his fingers as a visual aid to help Walcott see the exact count. That criticism is simply wrong as you can clearly hear him hit the canvas with his hand ten times. After McDonough had slapped the mat for the tenth and final time, Liston's right knee was still on the canvas. That is indisputably a knockout.

Timekeeper McDonough said he had in fact given a hand count but that Walcott never looked at him. McDonough, as it turned out, did his job perfectly. Getting Walcott to look at him was not part of his duties. Did Walcott know to look at the knockdown timekeeper in order to pick up the official count from him? Yes, he did. So why didn't he do so? Obviously because his attention was being diverted by Ali and Fleischer's post-knockdown shenanigans. The end of the Ali-Liston rematch was befuddling to many. The mass confusion stemmed from a confluence of seven separate but related incidents that occurred within seconds of each other, and combined to turn the fight into a fiasco:

1. Ali knocked Liston down and then proceeded to run around the ring like a wild man, refusing to obey Walcott's command to go to the farthest neutral corner.

2. Walcott neglected to call time, which would have stopped the official knockdown timekeeper's count.
3. Walcott was unable to get Ali to go to the farthest neutral corner.
4. Nat Fleischer illicitly imposed himself into the proceedings by calling Walcott over.
5. Walcott mistakenly left the action after Liston had risen to confer with Nat Fleischer when he should have only spoken with McDonough.
6. Walcott was unable to hear McDonough's count over the crowd because McDonough had no device such as a microphone with which to amplify his voice.
7. Walcott mistakenly listened to Fleischer and then waved off the fight.

Was Liston legitimately knocked out by Ali? Yes. Liston was on the canvas for more than ten seconds, according to the official timekeeper. That is unequivocally a knockout. This point is inarguable. Although an extremely bewildering set of circumstances occurred after the knockdown, which anyone would have had trouble following, as Walcott demonstrated, it still doesn't diminish the fact that Ali won the fight.

To fully understand the outrage over the outcome of the second fight between Ali and Liston, it is necessary to understand the drama and the controversy that preceded it. The original rematch between them was scheduled to take place at Boston Garden in Boston, Massachusetts, on November 16, 1964. The fact that a rematch was even taking place raised a self-righteous stink within the World Boxing Association (WBA).

Liston's Mob-appointed manager Jack Nilon had set up Inter-Continental Promotions Inc. to control the promotions of the closed-circuit viewings of Liston's title fights. The Mob believed, as did everyone else, that Liston would have many successful title defences. They were looking well past Cassius Clay, who was considered to be nothing more than an easy first defence for Liston. It's worth noting at this point that Blinky Palermo associate Sam Margolis and several other mobsters owned many shares in

Inter-Continental Promotions Inc.[2] This is not surprising as Liston was a mobbed-up fighter from the very beginning of his ring career. Nilon, by the way, resigned as Liston's manager in early September 1964.[3] Liston was an unpredictable and often uncontrollable character, even on his best days, and Nilon's already-nervous constitution could no longer withstand the stress that came with trying to control Liston on a daily basis. After Clay/Ali crushed Liston to capture the heavyweight title, Inter-Continental Promotions Inc. announced that it was promoting Ali's first title defence against Liston.

Clay and his management team were not happy with this deal, but they were forced to sign it prior to Clay's initial challenge of Liston, if they wanted a shot at the heavyweight title. Having challengers guarantee the champion a rematch should they win the title has been standard practice in boxing for well over one hundred years. The short, surreptitious clause in the contract was signed by Clay before both Liston fights had taken place. This was not revealed to the Florida State Boxing Commission prior to their first fight.[4]

The WBA did not permit title fight contracts that included rematch clauses (a rule they adopted in August of 1963) for their own idiosyncratic reasons, so this part of the original Clay-Liston deal was supposedly kept hidden from the press and public (although the WBA hierarchy were certainly well aware of it) until the Ali-Liston rematch was announced. Upon the announcement of the rematch, the WBA vowed they would ban or suspend any state that promoted the Ali-Liston rematch. The WBA (which also stands for Without Brains Attached) was rightly viewed by the boxing community as a group of mendacious, churlish clowns.

It was at the WBA's annual meeting in the last week of August 1964, at the Camellia Room of the Golden Triangle Motor Hotel in Norfolk, Virginia, where twenty-seven of the twenty-nine commission representatives voted to strip Muhammad Ali of their heavyweight title strap, further demeaning the worth of their brand, if such a thing was even possible. Of course, such outrageous and detrimental actions were made arbitrarily and without any concern for how it would adversely affect the long-term welfare of boxing, or how the sport (and the WBA) would be negatively perceived by its fans around the world. In truth, the commission consisted of old, white, bigoted men who were short on brains and long on bluster. Their biases and prejudices were well known. The meeting could have passed for a KKK symposium, judging by their comments.

The representative of the Ohio Athletic Commission, dentist Dr. A.J. Wagner, suggested that they throw Liston back into the gutter from whence he came. Why did Dr. Wagner (as uncivilized a man on civil rights as existed at that time) make such overtly racist comments about Liston belonging in the gutter? Because he believed that of all African Americans. Dr. Wagner then strenuously stated that the WBA should condemn Cassius Clay in the harshest manner possible for joining the Black Muslims. He finished his bigoted rant with a rather nonsensical comment suggesting they teach their own children to behave as criminally as Ali and Liston. This was a rather ironic statement as there were no bigger crooks in boxing at that time than the WBA.

To refer to Muhammad Ali as a "crook" simply because he chose to change his religious beliefs shows that Dr. Wagner was more concerned with the colour of the champion's skin than the merits of his abilities. How stupid were these crusty, odious old bastards? They actually elected the former athletic commissioner of Ontario, Canada, Merv McKenzie, as their new president. McKenzie was the boxing genius who somehow "forgot" to license anyone — fighters, seconds, managers, officials — for the Floyd Patterson–Tom McNeeley heavyweight title fight held in Toronto at Maple Leaf Gardens on December 4, 1961.[5] By the way, the referee for the Patterson-McNeeley bout was Jersey Joe Walcott.

Despite Ed Lassman's comments to the contrary, the outgoing WBA president knew all about the supposed "secret" rematch clause involved with the Clay-Liston contract.[6] He was not fooling anyone with his display of mock indignation. Lassman was also the head of the Miami Beach Boxing Commission, which was decidedly not kosher. This could only happen in boxing. That is why the timing of Lassman's threats and the subsequent stripping of the WBA title from Ali were rather disingenuous. If the Mob pressured Lassman to enforce their "no rematch" clause and strip Ali of the WBA heavyweight crown so as to benefit another of the Mob's fighters, it would not have been surprising — although there is no evidence to suggest this. Sad as it was, this whole shameful, sorry cockup seems to have been orchestrated by the WBA all on its own.

Clearly the Mob wanted to hedge their bets by having the WBA title awarded to one of their in-house fighters, Ernie Terrell, in case Liston came up short in his rematch with Ali. Terrell was managed by the Outfit in Chicago. They were determined not to be left out in the cold when it came to ownership of the world heavyweight title, or at least a portion of it. Of course, if Liston had emerged triumphant in his return against Ali, the Mob would have owned both heavyweight champions. The Mob's iron grip on the heavyweight title had been loosened somewhat by Ali's original victory over Liston, but it had not been completely erased. The WBA's self-serving rule prohibiting rematches was said to have been inspired by the contract Liston was forced to sign to get a title shot against Floyd Patterson, whom Liston twice knocked out in less than one round. Its motivation went back even further, to Patterson's three consecutive title fights with Ingemar Johansson. Liston's contract with Patterson was described by most boxing people as the worst contract ever seen in the business.[7] Liston was forced to sign the egregious contract when he challenged Patterson for the title. Liston received little of what he was owed from his Mob handlers for beating Patterson twice. To the Mob, Liston was simply there to serve as a functionary for the Mob's ulterior motives in the sport and elsewhere.[8]

The WBA did the Mob's bidding (inadvertently or otherwise) by unceremoniously stripping Ali of their title and awarding it to the winner of the Ernie Terrell–Eddie Machen fight. After Terrell (whom Ali later annihilated) beat Machen, the WBA dropped Liston from its rankings altogether, which was very short-sighted because next to Ali, he was the best heavyweight in the world.

Because of the overt pressure tactics applied by the WBA against various state boxing commissions, it became a rather onerous task to find a venue amenable to staging the Ali-Liston rematch. Many states meekly bowed to the despotic dictates of the WBA and simply refused to license an Ali-Liston rematch. Luckily for both fighters, professional boxing had very deep roots running through the state of Massachusetts. A deal was reached to hold the Ali-Liston rematch on November 16, 1964, at the

Boston Garden. Of course, the self-serving WBA instantly suspended the Massachusetts State Boxing Commission. This didn't stop Boston from going ahead with the fight.

Misfortune then reared its ugly head. A mere three days before the scheduled bout, Ali suffered an excruciatingly painful incarcerated inguinal hernia, which forced him to undergo immediate emergency surgery at Boston City Hospital. The fight, which felt cursed to begin with, was now postponed for six months, to allow Ali to fully recover from his surgery.[9] This was terribly disappointing to Liston, who was in phenomenal condition for the rematch. Liston, by his own admission, would never be able to get into such outstanding physical shape again. Boxing is as much of an exercise in mental strength as it is one of physical skill. The fault for Liston's inability to regain the excellent physical state that he had achieved for the original date of their rematch lies solely with him. Boxing is full of disappointments at all levels. It is how you handle such disappointments that determines the fate of your career. Needless to say, Liston didn't handle disappointments well.

In the interim, before the rematch was scheduled to take place, the charismatic, exiled Nation of Islam minister, Malcolm X, Ali's former close friend, confidant, and mentor, had been brutally assassinated at the Audubon Ballroom in New York on February 21, 1965.[10] The assassination of Malcolm X set off a never-ending wave of fear and rumour mongering that permeated the environment surrounding the Ali-Liston rematch. State and federal police were dispatched to protect both Ali and Liston 24-7, from possible retaliatory threats from supporters of Malcolm X, supposedly looking to avenge his murder. Both fighters (and especially Liston) had to be somewhat unnerved by the large, armed police presence in their respective training camps, at least as much as the fans were at the arena in Lewiston. Ali, as it turned out, was able to handle such chaos and turmoil rather gracefully, as he showed throughout his career, both in and out of the ring.

Still, the police and FBI thoroughly searched everyone entering the arena in Lewiston that night, irrespective of race, celebrity, or gender. The year 1965 was a very turbulent and violent one in American history. Ali's conversion to the Nation of Islam upset a lot of Americans, white and Black alike. Such consternation over Ali's religious conversion and subsequent name change were really no one's business but his own. The criminal sanctioning bodies and the Mob, which controlled boxing back then, were only upset because they could not exercise unfettered control over the new, undisputed world heavyweight champion. What did the WBA or organized crime really care about Ali's new name and religion? They didn't. They were only upset because they would not be able to financially exploit him further. This is what was at the true heart of their outrage.

Ali was exceptionally close with Malcolm X, who viewed Ali as his baby brother. They loved each other. Sadly, their brotherly friendship ended due to the vindictiveness of their mutual spiritual leader, the Honorable Elijah Muhammad. Muhammad had unceremoniously banished Malcolm X from the Nation of Islam after Malcom X had exposed the long-hidden secret that Muhammad had fathered eight children out of wedlock with his private secretaries. The revelations were true but eventually ended up costing Malcolm X his life. Ali was then forced to break ties and shun all contact with Malcolm X on the direct orders of Muhammad. Malcolm X's eloquence and charisma were always viewed by those loyal to Muhammad as a direct threat to his leadership. Shunning Malcolm X was a move that Ali would deeply regret forever.

It is no exaggeration to say that the assassination of Malcolm X very much overshadowed the upcoming fight. It almost seemed as if America was waiting with trepidation for another high-profile member connected to the Nation of Islam to be gunned down. Even the police were on edge. In fact, years later, Angelo Dundee recalled just how tense the atmosphere had become. Shortly after Ali had won the world heavyweight title and was preparing to face Liston in the rematch, Dundee and his brother, Chris, were walking together in Miami on the sidewalk, toward their Fifth Street gym. A black car with tinted windows pulled up to the curb. Two men in dark suits and dark sunglasses emerged from the car and identified themselves as FBI agents. They quickly hustled the Dundee brothers into their car and spirited them away.

The FBI agents then ushered the Dundee brothers into a supposedly "abandoned" warehouse. Inside they were greeted by other agents clad in similar fashion. They directed the brothers' attention to a long table upon which several dozen photographs of members of the Nation of Islam, all dressed in black suits with white shirts and red bow ties, had been placed. The FBI asked both Chris and Angelo Dundee to identify which of the African Americans in the photographs in front of them were part of Ali's entourage. Feeling flustered, and wanting to protect their fighter, Chris Dundee shrugged his shoulders and said, "I dunno. They all look alike to me." The Dundees had outwitted the FBI by using the FBI's own prejudices against them. The two men were then driven back to their gym and not bothered any further by the FBI.[11]

The persistent fear of a possible reciprocal assassination attempt on the life of Ali (which turned out to be an unsubstantiated rumour) was predicated on the belief that some of Malcolm X's followers intended to travel to Lewiston to murder Ali for shunning Malcolm X. This rumour had been generated by the press from beginning to end. It is true that the assassination of Malcolm X affected Liston adversely, too, but in a much different way than it affected Ali. Liston worried that members of the Fruit of Islam (FOI) might try to shoot both him and Ali, and since Ali was much faster than him, he and not the new champion would be the one to take the bullet. Such rumours emanated from the heightened hysteria and extreme paranoia that had been fanned by older members of the biased white press. Still, police protection was doubled, and tripled in some cases.

Did the Nation of Islam meet privately with Liston and threaten him with death if he won the fight? That was just one of many rumours circulating back then, and there exists no credible proof of any kind to substantiate it. Liston was backed by various Mob factions in Philadelphia, New York, St. Louis, and especially Chicago. It seemed as if almost every upper echelon Mob figure owned a piece of Liston. With such major backing from organized crime, why would Liston fear anyone? It is hard to believe that threats from a fringe religious sect could have convinced Liston to purposely botch his chance at fistic redemption. Liston was not just fighting to regain his world heavyweight title; he was fighting to regain his sense of self-worth. The heavyweight title defined Liston. It gave him a feeling of importance. Without it, he felt aimless.

A major factor working against Liston in both fights was that his main base of strength, the Mob, had seriously misread the situation with Ali. They guessed that the Nation of Islam would cower in fear and knuckle under to their verbal threats and strong-arm tactics — tactics that had always worked in similar situations. The Mob guessed wrong. The Nation of Islam had no reason to fear the Mob, and therefore, they had less than a scintilla of interest in doing *any* business with them. To them, the Mob was something to be ignored and reviled and, if necessary, eliminated.

The Nation of Islam's contempt for the Mob stemmed from the wretched, ruthless financial and physical abuse they had visited on African American boxers and businesses for over forty-five years. The Nation of Islam was the only group that could make such a publicly defiant stand against the Mob, because they had the money, the manpower, and the muscle to back it up all the way down the line. The Nation of Islam was resolute in their firmness to not allow Ali or themselves to be ensnared or intimidated by organized crime. In terms of sheer numbers, the Mob, in all its guises, was no threat to the Nation of Islam, which the outnumbered gangsters slowly came to understand.

A New Era

In the 1960s, politics, cultural mores, social activities, the arts, and professional sports were all experiencing massive foundational changes. There was a new, exciting, young, photogenic man occupying the White House — President John F. Kennedy. Kennedy was the youngest man ever elected president, and he assumed the presidency at a very auspicious time in American history. Everything seemed possible at the beginning of the decade. There was, however, trouble in the offing. There was the Bay of Pigs failure, the Cuban Missile Crisis, and then the shocking assassination of the beloved young president. Events were moving too fast in the United States. It's important to remember that these three cataclysmic experiences occurred before the civil rights and anti–Vietnam War movements had reached full speed. This was the backdrop against which the Ali-Liston rematch took place.

America had developed into one giant seething cauldron of constant change. The events that took place during 1960s were moving at breakneck speed, or at least faster than those affected by them could perceive their true and lasting impact. Americans of all ages and stripes were forced to quickly readapt to their changing landscapes or suffer the consequences of being permanently left behind and out of touch with the new realities that confronted them.

Clay's monumentally astonishing upset over reigning world heavyweight champion Liston (in their first fight) was one of those benchmark events of the decade. It was something that all Americans were told was a virtual impossibility, yet it happened. Boxing writers and the press in general were having trouble explaining how such an unlikely outcome could have happened. All but a handful of these writers had glibly written that Liston would devastate Clay within one round. These scribes were now in a rush to make sense of what had taken place. These older white journalists and their fellow American citizens had trouble accepting the reality of what transpired on the night of February 25, 1964, at the Miami Beach Convention Center.

Clay's comprehensive defeat of Liston was such an earth-shattering surprise that few people believed their first fight to be on the level. Looking back now, it might be hard to remember that Clay was given virtually no chance of defeating Liston. It was generally assumed that the only way Clay could win was if Liston purposely went into the tank. Clay's victory was such a shock to the system that the rematch clause was immediately activated to settle any doubts as to the first fight's legitimacy. The health of the sport of boxing has always depended on the success of the heavyweight division. It was thought that if the heavyweight division was exciting and successful, then that success would trickle down to boxing's other seven weight divisions. This was prizefighting's version of the obsolete financial theory of trickle-down economics. Liston was most decidedly not a box office draw.

Clay's win over Liston presented the Mob with an intriguing problem. Clay was not, nor would he ever be, a Mob-influenced boxer. He was firmly controlled by the Nation of Islam. After his rematch with Liston, the Mob would receive no more money from Ali, as he was free to fight whomever he chose. The Mob could do nothing after Liston succumbed to the new champion in Lewiston, Maine.

This was more than just a turf war between the Outfit and the Nation of Islam, two Chicago-based organizations. Ali's victory in his rematch with Liston signalled a paradigm shift in everyday American life. The once-nascent civil rights movement had begun to effect sweeping changes across America. Ali's defeat of Liston, combined with his later outspoken anti–Vietnam War views and his criticism of African American voter suppression, placed him at the forefront of newspaper headlines around the world on a daily basis.

Ali was, in essence, the new America that the old America did not want to recognize. He was young, religious, articulate, and incredibly appealing. He was the right man at the right time, and at the right turning point in American history. Ali himself summed it up best: "I am America. I am the part you won't recognize. But get used to me. Black, confident, cocky; my name, not yours; my religion, not yours; my goals, my own; get used to me."[12]

Each year, untold Americans change their names and their religions. As Olympic gold medallist Cassius Clay, he was loved by fight fans throughout the United States. After following his own moral and religious conscience, however, he became hated by many people throughout the United States, and faced an unprecedented political and social backlash, for doing something many other Americans did every single day: he changed his name and religion.

White America's hatred toward Ali had nothing to do with his name change or his new religion. Their hatred sprung from an African American having the audacity to assert his legal rights. The new champion faced a tidal wave of racism at home, not only from fight fans and reporters but also from the various autocratic sanctioning bodies as well. In the face of this unprecedented wave of bigotry aimed directly at him, Ali refused to bend or go back on his moral or religious persuasions. He was in the right and he knew it, and in time, the country would catch up to him and laud him for his courageous stand.

But in 1965, the old guard of white sportswriters who once tried to couch their prejudiced articles about Black athletes with clever racism were no longer so clever when writing racist diatribes against Ali. In some ways, the ruckus over Ali's name change and religious conversion made him a better fighter. The uproar made him work harder — it stiffened his resolve to improve on his already magnificent skills. The fury over his conversion to Islam created a predicament for the promoters of his rematch with Liston. Whereas in their first encounter, Liston was perceived as the villain and Clay was looked upon as the young Olympic hero in shining white trunks, now, in the minds of many press members and the public, their roles had been reversed.

For the first time in his long ring career, Liston entered the ring to face an opponent with the crowd behind *him*. This was the tense, angry backdrop against which Ali-Liston II occurred on May 25, 1965, in of all places, Lewiston, Maine, the maple syrup capital of the United States. No amount of deliciously sweet maple syrup, however, could remove the sour taste that long remained in the mouths of all those people who witnessed the much-anticipated rematch that night.

The Rematch

Liston knew that the rematch against Ali was his best chance at personal and professional redemption, and as such, he originally showed tremendous discipline and drive in preparing for the return bout. He wanted to show the world that he was not a quitter. Many boxing writers had known Liston since he first entered the pro ranks. To a man, they felt strongly that, at the beginning of training camp for the scheduled rematch, Liston was the best he had ever looked in his entire career. Everyone involved in boxing expected Liston to reclaim his dearly departed throne. Then the fight was postponed for six months. Liston fell apart emotionally and physically and, later on, looked awful in the weeks leading up to his clash with Ali in Lewiston. He looked lethargic. His timing and balance were terrible. The six-month delay had sapped Liston of his will to stay in shape. He became sullen and depressed. He felt the world was against him.

It was no secret that Liston barely trained for their first bout. He had taken Clay much too lightly. According to Liston biographer Paul

Gallender, "This fight became a primer on how not to prepare for a heavy-weight title defense. Judging by the number of guests at Liston's house, his victory party started two or three weeks before the actual bout. Sonny whiled away many evenings eating hot dogs, drinking beer, and dealing blackjack."[13]

Liston wanted everyone to know that he was a genuine tough guy, both in and out of the ring. And he was. Liston's Mob credentials spoke volumes as to his true character. He had the full support of organized crime, for whom he had been a head-breaker at various union strikes and a debt collector. Whenever some lowlifes borrowed money from the Mob but were recalcitrant in paying them back, Liston was the guy they sent to convince them to make good on their debts, plus interest to the Mob.

There was also the thorny issue of Liston's real age. Ali's trainer, Angelo Dundee, knew the truth about Liston's age and readily shared it with Ali prior to their first brawl. Dundee knew that Liston was "older than dirt" and had not trained hard for their first fight. More to the point, Liston never perceived Clay to be any kind of serious threat to his crown. Liston's ego had blinded him to what was truly in front of him.[14] He vowed not to make the same mistake in their rematch.

Liston's Prep for the Second Fight

Liston's newfound focus and superb conditioning were reflected in the betting odds, which once again favoured the former champion by a margin of thirteen to five (indicating that fight fans still had trouble believing that their first fight had been on the level). Liston fans simply could not fathom that their supposedly invincible hero was so soundly thrashed by some young kid who was likely less than half of Liston's real age.

Because of Ali's religious conversion to Islam, and the endemic racism directed at African Americans in the United States, public opinion was firmly against Ali in 1965. It was not until five years later, after he was unanimously exonerated by the Supreme Court, that public opinion caught up with Ali. His firm religious and moral stances, combined with his anti–Vietnam War views, turned him into a pariah in the U.S. heartland and among the mainstream (white) media, a reviled heavyweight king within his own empire.

There are more than a few boxing historians who still firmly believe the Mob fixed both fights with Liston, but that is nonsensical in the extreme. Why would the Mob voluntarily relinquish control of the most valuable prize in all of sports to a young kid under the sway of the Nation of Islam's leader, the Honorable Elijah Muhammad, without receiving substantial financial reimbursement and control over Ali's career in return? The Mob never allowed any fighter they owned (such as Liston or Terrell) to willingly give away a money-making machine like the heavyweight crown. The Mob had always controlled both fighters in every title match they promoted. When that was not possible, they would buy off the referee or the judges.

The Mob did not control Ali. This was a problem for the underworld. Their efforts to do so were strongly rebuffed by the Nation of Islam. When it came to prizefighting, the Mob left nothing to chance. Anyone that disagreed with their methods had their legs or arms broken. If you disagreed a second time, you caught a bullet. The Mob had never gracefully accepted no for an answer. All that ended when they encountered Muhammad Ali and the Nation of Islam.

The Mob had incorrectly assumed they could continue business as usual if Clay somehow won by simply muscling in on Clay's reign. Their mistake ended up costing them untold millions of dollars in future revenues. Ali's reign would be altogether different from the reigns of all previous world boxing champions. He declared his professional and personal freedom at a media scrum the day after winning the crown by declaring, "I don't have to be what *YOU* want me to be! I am free to be who *I WANT!*"[15]

Despite all the contrasting opinions about what a fighter needs to do to become a world champion, it is worth noting that the old boxing axiom of "styles make fights" is very true. Stylistically, Liston was tailor-made for Ali. He had only one mode of fighting, which he never deviated from. He would take two stutter steps forward, throw a double jab and then a straight right hand. Liston was deceptively quick when attacking, but because of the trepidation he instilled in his adversaries, he had not been forced to move quickly to catch his opponents. His ring foes, frozen by fear, simply stood there, waiting for Liston to destroy them.

In their first fight, Clay utilized his exquisitely fast reflexes and ring mobility, employing rapid lateral movement to frustrate and befuddle Liston. This forced the champion to repeatedly reset his feet, minimizing his leverage and taking away his superior strength advantage. Clay had taken away Liston's jab by circling to his left, forcing Liston to amateurishly lunge at Clay, which the challenger had no problem avoiding and exploiting.

By lunging at Clay, Liston was opening himself up to the challenger's lightning-quick counter shots. Whenever Liston leapt at Clay with a jab, he put himself off-balance, meaning any good, hard counter right hands by Clay would do significant damage. Clay buckled Liston's knees several times with straight right hands during their initial encounter. More importantly, Clay forced the older Liston to expend more energy than he had originally planned. Once Liston was tired, the fight became target practice for Clay.

Ultimately it was hubris that took down both Liston and the Mob. They had badly overplayed their hand against a superior force by underestimating both the tremendous resolve and overwhelming response of their formidable opponent. The Mob understood only intimidation and strongarm tactics, and the FOI (the Nation of Islam's security force) was more than happy to oblige them. Such a grave miscalculation ended up costing the Mob dearly when it came to controlling heavyweight boxing. Sure, the Outfit in Chicago had Ernie Terrell waiting in the wings, but it was Ali who was the gold mine at the box office.

The Mob, via Liston's manager, Jack Nilon, owned the rights to the film of their first fight and the live broadcast of their possible rematch. Clay's team had to concede on that point if they wished to secure a chance at the title. The problem, as outlined earlier, lay with the WBA's inane bylaw regarding rematches.[16] If fight fans and boxing scribes in attendance and around the world were absolutely flabbergasted when the supposedly invincible Liston quit on his stool during their first fight, they were now in for an even bigger shock. In their first bout, Clay had dominated the slow, lumbering Liston with supersonic hand speed and astonishing foot movement that would have put Rudolf Nureyev to shame. In the rematch, he knocked Liston out with one deep dish beauty of a counter right hand.

Controversy

The Ali-Liston rematch gave rise to a host of controversies that stubbornly persist to this day. Was the outcome of the rematch predetermined? Was Liston paid to take a dive? Did he bet his entire purse on himself to lose the fight by a knockout? Did he call close friends and family and tell them to bet on Ali by an early knockout only hours before the bout? Have people who claimed to have proof that the rematch was fixed ever provided any concrete evidence to back up their assertions?

A recently released FBI report from that time states that Liston's Mob handler, Irving "Ash" Resnick, told an associate, gambler Barnett Magids from Houston, Texas, that the fight was fixed and to bet everything on Liston within two rounds. Are any of these allegations true? Is the FBI report valid?

Is it possible that the FOI threatened Liston into tanking the fight?

The Decision

In any boxing controversy, it always comes down to what we know for sure. In this instance, what we know for sure is that the fight was stopped at 2:12 of the first round by referee Walcott. (The official time of the knockout was originally announced as one minute, but that was incorrect.) Recently, the FBI released their files on the fight. They show claims purported to reveal that the fight was fixed by Resnick and Magids.

Evan Hilbert of CBS Sports cited the *Washington Times* 1996 report of evidence developed by the FBI:

> "On one occasion, Resnick introduced Magids to Sonny Liston at the Thunderbird, [one of the Las Vegas hotels organized crime controlled]," the memo states. "About a week before the Liston and Clay fight in Miami, Resnick

called and invited Magids and his wife for two weeks in Florida on Resnick. Magids' wife was not interested in going, but Magids decided to go along, and Resnick was going to send him a ticket."

"Two or three days before the fight, Magids called Resnick at the Fontainebleau Hotel in Miami to say he could not come," the memo states. "On this call, he asked Resnick who he liked in the fight, and Resnick said that Liston would knock Clay out in the second round. Resnick suggested he wait until just before the fight to place any bets because the odds may come down.

"At about noon on the day of the fight, [Magids] reached Resnick again by phone, and at this time, Resnick said for him to not make any bets, but just go watch the fight on pay TV and he would know why and that he could not talk further at that time.

"Magids did go see the fight on TV and immediately realized that Resnick knew that Liston was going to lose. A week later, there was an article in *Sports Illustrated* writing up Resnick as a big loser because of his backing of Liston. Later people 'in the know' in Las Vegas told Magids that Resnick and Liston both reportedly made over one million dollars betting against Liston on the fight and that the magazine article was a cover for this."[17]

Of course, none of the allegations stated above have ever been verified. The story told by Magids simply does not hold up under the microscope. Resnick advising him to wait to place his bet until just before the fight began, to possibly get better odds on the bout, is a common move by most experienced bettors and does not in any way indicate that Liston was about to "go into the tank." If Liston made one million dollars on the fight by betting against himself, he never saw a nickel of it. After federal, state, and Mob taxes, Liston was left with little more than thirteen thousand dollars for his efforts. This was the same net amount he'd made in their first fight.

Of course, lack of evidence has never stopped anyone from making ridiculous claims regarding any boxing match. What Liston and the crowd in attendance did not know is that Ali entered the ring prior to their rematch with a broken rib as the result of a body punch from sparring partner Jimmy Ellis during training. The pain he felt from the fracture was eased by a shot of novocaine just before the fight.[18] If Liston had only known that, he might have fought in a much more aggressive manner.

It would have been almost impossible for Liston or Resnick to place any six-figure bets against Liston in their rematch with just one bookie. They would have had to lay their bets with a series of Mob bookies, and even then the news would have leaked out. Rumours of Liston preparing to tank the fight would have surfaced beforehand in the press and drastically lowered the odds favouring him, thereby substantially reducing any financial windfall he or Resnick would have received from such a bet.

The other pertinent question here is, who would have taken Liston's bet to begin with? He was notorious for welching on bets. He bet a lot at the Thunderbird Hotel and Casino, but it's important to remember that he was a Mob fighter playing with Mob money. Any money he lost at the gaming tables was just taken from his next fight purse. Moreover, why would the Mob willingly give up their control of the world heavyweight title by forcing Liston to lose deliberately? It makes no financial sense. They would have been able to steal much more money from Liston in a series of future bouts, after he regained the title, than from a one-time payout by bookies.

Is it possible that the FOI threatened Liston? Yes, but it's very unlikely. They didn't need to. They believed that Ali would win, although truth be told, the Honorable Elijah Muhammad wasn't so sure. Besides, Liston looked so bad in training camp immediately before the fight that it was hardly necessary to intimidate him. Did Liston owe money to the Mob? Yes. They stole most of his ring earnings throughout his career. It was not uncommon for the Mob to claim a fighter owed them money. They would rob a fighter like Liston of his purse and then claim the fighter owed *them*. They did that to hundreds of fighters. Mobster Frankie Carbo was in jail by this time, but he was still in control of boxing.

We know Liston was always broke and in constant need of cash. He was addicted to gambling and often borrowed large sums of cash from Resnick. Owing money to the Mob was not a wise financial strategy. If Liston had owed the Mob (and all indications are that he did), they would have just continued stealing his future ring earnings, thus forcing him to continue fighting long past his prime — which he did. The Mob would not have even bothered to tell Liston he owed them money, because it wasn't necessary to do so. Liston knew how the game was played.

If Liston had genuinely won a million dollars by betting against himself in his rematch with Ali, the Mob would have stolen that, too. What was he going to do, argue with professional killers that his accounts were settled? Not likely. Stories of the supposed millions earned by Liston and Resnick were simply apocryphal. Magids was a pathological liar and a compulsive gambler.[19] The two go hand in hand, like gin and tonic. There is no one-word answer to the question of whether the second fight between Ali and Liston was fixed. The truthful answer might very well be no … and yes. Some boxing insiders have claimed that Ali admitted to them privately that the second fight was fixed but without his prior knowledge, which was possible but not probable. Such claims have never been verified. Ali was unsure of what had happened himself, which is why he stood over Liston and menacingly screamed at him to get up.

Why did Liston get to one knee and then fall back on the canvas a second time? Maybe he was discombobulated from the hard shot he'd taken from Ali. Or maybe, just maybe, he was telling the truth. Maybe he was protecting himself because he thought Ali would hit him while he was on one knee or bump into him and knock him over. There is one thing that is certain: The moment Liston got up off the canvas is also the specific moment where the allegations of a fixed fight begin to lose traction. Because if the fight was fixed, why didn't Liston just stay down? Why did he get up and resume fighting? Fighters that go into the tank don't usually do that. Those fighters who get up and continue fighting and then go down repeatedly only confirm the obvious. Liston did not do that. By the time Liston arose, the knockdown timekeeper, McDonough, had already counted ten over him. The fight was officially over, although no one in the arena knew that except for McDonough and Fleischer. In other words, by the time Walcott came over to talk with them, the fight was already in the past.

The evidence of what transpired is the tape of the fight. To put it simply, Liston walked into a hard counter right hand. Liston's forward momentum made Ali's right hand more damaging. The fact that the tape shows Ali, after the fight's abrupt ending, standing in his corner, looking puzzled, should not detract from the fact that Ali did hit Liston with a crushing shot after slipping Liston's slow jab. Liston felt that punch. The knockdown was genuine.

Angelo Dundee had studied tapes of Liston's fights. Dundee noticed that Liston would often lunge forward when he threw his powerful jab. His head would be out over his front foot, effectively placing him off-balance. What does this mean? It means that because Liston's balance was awry, the full power of any counter shot he got tagged with would not be diffused through his massive tree trunk legs but rather absorbed solely by his head, which is exactly where Ali's powerful right hand landed. Dundee instructed Ali to slip Liston's jab, slide about an inch to his right to create an angle, plant his feet firmly, and throw a quick counter right hand. Dundee called the maneuver "Slip, slide and bang." It was the same series of moves that Ali would later utilize during his historic career against such fistic foes as Zora Folley, Cleveland Williams, Floyd Patterson, Karl Mildenberger, Henry Cooper, Brian London, Richard Dunn, Oscar Bonavena, and George Foreman.

One has to feel bad for Walcott, who was clearly out of his depth. The rules clearly state that the referee is supposed to pick up the count from the official timekeeper after the fighter scoring the knockdown has gone to the farthest neutral corner. Ali did not go to the farthest neutral corner; he was off in his own reverie. Walcott was confused as to what to do next. It was the world's most famous game of broken telephone. When Fleischer motioned for Walcott to come over, Walcott should have ignored him — Fleischer was just one more distraction preventing Walcott from doing his job correctly.

Under the rules of the Maine State Boxing Commission, Walcott had the authority to stop the count (which would have forced McDonough to stop his knockdown count) until Ali went to a neutral corner and order was restored. The moment Liston hit the canvas, the first thing Walcott should have done, after Ali refused to listen to him, was immediately call time.

Secondly, he should have ordered Ali to go to the farthest neutral corner and then read him the riot act. The third and final task for Walcott would have been to call time in and pick up the count from the knockdown timekeeper and start counting again over Liston.

It is easy to tell by Ali's post-fight reaction that he did not know how the fight would end prior to entering the ring that night in Lewiston, Maine. If the fight was fixed, Ali was certainly not in on it. It is because the fight was never fought to a satisfying climax that the boxing world will always have questions regarding how it ended.

Significance

The second Ali-Liston fight was significant for many reasons. Ali was robbed of his chance to score a legitimate knockout over Liston, partly by his own antics. This would have quelled the doubts of all those fans who still did not believe their first fight was legitimate. It also would have been more enjoyable for boxing fans and the media had Ali been able to score a knockout similar to the one scored by former Liston sparring partner Leotis Martin four years later, in December 1969 in Las Vegas.

The way the second Ali-Liston fight ended was a great disappointment to everyone involved and further sullied pro boxing's already dismal reputation. The bout's ignominious conclusion cast a dark shadow over what many fans perceived as a dubious outcome. It was but one more in a series of black clouds hovering over the sport. By 1965, fans were getting fed up and had started to aggressively push back by switching their allegiance to other sports. Boxing tickets in 1965, like today, weren't cheap. To pay good money to watch a fight end in controversial fashion, in less than one round, was something that casual and long-time fans could no longer tolerate.

A host of fans, writers, and boxing figures still believe the second Ali-Liston bout to have been fixed. That is the prevailing opinion that has come down through the years. Some so-called experts will call you crazy if you dare to disagree with such a claim. Many possible theories have been posited, as seen above, as to how the fight was supposedly fixed. None of these assertions contains any substantive proof. What is significant here is that

Liston kept fighting, even as his skills greatly diminished. This shows that he gained nothing (financially) from losing his rematch with Ali, other than the criticism of fight fans and the media.

The significance of Ali-Liston II is more a question of who benefitted the most from its outcome rather than if the fight was possibly fixed. A fix is easier to perpetrate if both fighters are in on it. If both boxers do not agree to a fix, then the Mob is forced to exert their influence elsewhere. There is no evidence of that happening here. This fight had enough trouble finding a home. Any miniscule hint of Mob involvement beforehand would have put the kibosh on the event altogether. The fight ended abruptly because of a series of events occurring simultaneously, which confused referee Walcott. That is, truly, the only controversy that can be proven factually regarding this bout. Ultimately, the fight was indeed legitimate, as was Ali's claim as the only heavyweight champion of the world.

CHAPTER 10

KEN BUCHANAN VS. ROBERTO DURÁN

Fight: Roberto Durán vs. Ken Buchanan
Weight Class: Lightweight
Title at Stake: WBA world lightweight
Date: June 26, 1972
Location: Madison Square Garden, New York
Outcome: Durán wins the WBA title by thirteenth-round KO
Referee: Johnny LoBianco

Background

The 1972 world lightweight title fight between the classy, undisputed defending champion, Scotsman Kenny Buchanan, and the hungry, feral challenger from Panama, Roberto Durán, produced enough controversy to last hardcore fight fans a lifetime. Buchanan, known as "The Fighting Carpenter" and "King Ken," was fouled twice by Durán at the conclusion of the thirteenth round. Durán, by his own admission, deliberately struck Buchanan low and after the bell. Those two brazen fouls cost Buchanan much more than the lightweight title on that sunny June day in New York City. Durán's blatant fouls resulted in permanent testicular injury to the Scotsman. More than fifty years later, Buchanan still sported the physical and emotional scars from having his title taken in so unjust a manner.

Durán — a.k.a. Manos de Piedra (Hands of Stone), a.k.a. El Cholo, a.k.a. Rocky — was comfortably ahead on all three scorecards at the end of round thirteen, although that does not mitigate the severity of his fouls. Many boxing scribes believed Durán likely would have stopped Buchanan before the fifteenth round. Given Buchanan's incredible iron will, that was far from a sure thing. Astonishingly, even after rising from the canvas in excruciating pain, and still clutching his groin, Buchanan indicated he wanted to fight on. Buchanan was one super tough Scotsman. With the champion on his feet and willing to continue, referee Johnny LoBianco, in a moment of infamy that will live forever, waved off the fight, shamelessly awarding the lightweight title to Durán.

Some scribes have posited that if the fight had been allowed to continue, LoBianco might well have stopped the bout in rounds fourteen or fifteen, to save Buchanan from further punishment. After the fight was over, however, LoBianco admitted to blow-by-blow announcer Don Dunphy that he had not considered stopping the fight. It is quite conceivable, if not probable, that a referee more familiar with the rules of the NYSAC might have disqualified Durán, resulting in Buchanan retaining his title. At the very least, Durán should have had a minimum of two points deducted from his score for hitting Buchanan low and after the round had ended. LoBianco was trying to separate the two fighters after the bell when the double foul occurred. A two-point swing in one round would have made the fight much closer on the scorecards. Would it have been enough to allow Buchanan to save his title on points? Probably not, but that is not relevant to this specific incident.

At the time of this fight, Buchanan was recognized as the undisputed, universally recognized lightweight champion of the world. He held both the WBC and WBA belts. He entered the fight with Durán as a two-to-one favourite.[1] Buchanan had previously won the WBA belt by defeating Durán's fellow countryman, Ismael Laguna, on September 26, 1970, by split decision, in San Juan, Puerto Rico, at Hiram Bithorn Stadium.[2] He beat Laguna once again in their rematch, by unanimous decision, on September 13, 1971, at Madison Square Garden.[3] Buchanan annexed the WBC title by scoring a unanimous decision victory over Ruben Navarro in Los Angeles, on February 12, 1971.[4] Buchanan was twenty-six years old and in the prime of his career. Boxing experts agreed: he had a long title reign in front of him.

Ken Buchanan

Kenny Buchanan, MBE, was born in Edinburgh, Scotland, on June 28, 1945. His parents, Tommy and Cathy Buchanan, were always supportive of his boxing ambitions. The most ardent supporters of his nascent boxing career were his aunts, Joan and Agnes. These aunts bought him a pair of boxing gloves for Christmas when he was seven years old, and his love for the sport grew exponentially. Buchanan grew up poor but in a caring, affectionate household with a large, extended family.[5]

Buchanan loved to scrap as a youngster, and after seeing the movie *The Joe Louis Story*, starring former heavyweight fighter Coley Wallace, he joined one of the many local amateur boxing clubs in Edinburgh. Buchanan made his professional debut in September 1965 at the world-famous National Sporting Club in Piccadilly, London, scoring an emphatic second round TKO over his opponent, Brian "Rocky" Tonks.[6] Buchanan was the sixth Scottish-born fighter to hold a universally recognized world boxing title, and the second Brit since Freddie Welsh to hold the world lightweight crown. He was considered the underdog when he upset Laguna in Puerto Rico by split decision, to capture the WBA version of the world lightweight title.

It was thought that Buchanan, one of the best-conditioned athletes in the world, would fade in the intense afternoon Puerto Rican heat. That did not happen. Buchanan got stronger as the fight wore on. Buchanan was able to land his long left jab regularly while slipping then countering Laguna's jabs with powerful right-hand counters. Buchanan also threw his right uppercut often and effectively. Buchanan proved to be the faster and more accurate puncher. His unerring jab kept Laguna off balance for the majority of the fight. Laguna was an exceptionally skilled ring technician, but on this day, Buchanan's skills won out.

Scotland and indeed all of Britain were immensely proud of Buchanan's unexpected victory over Laguna. Buchanan is widely considered to be the greatest Scottish fighter of all time, next to the incomparable world flyweight champion Benny Lynch.

Roberto Durán

Unlike Buchanan, who was born into a large, loving family, Roberto Durán was born on June 16, 1951, amid squalor, poverty, and violence, in Guararé, Panama. His birth was the result of a brief encounter between Clara Samaniego and Mexican American Margarito Durán Sánchez. Durán grew up destitute in an ultra-violent slum known as El Chorrillo, in an area ironically named "The House of Stone," or "La Casa de Piedra."[7] Durán's father was absent during his childhood. Durán learned early on how to protect himself and fight to win. For Durán, not winning a street fight meant not eating that day or not having a place to sleep. He almost always won.

Durán's childhood was grim, hard, and ugly. Everyone fought in the slums of El Chorrillo. It was a way of life. They fought with their fists and they fought with weapons, which sometimes turned deadly. They fought to prove their manhood. They fought over girls. They fought for many reasons, but most of all, they fought for pride. Durán's neighbourhood featured gang fights and one-on-one fights with other angry street urchins from various impoverished and crime-ridden neighbourhoods. Durán often went many days without food or shelter as he was usually away from home, involved in some sort of fracas. His childhood was the quintessential breeding ground for a future all-time boxing great. He proved that poverty makes fighters of us all.

Durán's rough upbringing toughened him up immeasurably and turned him into a relentlessly brutal war machine in the ring. He never asked anyone for mercy, nor did he extend it to anyone he ever faced in the squared circle. To Durán, boxing was no different than a bullfight — someone had to win and someone had to die. And Durán always had to win. He had a primal hunger to succeed that burned brightly within him from birth. His dark eyes were always aglow with rage at some perceived slight, real or imagined. He seemed to sport a perpetual wolf-like sneer upon his lips. Durán's lupine countenance let his ring rivals know that boxing was more than just a sporting contest. For Durán, boxing was his *raison d'être*.

Durán took up boxing at the very young age of eight and excelled in it from the beginning. He had finally found a place he could call home. He enjoyed a very brief amateur career, finishing with a record of sixteen wins and three losses. He turned professional at the age of sixteen, in 1968. Durán entered the pro ranks with a unanimous decision win over Carlos Mendoza on February 23, 1968. He ran off thirty-one consecutive victories to start his career, including a spectacular knockout win over future world featherweight champion Ernesto Marcel, and a particularly brutal knockout of former super featherweight world champion Hiroshi "Royal" Kobayashi.

Durán was wise beyond his years. He understood that because he was not tall and had short arms, it would be more advantageous for him to fight his opponents on the inside, at close range. Durán perfected the art of slipping and deflecting his opponent's punches with his body. By denying his opponents sufficient punching room, he prevented them from getting significant leverage on their shots. With help from Hall of Fame trainers Ray Arcel and Freddie Brown, Durán turned his physical drawbacks into strengths, which is the sign of a very smart fighter.

Durán's memorable debut at Madison Square Garden in New York on September 13, 1971, featured a sensational one-round knockout of Benny Huertas, which brought him to the attention of American fight fans. His thirty-second professional bout was for the WBA world lightweight title, held by the imperturbable Ken Buchanan. As different as they were, both in the ring and out, there were some basic similarities between them. Both men experienced hardscrabble upbringings, and boxing was their one opportunity to provide financial security for themselves and their families.

Both belligerents started out as street fighters. Durán was the fourth Panamanian to win a world boxing title (after "Panama" Al Brown, Ismael Laguna, and Alfonso "Peppermint" Frazer). He was a silent stalker inside the ropes, always looking to inflict maximum hurt on his opponents. Some fighters switch into higher gear as a fight progresses; Durán started his fights in a higher gear. His passion for ring conquests was unquenchable. He fought often because combat nourished his soul.

Both men were charismatic characters. Buchanan and Durán enjoyed legions of loyal fans all over the world. More importantly, they packed stadiums and arenas full of boisterous, overflowing crowds. Both men were paid well for their fistic talents. The differences in their respective boxing styles were reflected in their unique and distinct personalities.

Buchanan was a perfectionist, a technically flawless boxer who could bang a little but mostly won his fights by decision. His ring skills and strategies were built for distance. He was, at all times, a gentleman. His most potent ring weapon was his whipping, pinpoint jab. For Buchanan, his entire ring arsenal was set up by his left jab. If you could nullify his jab, you could beat him. He was also hailed for his ability to out-think his opponents. He possessed an unusual knack of anticipating his opponent's actions and countering them with long right hands and short left hooks upstairs. At the time of his fight with Durán, Buchanan was the most technically skilled lightweight in the world.

Buchanan's and Durán's pugilistic talents were heavily in demand in the boxing-mad hotbed of New York City. Buchanan's fan base in New York was loud, supportive, and tartan loyal. Durán's New York fan base was, much like Durán, pugnacious, boisterous, and always looking for a fight. In prizefighting, it simply doesn't get better than being a world champion and fighting in New York.

Buchanan's title reign brought temporary peace (through unification) to the previously split lightweight division. Or so it was believed. Of course, it is rather important to note that we are talking about prizefighting, where the rapacious nature of the unrepentant thieves running the Alpha Bet sanctioning bodies (cabals) was only exceeded by their chicanery. For many years, the Alpha Bet Boys collected usurious fees from unscrupulous managers to ensure their fighters were highly ranked, irrespective of their fabricated ring records. For example, Buchanan defended the unified lightweight world title four times until the WBC unceremoniously stripped him of their title for refusing to face their mandatory challenger, Spain's Pedro Carrasco. It was a typical brazen money grab by the WBC. Sadly, it still goes on today.

The WBC wanted Buchanan to pay them a huge sanctioning fee for the "privilege" of defending their lightweight title against Carrasco, who merited neither his high ranking nor a title shot. Buchanan possessed two things foreign to the WBC: personal integrity and class. Buchanan did the honourable thing by allowing Durán, the number-one-ranked lightweight in the world, a crack at the title. Buchanan knew that his prime earning power existed only for as long as he was the champion. And let's be honest here: there was a hell of a lot more money to be made facing the exciting and explosive Durán than Carrasco.

Carrasco's WBC ranking was dubious at best. He had built up his record by fighting men with more losses than wins on their respective ledgers.[8] The WBC knew that Durán was the best lightweight on Earth next to Buchanan. The WBC chose Carrasco knowing full well that Buchanan would turn them down, thereby giving them a flimsy pretext to strip him of their worthless title. (Even today, unified titles rarely remain unified for very long. Why? There's more money to be made in each weight division from disunity, with each Alpha Bet cabal crowning their own champions. The fans do not like multiple champions in each weight division, but since when have sanctioning bodies ever given a good goddamn about what fans like?)

However, as the immortal Muhammad Ali once remarked, "World titles can only be won or lost in the ring," and not in the boardrooms of crooked sanctioning bodies. In the eyes of the fans, Buchanan was still the lightweight champion of the world. Durán had cut a wide swath through the lightweight division, leaving a trail of fallen, quivering bodies in his wake. No one had seen such ferocity in the lightweight division since the days of the great Ike Williams. Durán never waited for things to unfold in the ring. He preferred to create his own opportunities by always forcing the action. In that sense, Durán's fight strategy was reminiscent of a superior homily uttered by British writer John Milton but popularized by baseball's Branch Rickey: "Luck is the residue of design."[9] In other words, Durán made his own luck with his fists. His desire for victory seemed to emerge from the very depths of his being. In his prime, he was likened to an inexhaustible ball of rage, cornering his opponents like a forest fire, growing in intensity, violently consuming everything in its path.

Durán broke most of the boxing norms. He actually got stronger and threw more blows in later rounds. The media and Buchanan misidentified Durán as nothing more than a one-dimensional slugger. Yet, there was so much more to Durán than his prodigious power. The Panamanian whirlwind was an extremely well-schooled fighter. He was the only real threat to Buchanan's lightweight title supremacy. Durán vs. Buchanan was *the* fight that fans wanted to see. Amazingly, the precocious Durán was just twenty-one years old at the time he faced the twenty-six-year-old Buchanan. Durán had no wear or tear on him. He had yet to enter his prime. It is not hyperbole to say that Durán enjoyed a longer prime at the top of his field than any other boxer in history.

Bad Blood

For several reasons, bad blood existed between Buchanan and Durán prior to their fight at Madison Square Garden. Buchanan had committed the unpardonable sin of beating Durán's hero, Laguna, to win the lightweight title. Buchanan repeated this feat one year later, in their rematch. The defeat of his hero incensed Durán. He felt he needed to avenge Laguna and restore the pride of the Panamanian people. Durán's motives were not entirely selfless; he was eager to supplant Laguna as Panama's number one sporting hero.

Durán's entire boxing career can be summed up in one word — respect. He felt that Buchanan did not respect him as a fighter. This lit a fire in Durán that could only be extinguished with Buchanan's blood. This burning rage encouraged Durán (who loathed training) to get up early each morning and faithfully do his roadwork before later entering the gym to attack his sparring partners as if they owed him money. What separated Durán from most fighters was his singularity of vision. Knocking out his opponent was never good enough for Durán. He needed to vanquish them as men, to emasculate their manhood.

Respect is something that is earned in the prize ring. Durán planned to earn Buchanan's respect with his *manos de piedra* (hands of stone). Buchanan felt that Durán had yet to fight a bona fide lightweight contender, which was incorrect. Durán bristled upon hearing Buchanan's comments. Durán's ring accomplishments were impressive and merited attention and admiration. Buchanan's blatant disregard for his accomplishments only made Durán work harder in training. Durán predicted he would knock Buchanan out within nine rounds. Buchanan laughed at Durán's bold prognostication — he unwisely never missed an opportunity to denigrate Durán's boxing skills.

To anyone familiar with Durán's fiery temperament, this was the wrong approach to take with him. Buchanan and Durán possessed two distinctly different personalities, which manifested themselves in their ring styles. The cerebral Buchanan was mentally and physically tough and always in control of his emotions. Durán, meanwhile, wore his emotions on his sleeve and used hatred to fuel his ring antics. If Buchanan was the cagey, sly fox, Durán was the rabid dog, forever snapping at your heels.

When boxing writers discuss killer instinct, they are talking about Roberto Durán. No fighter in the annals of boxing, going back over three hundred years, possessed more killer instinct than Durán. All of his opponents knew they were putting their lives in jeopardy just by getting into the ring with him, which is why, strategically, it made no sense for Buchanan to purposely antagonize him.

Buchanan's negative comments about Durán were only designed to throw him off his game. But Durán took them personally. Most fighters do not fight well when they are angry — Durán was the glaring exception to this rule. The angrier Durán was, the deadlier he became. Buchanan told the press that he believed Durán didn't know how to pace himself properly for the fifteen-round distance — he assumed Durán's stirred-up emotions would tire him out in the early rounds, leaving him susceptible to Buchanan's pinpoint jabs and counter right hands. It was a costly error in judgment. Against Buchanan, Durán got stronger and meaner and dirtier with each passing round. Durán hit Buchanan numerous times after every round, but referee LoBianco never warned him. Much to Buchanan's chagrin, Durán's tempo increased alongside his ferocity and punch output with each round.

Durán never lost focus during the fight due to his outstanding preparatory work, designed by venerable trainer Ray Arcel. Arcel was a recognized master of getting fighters in top shape, mentally and physically. He had trained many undisputed world champions, including lightweight king Benny Leonard, the only man who could usurp Durán's title as the greatest lightweight champion of all time. For someone as brilliant as Arcel to be involved with Durán should have been a clarion call to the boxing community at large that Durán was a special fighter indeed. It is worth mentioning that in 1972, Durán was not well known in boxing circles, and certainly not by the general public. But all that was about to change.

Buchanan's game plan involved putting his four-inch reach advantage (seventy to sixty-six inches) to good use by employing his jab to keep the fight on the ring perimeter. Buchanan felt strongly that he could keep Durán at bay by doubling and tripling up on his long left jab. It didn't work. Durán was stronger and faster than Buchanan expected, and he excelled at sliding under the taller man's jabs while mercilessly pounding his body and head. Durán was equally adroit at counterpunching the Scotsman from a distance. Buchanan seemed gobsmacked at times by the depth of Durán's ring skills. In later rounds, Durán began to effectively time and counter Buchanan's jabs, taking away the champion's best weapon. Buchanan became hesitant to use his jab lest he get dropped with a straight right-hand counter. Durán's ceaseless body attack started to pay big dividends in the later rounds.

Durán showed Buchanan he could fight well in a wide range of ring styles; he was never beholden to one particular mode of prizefighting. Some boxers have difficulty adapting to various ring styles, but Durán had no problem adapting to any ring style over the course of a fight. He liked to improvise in the ring. Conversely, Buchanan was a technical boxer. It was the only style that suited him and the only style with which he felt comfortable. Fighters who could not adapt against Durán rarely won. As Sugar Ray Leonard confirmed years later, Durán was difficult to nail with a flush shot on the inside because he did so many things well, such as slipping and blunting punches with his forearms and shoulders. Durán's head and shoulders were always in motion, never providing his opponent with a static target. Durán frustrated his opponents with his defensive dexterity. He was adept at catching body shots with his elbows, and he knew how to roll with punches, to lessen their impact. He was a highly skilled technical boxer and puncher. Durán also possessed a cast-iron chin (Thomas Hearns's straight right hand notwithstanding).

Durán employed a dizzying array of head, shoulder, and even foot feints. Even more frightening, he carried his power into every higher weight division he entered. He liked to double up on his crunching left hook, throwing it first to the liver and then to the head; either shot could end your night. Durán excelled at cutting off the ring and forcing his rivals to fight his fight, which contributed to their inevitable defeat. Durán never apologized for his actions in the ring. He also never hesitated to use everything at his disposal to destroy his opponents — head-butts, elbows, forearms, and low blows were all part of his repertoire. Boxing was war in its purest form. Rules were for wimps. Durán considered any fighter complaining about fouls to be looking for an easy way out and therefore deserving of no respect, in the ring or out. Both Buchanan and Durán had never faced anyone quite like the other. Each wanted to win, but only one man could. Buchanan desired to win within the rules of the sport; Durán pursued victory by any means necessary.

Buchanan was not known as a knockout puncher. It was always the cumulative effect of his blows that enabled him to stop 44 percent of his opponents.

Durán sometimes stopped his opponents with an accumulation of punches, but he could also take a man out with one shot from either hand in any round, which is why 68 percent of his opponents never saw the final bell.

Both men were complete fighters within the confines of their own unique styles. Both warriors shifted effortlessly from offence to defence and back. Although Buchanan wouldn't admit it beforehand, Durán was definitely his equal in terms of technical skill, and most definitely his master when it came to firepower. Durán's star was just starting to ascend, while Buchanan's had already reached its zenith and was starting to lose velocity and elevation — though he did not know it at the time. The critical difference between Buchanan and Durán was in their attitudes — Durán disdained ring niceties, like touching gloves before the fight and at the start of the last round.

Durán never cared much for rules, which is why, offensively, he held his rivals against the ropes with his shoulders while goring and mauling them up close. He liked to immobilize his opponents before methodically battering them into submission with a two-fisted full body attack. Arcel told Durán to approach each opponent as if he were a lumberjack. It was an apt metaphor — Durán kept chopping away at the tree in front of him, knowing that eventually it would succumb to his will. He enjoyed taking time to punish his foe. He liked to bring the pain.

Although known as a complete fighter, Buchanan did have one noticeable ring flaw: he was a notoriously slow starter. He needed time to get into the flow of a fight. Time, however, was a luxury that Durán would not allow him. Durán always flew out of his corner in every round as if you had insulted his sister. Buchanan wasn't easily rattled during a fight, but that would change when pitted against Durán. The champion preferred to be patient and methodical in his attack — he didn't like taking unnecessary risks in the ring. But patience was a virtue Durán had never possessed, inside or outside of the squared circle.

Buchanan would have to be in mid-fight form from the opening bell.

Buchanan exhibited a steely demeanour inside the ring. He seemed to be above the fray, as if on a higher plane. Arcel had devised a plan for Durán to ruffle the champion's feathers and bring him back down to earth. Arcel knew from his past experience that Durán's constant aggression and liberal use of his head and elbows would prick Buchanan's stiff upper lip — his plan was to upset Buchanan by disrupting his rhythm and composure. With the exception of Gene Tunney, no fighter displayed more self-control between the ropes than Buchanan. He was the personification of grace under pressure. Yet no fighter was better at getting under an opponent's skin than Durán. And Arcel knew this.

At the packed press conference in New York, Buchanan perhaps displayed too much confidence by refusing to watch the highlights of Durán's fights. The champion blissfully ignored clips of his opponent's previous victories while calmly eating his lunch. Durán could weather just about anything except personal disrespect. Buchanan's grand self-assurance strengthened Durán's resolve to earn the champion's respect by beating it out of him, round by round, punch by punch, head-butt by head-butt, low blow by low blow. Buchanan's mistake was that he failed to realize that for Durán, the fight had started long before they ever entered the Madison Square Garden ring.

Durán's brilliant brain trust of Arcel and Freddie Brown formulated his no-holds-barred ring strategy, which proved extremely effective against Buchanan and so many other elite fighters in subsequent fights. Arcel knew all the little tricks of the trade that would help a fighter succeed. For instance, at the beginning of each round, Arcel placed his arms under Durán's armpits and lifted him up off the stool. This helped preserve Durán's leg strength throughout the bout.

Durán's fight plan was almost military in its precision. He never allowed Buchanan a chance to relax or extend his arms. Durán crowded the champion in each round, never allowing him enough room to punch effectively or manoeuvre. Durán never allowed Buchanan into the fight. By design, Durán planted his head on Buchanan's chest in the first round and kept it there for the whole fight. Arcel and Brown's strategy worked to perfection. Durán was constantly feinting Buchanan and giving him different angles with which to contend. This was a skill Durán was not supposed to have, according to Buchanan. Arcel had been in boxing for almost six decades and he'd readily shared his wealth of knowledge with Durán, instructing him to move his head up, under Buchanan's chin, thereby forcing Buchanan to lift his head up, whereupon Durán was able to consistently nail him with left hooks. It was an old-time move but extremely effective.

Buchanan was never able to establish a good rhythm in the fight. He was like a shark — he needed to be constantly moving and employing angles in order to be an effective fighter. He was incapable of fighting well off the ropes. Durán immobilized Buchanan against the ropes by putting his lead left foot between Buchanan's feet. This manoeuvre effectively stopped the champion from spinning off the ropes and out of harm's way. Buchanan had been trained by the great Gil Clancy. Clancy wanted Buchanan to use his legs to continuously circle and turn Durán, which would force Durán to constantly reset his boxing stance. He aimed to frustrate the challenger into making foolish, desperate lunges, exposing his chin in the process. Buchanan wanted to use the young Panamanian's own momentum and anger against him, hoping to eventually tire him out. This strategy failed enormously — Durán never permitted Buchanan the chance to establish the necessary distance required to get his shots off.

Durán jumped on Buchanan in round one, scoring a flash knockdown. Buchanan was not dropped, rather his gloves touched the canvas briefly after Durán tagged him on his back, when he was off balance. It should have been ruled a slip. Referee LoBianco, incredibly, ruled it a knockdown. This was not one of LoBianco's stellar nights as the third man in the ring.

Later in the first round, Buchanan caught an off-balance Durán with a hard right hand, causing him to fall back into the ropes. According to NYSAC rules, if a fighter is held up by the ropes after receiving a punch, it is considered a knockdown. LoBianco did not see it that way, and Durán soon recovered. From the first round until the thirteenth, Durán committed dozens and dozens of obvious fouls that LoBianco, with one exception, steadfastly ignored.

Durán managed to stay on top of Buchanan round after round, completely negating the champion's necessary mobility. The problem for Buchanan was that he had no plan B. How do you counter a tidal wave? You can't; you can only succumb to it. Durán's ceaseless body barrages took the steam out of the champion's legs and punches. Buchanan briefly managed to tag Durán with some hard head shots. He said after the fight that he had never hit any man harder, yet the challenger just smiled and shook his head. The champion was quickly becoming demoralized. In the end, Buchanan did not possess enough power to earn Durán's respect. Buchanan had little left to offer — at this point, he was just hoping to last the fifteen-round distance. He had fought to the best of his abilities but was exhausted and trailing badly on all three scorecards going into the thirteenth round.

Controversy

Why didn't referee LoBianco warn or deduct points from Durán for his deliberate use of head-butts, elbows, forearms, hitting on the break, punching after the bell, and low blows throughout the fight? Why did LoBianco willingly ignore the NYSAC rules, as outlined in sections 211.47 and 211.48, as they pertained to fouling an opponent?[10]

Why did LoBianco not disqualify Durán after the thirteenth round and rule the fight a no-contest?

Was LoBianco unaware that Durán's use of his shoulders (while common) was strictly forbidden by the NYSAC? Why did LoBianco not disqualify Durán for brazenly hitting Buchanan after the bell and well below the belt at the end of round thirteen?

Perhaps the most pertinent question to be asked is, if LoBianco did not believe that Durán had fouled Buchanan, why then was the champion rolling around on the canvas, writhing in extreme pain? Did LoBianco think Buchanan was feigning an injury? In other words, if no foul had been committed, and the punch did not count in LoBianco's assessment, why then stop the fight? Shouldn't that have been a no-contest decision?

Furthermore, if in LoBianco's mind nothing untoward occurred, why then did he award the lightweight world title to Durán at the start of the fourteenth round even though Buchanan was ready to continue? Wasn't LoBianco bound to strictly follow the bylaws of the NYSAC as outlined in their rulebook? Finally, what was LoBianco's reasoning for penalizing Buchanan and rewarding Durán?

The Decision

To the utter astonishment of blow-by-blow announcer Don Dunphy, the maladroit LoBianco only warned Durán once during the entire thirteen foul-filled rounds. LoBianco told Durán in round thirteen to keep his punches up. It was not an official warning, though. Durán ignored LoBianco, and the rules, and just kept on fouling Buchanan. LoBianco blithely chose to ignore the NYSAC bylaws regarding fighter conduct during the entire fight.

As the tape of the fight shows, the bell clearly sounded several times to end the thirteenth round. It was at this time that referee LoBianco committed several sins of omission that will live forever in the boxing hall of shame. At the end of round thirteen, the bell clanged seven times to indicate that the round was indisputably over. Seven clangs means seven seconds had passed from when Durán hit Buchanan with a right hook well below the beltline. Buchanan, writhing in agony, slumped to the canvas and his eyes rolled into the back of his head. Buchanan's cornerman, Clancy, practically had to carry Buchanan to his corner. Clancy later claimed that Durán had kneed Buchanan in the groin.

Clancy's assertion must be taken seriously because from his position in Buchanan's corner, he was perfectly placed to see exactly what had just transpired. If Durán had in fact kneed Buchanan, should he not have been disqualified according to section 247.11(a) 2 of the NYSAC rulebook, which states that using a knee against an opponent is a disqualifiable offence?[11]

The debilitating effect of Durán's constant fouls on Buchanan was rather telling. The lightweight king's strength and stamina were fading fast in the later rounds. It was disappointing that a world title bout was marred by Durán's fouling and the adamant refusal of an inept referee to do anything about it. It was abundantly clear to everyone in Madison Square Garden that day that LoBianco was there as an observer and not as a referee. After the fight, *Sports Illustrated* reported, "Duran … used every part of his anatomy, everything but his knee, and he would be accused of that breach of etiquette, too." Buchanan accurately remarked after the fight, "I had no protection from the referee tonight."[12] LoBianco was an empty bow tie that night and nothing more.

Durán was hitting Buchanan each time LoBianco broke up a clinch between them. This is strictly against the rules and yet Durán was not warned even once for this infraction.

Buchanan needed a knockout to retain his title. It was evident to the champion and everyone watching the fight that this was not going to happen. For Buchanan the fight had become a matter of survival. Losing the title was a foregone conclusion — the only thing left for Buchanan to successfully retain was his pride.

On the tape of the fight, six separate but distinct actions occurred in rapid succession after round thirteen ended. These actions are what make this fight one of the most controversial in ring history.

1. The bell clanged to end the round.
2. Referee LoBianco attempted to restrain Durán from behind because Durán had been punching Buchanan after the bell in every round.
3. Durán freed his right hand and punched Buchanan's testicles.
4. Buchanan fell to the canvas in excruciating pain.
5. Buchanan rose and indicated he wanted to continue.
6. LoBianco lost control of his senses and the fight.

LoBianco's mishandling of the fight after round thirteen certainly cast a lingering shadow over the legitimacy of the beginning of Durán's title reign. The salient point in LoBianco's mind was not that Durán's shot was low, but rather that Buchanan was struck after the round had *ended*, so the placement of the punch could not be considered an infraction.

Dunphy interviewed LoBianco only seconds after he had inexplicably stopped the fight and awarded the title to Durán. LoBianco stated that Buchanan was hit after the bell and that the blow should not have counted. He then added that Buchanan was clearly in no condition to continue, which is why he stopped the fight and bestowed the lightweight crown on Durán. That makes no sense whatsoever.

If LoBianco did not count the blow because it landed after the bell, then there was no reason to stop the fight and award the title to Durán. If, as LoBianco ruled, Buchanan could not continue, the fight was, by definition, a no-contest. There was simply no logic to LoBianco's reasoning or actions. They were specious at best. LoBianco compounded his error by ridiculously claiming that it was not a low blow but rather a punch to the lower part of the abdomen. He must have been absent from school the day they taught anatomy in health class. The lower part of the abdomen is the groin. Punches to the groin are not considered legal in boxing. We can only take LoBianco at his word, which raises another question: If, as he claimed, he did not count the late blow, why then did it matter where it landed?

LoBianco was unfortunately not finished spewing twaddle. He nonsensically added that it was impossible to be hurt by a low blow on the cup in a boxing match. Apparently, Durán's foul inflicted more damage than originally thought. It not only fractured Buchanan's right testicle, it also short-circuited LoBianco's brain. This was boxing's version of the Warren Commission's magic bullet theory. Obviously LoBianco had never engaged in a boxing match or a football game. Buchanan was struck under his cup in an exposed and unprotected area. LoBianco's comments about the impact of the blow only served to contradict what he had just said about omitting the blow. Why make an inane comment regarding Buchanan's jockstrap if the punch was not officially counted?

Also, if Buchanan was kneed in the groin, as was claimed by his trainer Clancy, then Durán had committed a flagrant foul, which should have resulted in his immediate disqualification according to NYSAC rules. This was never addressed. That Buchanan had been fouled was certain. How do we know this? Because Buchanan suffered a ruptured testicle. Doctor A. Harry Kleiman of NYSAC examined Buchanan after the fight and said, "He has a swelling of the right testicle. He's in extreme pain." Years later, Buchanan said the low blow "dented my protector and metal burst into my right ball. I was peeing blood for days."[13]

In his defence, LoBianco could not have known the true extent of Buchanan's testicular injuries at that moment. But to be so oblivious to the fact that Buchanan had suffered grievous harm required a concerted effort. LoBianco's incomprehensible ramblings to Dunphy post-fight only exacerbated an already bad situation. Given everything that had transpired, LoBianco had several specific options as outlined in the NYSAC rulebook from which he could select a proper outcome for the fight. Since striking an opponent after the bell is considered a major foul, LoBianco could have disqualified Durán and awarded the bout to Buchanan, thereby allowing him to rightfully retain his title.

LoBianco could also have deducted one or more points from Durán. That would not have changed the situation, but it would have been the right thing to do. LoBianco chose to neither deduct a point from Durán nor disqualify him for deliberately striking Buchanan below the belt after the bell.

LoBianco was an experienced, veteran referee and should have deduced that something covered in the NYSAC rulebook had just taken place. He was bound by law to strictly adhere to the NYSAC rules when refereeing a fight. At the very least, the fight should have been declared a no contest — that would have been the sensible thing to do.

There are two sections in the NYSAC rules governing boxing that apply directly to the outcome of this fight, and had they been followed properly, it is unlikely the fight would have ended in controversy. Section 211.48 discusses injuries sustained by fouls and how to rule on them. It's all there in black and white. These rules are codified and unequivocal:

1. If an intentional foul causes an injury, and the injury is severe enough to terminate the bout immediately, the boxer causing the injury shall lose by disqualification.

2. If an intentional foul causes an injury and the bout is allowed to continue, the referee will notify the authorities and deduct two (2) points from the boxer who caused the foul. Point deductions for intentional fouls causing injury will be mandatory.

3. If an intentional foul causes an injury and the bout is allowed to continue, and the injury results in the bout being stopped in any round after the fourth (4th) round, the injured boxer will win by TECHNICAL DECISION if he is ahead on the score cards or the bout will result in a TECHNICAL DRAW if the injured boxer is behind or even on the score cards. Partial or incomplete rounds will be scored. If no action has occurred, the round should be scored as an even round.

4. If a boxer injures himself while attempting to intentionally foul his opponent, the referee will not take any action in his favor, and this injury will be the same as one produced by a fair blow.

5. If the referee feels that a boxer has conducted himself in an unsportsmanlike manner, he/she may stop the bout and disqualify the boxer.

All of the possible outcomes for how the fight was supposed to end are unambiguously stated above. Rules 1, 2, 3, and 5 are all applicable to the Buchanan-Durán brawl. Hitting Buchanan after the bell was an intentional foul. Buchanan was injured. He was behind on the scorecards. LoBianco ruled that Buchanan could not continue. Therefore, the bout should have been declared a technical draw according to the NYSAC. This remains one of boxing's biggest travesties. LoBianco's unfathomable decision to ignore the explicitly stated NYSAC rules and give the win to Durán was an unmitigated farce. It is one of the top ten worst referee decisions in boxing history.

LoBianco's actions were disgraceful to Buchanan, to the fans, and to the great sport of boxing.

Ironically, Durán denied himself the knockout win he had so coveted by his own illegal actions. His victory over Buchanan remains tainted. The only other option open to LoBianco was to total up the scorecards for the first thirteen rounds to determine the winner, which would have been Durán. Unfortunately, amid all of the confusion over how the round ended, the judges neglected to score the thirteenth round. Of course, that route became unnecessary once Buchanan forcefully stated to LoBianco that he could continue and, indeed, insisted on doing so. Clancy, Buchanan's chief second, emphatically told LoBianco that his fighter wished to continue. LoBianco ignored them both as well as the rules, which makes him as complicit as Durán in Buchanan's unjust downfall. The manner in which this fight ended was a travesty and a deep embarrassment to boxing.

We do not know what, if anything, was going through LoBianco's mind at that moment. All we have to go by is what LoBianco said on camera to Dunphy. He did not penalize Durán because he believed that no foul of *any* kind had taken place, even though he readily admitted that the punch in question occurred after the bell. The only logical response to that comment is, why then stop the fight when Buchanan was willing to continue at the start of round fourteen? LoBianco was a very well-respected referee, and there is no indication or evidence of any kind to suggest that his actions were in any way deliberately untoward or anything other than gross incompetence.

If a referee disputes that a foul was committed and believes that the blow landed was a legitimate punch, he can continue counting over the stricken fighter. However, that did not happen here. LoBianco's claims about the placement of the blow on Buchanan's body are irrelevant because *any* blow landed after the bell has rung, whether it be low or legitimate, is by definition an illegal punch. This pertinent fact seems to have eluded LoBianco.

Thanks to shoddy officiating, Buchanan could not have been robbed of his title any better if he'd had a gun to his head. The most plausible explanation is usually the simplest. In this instance, the only credible answer is that LoBianco, under pressure, screwed up big time. At the very least, and leave it to pro boxing to always do the very least when something afoul is afoot, the NYSAC should have mandated an immediate rematch.

Significance

The significance of this fight is that Roberto Durán was awarded the world lightweight title, his first title win. He subsequently went on to become the greatest lightweight champion in boxing history. Even though Durán's title victory was circumspect, he went on to dominate the lightweight division in the 1970s, destroying each challenger to his lightweight throne with vicious efficiency. He made headlines constantly, both in and out of the ring. Durán's incredible success at lightweight culminated with him moving up in weight, to capture the world welterweight title from Sugar Ray Leonard in Montreal on June 20, 1980. Durán also won titles at junior middleweight, middleweight, and super middleweight.

Buchanan continued boxing successfully after the Durán fight, recapturing the European lightweight title. Durán did in fact agree to give Buchanan a rematch several times, but his manager, the wily Carlos Eleta, always found a reason to cancel any scheduled rematch with Buchanan. Buchanan knew that Durán's total belief in himself was such that he would never avoid giving anyone a rematch. It was Eleta who did not want to risk giving the always-dangerous Buchanan another crack at the lightweight title. In essence, Eleta scotched the Scotsman.

Durán's win over Buchanan launched him into boxing's big time. He started to receive huge paydays for his fights. He was an elite-level fighter in his prime. He was also the best fighter, pound for pound, in the world. He went on to clean out the lightweight division several times over. Durán's greatest ring skill was his ability to make his opponents fight his fight. It was very difficult to take him out of his natural rhythm, although Sugar Ray Leonard managed to accomplish that feat in their second bout.

In prizefighting, a fight can only be judged by what happened and not by what might have or should have happened. Incredibly, the controversy surrounding this bout did not end that evening. *Sports Illustrated* reported: "Later in the week, slow-motion replays of the television film seemed to convince LoBianco that the Scot was hit below the belt." Big deal. LoBianco's *ex post facto* admission was one week too late to help Buchanan.

The brilliant *New York Times* columnist Walter "Red" Smith remarked in his column of June 28, 1972:

> The match ended untidily, in such disorder that two of the three officials forgot to score the last round. Buchanan lay writhing, face contorted and limbs twitching involuntarily. Nobody in position to see could doubt that his suffering was genuine and the examining physician said later that there was physical evidence of damage in foul territory.
>
> Still, under the stern code that governs this rowdy business in New York, LoBianco had no choice but to declare Duran [*sic*] the winner. In the United Kingdom, where Buchanan learned his trade, boxers still are disqualified for illegal punches, but for something like 40 years on these shores boxers have been encased in mail designed by an armorer named Foulproof Taylor and anything short of pulling a knife is regarded indulgently.

Some American boxing referees were perhaps a bit more lenient during that time period when it came to calling fouls in title matches. That was more of a personal preference than a specific American style of refereeing. The American ethos concerning boxing has always been that it is a fight, and in a fight, fouls happen. It is part of the sport. If you don't approve of what your opponent is doing, then foul him back.

The conclusion of the Buchanan-Durán bout did not take place on June 26, 1972. There was no clear postscript to this fight until, surprisingly, March of 2002.[14] Durán travelled to England then, ostensibly to make peace with both his past and Buchanan. After an emotional hug between the two warriors, Durán admitted to hitting Buchanan low after the bell for the thirteenth round had sounded. And in what can only be described as a totally uncharacteristic move, Durán publicly apologized to Buchanan for his actions. Both men embraced and wept, as did the audience while applauding loudly. It took thirteen rounds plus thirty years and a ruptured testicle for Buchanan's fight with Durán to officially come to an end. It was a hard-won victory for both men.

CHAPTER 11

MIKE TYSON VS. EVANDER HOLYFIELD II

Fight: Mike Tyson vs. Evander Holyfield II
Weight Class: Heavyweight
Title at Stake: WBA heavyweight
Date: June 28, 1997
Location: MGM Grand, Las Vegas, Nevada
Outcome: Holyfield victory by third-round disqualification
Referee: Mills Lane

Background

The first fight between WBA heavyweight champion Mike Tyson and challenger Evander Holyfield ennobled boxing. Their second battle disgraced it. Their infamous rematch was originally supposed to take place on May 3, 1997. It had to be rescheduled for June 28, 1997, because Tyson had suffered a cut over his left eye due to an accidental head-butt from a sparring partner, while training. Such mishaps are not unusual. Very few fighters ever enter the prize ring 100 percent healthy.

The long-awaited Tyson-Holyfield rematch that took place at the MGM Grand in Las Vegas is commonly referred to as the "Bite Fight" because of the shameful and astonishing manner in which the bout ended. However, it must be noted that there was a lot going on in their second scrap prior to Tyson chomping down on Holyfield's ear, which eluded the casual observer. Some of the animosity between the two combatants stemmed from their hellacious, hard-fought first bout, where both men liberally employed a variety of foul tactics. Such manoeuvres have long been a staple of professional boxing. In fact, fouls are so ingrained in boxing's ethos that many top trainers of the past readily taught their fighters how to commit these misdeeds without drawing notice from the referee. After all, it's a fight, not a spelling bee.

Even though fouls have always been ubiquitous to boxing, each fighter has a finite limit as to how many illegal blows he is willing to absorb before resorting to similar tactics, to dissuade his opponent from fighting outside of the accepted rules of the sport. Fighters understand and accept accidental fouls — such things happen all the time during a match. Deliberate fouls are another matter entirely. Deliberate fouls are considered verboten because they are a clear, unequivocal sign of disrespect from one fighter to another. One of boxing's oldest and most immutable rules is that you cannot take liberties (physically or verbally) with a prizefighter under any circumstances, in or out of the ring. It just isn't done. This tacit rule applies to everyone who comes into contact with professional fighters, including other professional fighters.

Most prizefighters are, by nature, very private and used to being on their own for long stretches of time while training. Some pugs (pugilists) will let you tease them verbally, up to a point; however, that is extremely rare, and there will come a time when a fighter will give you an unmistakeable sign (a malevolent look or a few choice words) to let you know that you have crossed a line and that you should back off. Unfortunately, some people miss these signals or just ignore them at their own peril. Becoming physical with a fighter, even in a playful sense, is dangerous in any situation. It's akin to becoming playfully physical with a grizzly bear. It just isn't done. Yet there are many stories of people crossing the line with professional pugilists.

Regardless of the trash talk fighters engage in before bouts, most boxers have an innate sense of respect for their opponents. It takes a lot of skill, discipline, and courage to try and make a living as a prizefighter. But that respect can, at times, be severely tested if one fighter continually and deliberately fouls his rival. In most cases, his opponent will give it back to him even more viciously. It is really the only foolproof, time-honoured method of bringing your foe's fouling to a halt. Referees are only human — sometimes they miss fouls being committed. Inside the squared circle, when the battle gets heated, all fighters are on their own. You have a problem with your opponent fouling you? Stop complaining and fix it yourself! Throughout boxing history, fighters have often looked to the referee for help and woken up later to regret it.

It is no secret that Mike Tyson won the majority of his fights with a combination of blazing speed, unfathomable power, and intimidation. The latter was a major contributing factor in some of Tyson's biggest wins — many of his opponents were mentally beaten prior to stepping into the ring to do battle with him. Not all of Tyson's opponents were able to be cowed into submission, however; James "Buster" Douglas proved to be immune to Tyson's bullying tactics. Evander Holyfield was also incapable of being browbeaten by any man. In fact, Holyfield's goal was to intimidate Tyson, throwing him off of his game mentally, just as he did in their first fight.

Holyfield used his superior height, reach, strength, and power to dominate Tyson in the first two rounds of their rematch. Holyfield effectively blunted Tyson's attacks by clinching him tightly and walking him to the ropes. Tyson knew he had a large problem in front of him once again. He was forced to admit to himself that he could not scare or outmuscle Holyfield. Tyson must have been haunted by the fact that he could not physically or strategically alter this equation. He was like a drowning man flailing away in the middle of a lake — the more he tried to save himself, the closer he came to drowning. All he could hope for was that Holyfield would tire or that he could catch him with a knockout shot. Neither eventuality came to pass.

It would be fair to say that both men were masters of the art of fouling. Holyfield was definitely guilty of excessive holding, head-butting, low blows, and using his forearms, shoulders, and elbows as weapons. Tyson also used his forearms and elbows to inflict damage on Holyfield in their second fight. Holyfield was particularly adept at physically controlling Tyson. The former champ was becoming annoyed with his inability to rough up Holyfield on the inside. Tyson had employed similar borderline tactics against his previous ring foes with great success. But Holyfield's superior strength immobilized Tyson's efforts. Tyson's famed fight focus was beginning to fade.

Tyson rushed straight toward Holyfield at the opening bell of their rematch. Holyfield slickly sidestepped and slipped Tyson's bull-like rushes. Early in round one, Holyfield rocked Tyson with a short, thudding right hook to the head. "Iron Mike" retreated to the ropes to cover up. Tyson's frustration grew as he tried to impose his will on Holyfield without success. Round one of their rematch was a continuation of round eleven from their first fight. Tyson was only able to get off one punch at a time before Holyfield clinched him. He would need to land multiple combinations if he hoped to get his title back, and the odds of him doing so were growing longer with each passing round.

To be sure, many controversial fights from boxing's past ended in sheer pandemonium. The fourth fight between featherweight greats Willie Pep and Sandy Saddler at the Polo Grounds on September 26, 1951, was a ceaseless foul-fest for nine rounds. Referee Ray Miller stopped the fight and awarded it to Saddler on a technical decision when Pep quit after the ninth round due to a horrific cut over his right eye. The NYSAC revoked Pep's boxing license and suspended Saddler indefinitely.

One of the most notorious foul-filled free-for-alls in boxing history took place on November 15, 1940, at Madison Square Garden in New York, between Al "Bummy" Davis and Fritzie Zivic. Zivic is recognized as the dirtiest fighter in modern boxing history. He dropped Davis in the first round; in the second, Zivic deliberately thumbed Davis in his eyes multiple times. Thumbing an opponent is considered the most egregious foul, because by blinding your opponent, you are deliberately depriving him of his livelihood. Davis was not a docile man by any means. He was a hellraiser who always entered the ring with a nasty disposition. Davis responded to Zivic's provocations by landing ten consecutive low blows on Zivic. When Zivic fell to the canvas, Davis started to kick him in the head and groin. Davis then kicked and punched referee Billy Cavanaugh. Davis tried to pull Zivic up off of the canvas, to continue the fight. Cavanaugh disqualified Davis at the 2:34 mark of round two, awarding the fight to Zivic. The fans rioted, and Davis required a police escort to leave the ring in one piece. He was suspended for life by the NYSAC but was later reinstated on July 7, 1941, for a rematch against Zivic. Zivic stopped Davis by a knockout in the tenth round of their rematch.

Incredibly, the second bout between Tyson and Holyfield was wilder than the Zivic-Davis and fourth Pep-Saddler imbroglios. The debacle that was their second bout found its origins in their first ring encounter. There was bad blood between the two warriors, going back to their amateur days. There was, however, more to the "Bite Fight" than past disputes. Tyson was perturbed with how Holyfield had used his head as a weapon in their first encounter. Holyfield was well known for this tactic. Neither Tyson nor Holyfield invented these fouls, but they certainly made good use of them. Tyson was clearly upset with Holyfield's ability to overpower him with seemingly little effort. Tyson was powerless to resolve this situation in his own favour.

Only seven months earlier, on November 9, 1996, Tyson had defended his WBA world heavyweight title for the first time against Holyfield. Holyfield was a huge underdog at twenty-five to one. Their first go-round was supposed to be an easy fight for Tyson, a sort of gift for the first defence of his second reign as WBA heavyweight champion. Frustration played a major role in both of their fights due to myriad unforeseen events. Their first brawl had been rescheduled several times — they were originally slated to fight on June 18, 1990, in Atlantic City, New Jersey. This was to be a big money fight, with Tyson earning twenty-two million dollars and Holyfield taking home eleven million. The fight never took place thanks to Buster Douglas. Douglas pulled off arguably the single greatest upset in boxing history when, as a forty-two to one underdog, he knocked out Tyson in the tenth round of their fight on February 11, 1990, in Tokyo, Japan.

The heavyweight title then became a game of musical chairs. On October 25, 1990, Holyfield knocked out an uninterested and out-of-shape Douglas in three rounds to become the new heavyweight king. A contract was then signed for Holyfield to face Tyson on November 8, 1991, at Caesars Palace in Las Vegas, in one of the most anticipated heavyweight title fights in years. As champion, Holyfield was promised thirty million dollars and Tyson was guaranteed fifteen million. Fight fans around the world were thrilled that they would finally get to see Tyson and Holyfield go at it.

Then events overtook sport when in July 1991, Tyson was arrested and charged with raping eighteen-year-old Desiree Washington, a contestant in the Miss Black America beauty pageant. The fight with Holyfield was still on, although many felt that proceeding with the match was in poor taste. Then again, when has poor taste ever bothered the mealy-mouthed lowlifes that control boxing? Still more bad news was to follow, however. On October 19, 1992, Tyson injured his ribs while sparring, and the Holyfield fight was indefinitely postponed. Tyson's rape trial began on January 27, 1992, in Indiana. On February 10, 1992, Tyson was found guilty of rape and sentenced to six years in the Indiana Youth Center in Plainfield, Indiana. He was released from prison in March 1995, after serving less than three years.

On March 16, 1996, Tyson knocked out overmatched Brit Frank Bruno in three rounds to recapture the WBC heavyweight title. On September 7, 1996, in the easiest fight of his career, Tyson dropped a terrified Bruce Seldon twice before stopping him in the first round to regain the WBA belt. Tyson then gave up the WBC strap rather than defend it against Lennox Lewis. At that time, Lewis was the best heavyweight in the world. He was a brilliantly skilled boxer who carried crushing knockout power in both hands. Unlike Seldon, Lewis feared no man. Tyson was wise to avoid him.

Tyson made the first defence of his WBA belt against Evander Holyfield. Holyfield was given virtually no chance whatsoever by the oddsmakers of beating Tyson. He had lost three of his previous seven bouts and was suffering from a non-compliant left ventricle, which almost forced him to retire from boxing. The heart problem was eventually corrected. Holyfield ignored the detractors and kept on fighting.

The first Holyfield-Tyson extravaganza occurred on November 9, 1996, at the MGM Grand in Las Vegas. Their original bout laid the groundwork for the madness that ensued in the third stanza of their rematch. A crowd of sixteen thousand hardcore fight fans produced a live gate of just over fourteen million dollars. Pay-per-view buys generated an additional seventy-nine million dollars. It was a great, action-packed heavyweight fight. To the surprise of everyone in attendance, including the champion, Holyfield smartly kept turning and spinning Tyson throughout the fight. Holyfield frustrated Tyson time and time again, with his quicker hand speed and superior boxing skills. Tyson certainly got his shots in, but Holyfield took them well and countered quickly with stiff, hard, short punches of his own.

The bigger Holyfield used his strength to bully Tyson around the ring. Holyfield was also very adept at picking off Tyson's shots. Tyson's defence was lacking as he was getting tagged consistently with short right hands flush on the chin. Tyson was having great difficulty fighting while backing up. That was not his game. He was much more effective coming forward, but Holyfield did not allow him to do so.

Near the end of the second round, Holyfield hurt Tyson badly with a right hook. Tyson was literally out on his feet. How he remained upright was anybody's guess. In the sixth round, Holyfield caught the uncharacteristically off-balance Tyson with a right hand and dropped him. It was a huge psychological turning point for Holyfield. He had shown the world that Tyson was indeed mortal, and more importantly, he had shown Tyson that intimidation would not be a factor in this fight. A few seconds earlier in round six, referee Mitch Halpern called time to tell the judges about an accidental head-butt delivered by Holyfield against Tyson. Tyson had rushed in head first and their heads clashed. Halpern warned both men to watch their heads.

The problem for Tyson was that Holyfield had been leading with his head in every exchange from the first round on. Holyfield's head was a potent part of his repertoire in most of his fights. Contrary to what Team Tyson said post-fight, Halpern had indeed warned Holyfield about butting after Tyson was cut. In round seven, Tyson rushed in at Holyfield, resulting in another severe head-butt, which buckled Tyson's legs. Tyson was confused, frustrated, and discouraged as the fight began slipping away from him.

Near the end of round ten, Holyfield caught Tyson with a crushingly concussive right hand, forcing the champion to the ropes. Tyson was helpless as Holyfield pounded away, but the bell soon ended things. Tyson gingerly walked back to his corner in a daze. In the eleventh round, Holyfield poured it on and finished Tyson off, with referee Halpern wisely stopping the fight at the 2:23 mark. Tyson was unable to defend himself. It was named the Fight and the Upset of the Year by *Ring* magazine.

No one believed that Holyfield would last more than three rounds against Tyson. The oddsmakers had not taken Holyfield's ring intelligence and innate toughness into consideration. "The Real Deal" refused to be intimidated, outsmarted, or outmuscled by the supposedly stronger Tyson. Holyfield's six-inch reach advantage allowed him to fight effectively from the outside. On the inside, Holyfield smartly shortened up his shots. He constantly proved to be the more formidable of the two, having no problem shoving Tyson around the ring. Tyson never dealt well with ring adversity because other than his loss to Douglas, he had never been forced to deal with setbacks in his previous matches.

The later rounds of their first fight led directly to what happened in their second bout. Tyson was extremely annoyed that Holyfield was landing numerous low blows, head-butts, and forearms in every round. Tyson was definitely no saint in the prize ring, as evidenced in his prior bouts, but against Holyfield, even fouling didn't work. Holyfield simply could not be ruffled, and Tyson did not possess enough strength to back him off. Tyson entered their rematch determined to show the world that Holyfield got lucky in their first melee. Of course, great fighters make their own luck through hard work and determination.

Mike Tyson and Evander Holyfield must be viewed within the context of the decade that shaped them and their ring attitudes, the ultra-turbulent 1960s. Both men came from impoverished backgrounds, in different states, in mostly all African American neighbourhoods that had been deliberately neglected by state and federal governments. Both warriors and their families were victims of the institutionalized racism directed specifically toward African Americans. Such systemic racism made a mockery of the American Constitution.

The 1960s moved along at supersonic speed, with events occurring much faster than the ability of most Americans to absorb them. Tyson and Holyfield were both products of these changes as their families were directly impacted by the civil rights movement and its leaders, in particular Muhammad Ali. Both Holyfield and Tyson started their lives with less than nothing. Tyson perhaps more so because Holyfield at least had his mother's love to support him. Holyfield's mother adored him and constantly instilled him with pride and confidence. Tyson rarely if ever saw his mother and almost never received any affection except from his older sister. He was largely a product of the often-brutal streets of New York and had been from a very young age.

Above all else, the 1960s were an ultra-violent, bloody, war-filled decade. There was violence on every street in every state in America. Given the soaring murder rates, multiple political assassinations, and the implacable Berlin Wall of anti–African American bigotry, it is a miracle in and of itself that both Holyfield and Tyson even survived into adulthood. When you consider the trials and tribulations they were forced to overcome during their childhoods, boxing was probably the safest route they could have chosen for success and security.

The Real Deal

Like many previous heavyweight champions, Evander Holyfield's life is the embodiment of a Horatio Alger rags-to-riches story. Looking back, Holyfield's life story appears extremely improbable. Then again, Holyfield has made a very successful career out of making the improbable possible. Has he kept most of the money he earned in the prize ring? No, but very few boxers do, for a variety of reasons. He was the youngest of nine children, born on October 19, 1962, in Atmore, Alabama. The family moved to Atlanta, Georgia, when Holyfield was still young. He came from a terribly poor family. Their dire financial straits forced them to live in a crime-ridden area of Atlanta known as the Bowen Homes Housing Projects.[1] Holyfield took up boxing at the very young age of seven. He was told all along the way that he would never amount to anything in the sport. But his mother's unwavering confidence in him helped Holyfield to develop an unshakeable belief in himself. From a young age, Holyfield mastered the very demanding emotional and mental aspects of boxing. He always exhibited an incredible amount of self-discipline and focus when it came to pugilism. Mentally, Holyfield may have been the toughest fighter ever to have lived.

Holyfield faced various setbacks on his eventual road to boxing success, but he never allowed any defeats he suffered to dissuade him from achieving his original goal of universal fistic supremacy, which he attained many times over. Holyfield qualified for the Junior Olympics in 1975 at age thirteen. Then in 1983, at the age of twenty-one, he qualified for the Pan American Games in Caracas, Venezuela, where he emerged with a silver medal in the light-heavyweight division. Holyfield was cheated of the chance to fight for the gold medal at the 1984 Los Angeles Olympic Games after he was disqualified by a horrendously incompetent referee in his bout with New Zealander Kevin Barry. Holyfield had to settle for the bronze medal. What happened to Holyfield at the Olympics acutely highlights the fact that the pro game does not have an exclusivity contract with corruption. Just ask Roy Jones Jr. or Michael Conlan about the integrity of boxing officials in the Olympic Games.

Holyfield accepted his Olympic misfortune with integrity and class, which earned him worldwide praise and respect. Such incredible aplomb became a hallmark of Holyfield's professional prizefighting career. He never used foul language or made wild claims or accusations during his ring career. He simply went about his business, plying his trade as one of the greatest-ever world heavyweight champions.

The amateur pedigrees of both Holyfield and Tyson prepared them well for success in the pro ranks. As Lennox Lewis stated about Holyfield and himself years later, "Me and Evander's extensive amateur experience brought us to the top of our games. In a sport where there are no guarantees, and even one mistake can end in disaster, it's important to play the odds. So, although we have both had setbacks in our careers, there was very little chance that the success we sought in the sport of boxing would not be reached based on our experience."[2] In other words, nothing prepares a fighter better for a pro career in boxing than a deep amateur pedigree.

Holyfield began his pro career in the light-heavyweight division on November 15, 1984, at Madison Square Garden by scoring an impressive six-round decision over Lionel Byarm. This was followed by victories over Eric Winbush, Fred Brown, and Mark Rivera. Holyfield then moved up to the cruiserweight division where he scored four victories in a row, over Tyrone Booze, Rick Myers, Jeff Meachem, and Anthony Davis in 1985.

In 1986, Holyfield beat Chisanda Mutti, Jesse Shelby, and Terry Mims to set up a shot at the WBA cruiserweight world champion, the formidable Dwight Muhammad Qawi.[3]

Qawi was a dominant and much-feared light-heavyweight and cruiser-weight world champion. He was a gifted ring technician, superbly skilled in every facet of the sport. Qawi only stood five foot six, but he fought from an exaggerated crouch, making himself even less of a target to his ring foes. Qawi was a master at ducking and slipping shots as well as catching them on his forearms and shoulders. He possessed a solid chin and waded into his opponents with unbridled fury. The key to beating Qawi was in backing him up. No one (with the exception of Michael Spinks) had been able to do that in any of his previous matches — Qawi was a huge obstacle to tackle, especially for a former Olympic medalist like Holyfield, with only twelve pro fights under his belt. Many other cruiserweights gave Qawi a wide berth rather than face him in the ring.

Holyfield engaged Qawi at the Omni Coliseum in Atlanta, Georgia, on July 12, 1986. Except for the flyweight and bantamweight classes, most heavier fighters usually have a minimum of twenty to twenty-five fights under their belt before challenging for a world title. Holyfield was a different breed of fighter. The Real Deal displayed incredible poise and grit in beating Qawi by split decision over fifteen hard-fought rounds to capture the WBA world cruiserweight title. The fight was a gruelling toe-to-toe phone booth war, fought entirely at close range. Holyfield absorbed a tremendous amount of body and head punishment that would have stopped a lesser man; however, in the eyes of two of the three judges, Holyfield dished out more punishment than he received. By defeating Qawi, Holyfield became the first American Olympic medalist from the 1984 Olympics to capture a world title. Then on May 15, 1987, at Caesars Palace, Holyfield captured the IBF world cruiserweight title by scoring a TKO victory over Rickey Parkey at the 2:44 mark of round three. Then, on December 5, 1987, Holyfield knocked out Qawi in their rematch held at the Convention Center in Atlantic City, New Jersey, at the 2:30 mark of round four.

In his very next fight, on April 9, 1988, against Carlos De León at the Caesars Palace Sports Pavilion, Holyfield added the WBC cruiserweight title to his trophy case by knocking out the highly regarded defending champion at 1:08 of round eight. Holyfield was now the unified world cruiserweight champion. He was just reaching his fistic prime.

The problem for Holyfield was that there were no significant paydays to be had in the cruiserweight division. The cruiserweight division was really just a transfer station for him on his way to the prestigious heavyweight division. By July 1988, the time had arrived for The Real Deal to move up to the heavyweight ranks and challenge the big boys for the big money. Holyfield made a huge splash in the heavyweight division. In quick succession, he stopped James Tillis, Pinklon Thomas, Michael Dokes (by a particularly savage tenth-round knockout), Adilson Rodrigues, Alex Stewart, and Seamus McDonagh. It was time for Holyfield to ascend to the top of the heavyweight mountain in a mega super fight with the undisputed world heavyweight champion, Mike Tyson. Unfortunately, fate, as it often does, unexpectedly reared its ugly head and laid siege to the best-laid plans of boxings' promoters and managers.

On February 11, 1990, the unheralded James "Buster" Douglas flipped the script for heavyweight boxing upside down. It was a plot twist that no one saw coming. Douglas pulled off the biggest upset since Clay-Liston in 1964, by knocking out Mike Tyson at the 1:22 mark in round ten at the Tokyo Dome in Japan, to win the WBC/WBA and IBF world heavyweight titles. Douglas was supposed to be nothing more than a bit player in the ongoing saga of Mike Tyson; an easy tune-up bout for the undisputed heavyweight king. Somebody neglected to tell Douglas that he was there just to act the patsy against Tyson.

Fight fans had long been clamouring for a Tyson-Holyfield title fight. The hundreds of millions of dollars such a fight would earn had promoters salivating in their sleep. Such multi-million-dollar dreams flew out the window when the hand of Douglas was raised in victory over Tyson — the boxing world would have to wait another six long years for the much-anticipated Tyson-Holyfield clash to occur. It was now time for Holyfield to face Douglas for the unified world heavyweight title. The fight took place on October 25, 1990, at the Mirage Hotel and Casino in Las Vegas, Nevada.

It was not much of a fight as Douglas entered the ring out of shape and uninspired. A superbly conditioned Holyfield easily knocked out Douglas in one minute and ten seconds of the third round to capture the undisputed world heavyweight crown. Holyfield defended the title three times before losing it to Riddick Bowe by decision on November 13, 1992. Holyfield defeated Bowe in their rematch almost one year later, on November 6, 1993, to recapture the WBA/IBF world heavyweight titles. The WBC title was not at stake as Bowe had been stripped of it for refusing to defend it against Lennox Lewis. Holyfield then lost the IBF/WBA titles to Michael Moorer by a majority decision on April 22, 1994.

Holyfield refused to accept the defeat to Moorer and the loss of his titles as the final statement on his career. Undeterred in both strength and spirit, Holyfield started all over again, and from 1996 to 1999, he won five fights in a row, including the two over Mike Tyson, to regain the WBA world heavyweight title. He defeated Moorer in a rematch on November 8, 1997, to regain the IBF heavyweight strap.

Iron Mike

Historically speaking, poverty and broken homes have produced more world champion prizefighters than privilege and stable upbringings. This is evidenced in the careers of Jack Johnson, Sam Langford, Jack Dempsey, Floyd Patterson, Roberto Durán, Sonny Liston, and so many others. The best modern-day example of this is Michael Gerard Tyson, born June 30, 1966, in Fort Greene, Brooklyn, New York. He was the youngest of three siblings. His older brother, Rodney, was born in 1961. His older sister, Denise, died tragically of a heart attack at the age of twenty-four in February 1990. Tyson's mom, Lorna, was born in Charlottesville, Virginia. Tyson's birth father was a local cab driver named Purcell Tyson who was originally from Jamaica. The man he knew as his father, however, was a local pimp named Jimmy Kirkpatrick. Kirkpatrick was born in Grier Town (now Grier Heights), North Carolina, which was eventually annexed by Charlotte. Growing up, Kirkpatrick was considered a hot baseball prospect.

Kirkpatrick left Virginia and settled in Brooklyn, where he met Lorna Mae (Smith) Tyson, Mike's mother. Kirkpatrick spent his days in pool halls, gambling dens, and hanging out on street corners. Tyson remarked about his pop, "My father was just a regular street guy caught up in the street world."[4] Kirkpatrick deserted the Tyson family when Mike was born. Mike's mother was left to fend for herself while raising her three young kids. Jimmy Kirkpatrick died in 1992.

Tyson grew up in the tough and ultra-violent New York neighborhood of Bedford-Stuyvesant. The neighbourhood motto, "Bed-sty, do or die," gives you an idea of the dangers inherent in that area at that time. Tyson's family was so poor that they were forced to move to Brownsville when the future world heavyweight champion was just ten years old. Brownsville was where Murder Incorporated (the assassination arm of the Mafia) was born forty-four years earlier.

Tyson had a fondness for pigeons from a very young age, a passion he carried into adulthood. It's possible that Tyson admired the fact that pigeons, unlike poor people, could come and go as they pleased. Tyson's very first street fight involved one of his birds. An older boy decided to upset Tyson by decapitating his most prized pigeon. An eleven-year-old Tyson beat the older and bigger youth into submission.[5] No one on the streets ever messed with Tyson again — he had made his bones as a savage street fighter. Without any parental guidance, or a school system to keep him occupied, Tyson was arrested thirty-eight times for various crimes by the age of thirteen. He had a high-pitched voice like Jack Dempsey and he spoke with a lisp. Anyone foolish enough to ridicule his speech impediment or the timbre of his voice received a brutal beating. He was sentenced in court to the Tryon Reformatory School for Boys. While at Tryon, Tyson continued to act up and get into fights. After going to the gym and watching others box, Tyson became interested in the sport. One of the centre's juvenile detention counsellors, Bobby Stewart, was a protege of the immortal International Boxing Hall of Fame trainer Constantine "Cus" D'Amato. Stewart demanded Tyson behave for twelve weeks in order to see if he possessed the self-discipline necessary to succeed in boxing. Tyson kept his word regarding his good behaviour, and Stewart started teaching Tyson the art and science of boxing. Stewart could see from the outset that Tyson was a boxing prodigy. At thirteen, he was easily beating men twice his age. Tyson had speed, phenomenal power, exquisite reflexes, and an unconquerable will to win. He learned Stewart's lessons quickly and incorporated them into his ever-burgeoning ring arsenal. It was evident to Stewart, even after training Tyson for just a few months, that the young phenom required more advanced teaching in all aspects of boxing — mental, physical, and emotional — which was more than Stewart could give him in that setting.

It wasn't long before Stewart brought Tyson to D'Amato. D'Amato had guided Floyd Patterson to the world heavyweight title and José Torres to the world light-heavyweight title. These were major accomplishments because both Torres and Patterson had started their careers as middleweights. Patterson had super-fast hands but a chin made of Waterford crystal, which was easily and often shattered. D'Amato guided both men through the Mob-infested waters of pro boxing all the way to undisputed world titles. Patterson held the heavyweight title from 1955 to 1962. How did he accomplish this? By assiduously avoiding Sonny Liston for seven long years.

D'Amato was a finishing school for Tyson's fistic ambitions. D'Amato always felt that the perfect heavyweight fighter would be a combination of Patterson's speed combined with Liston's power and intimidation tactics. Tyson knew he had a lot to live up to in D'Amato's eyes. Tyson was an intuitive and smart young man. He knew his future lay in the prize ring. D'Amato assigned Teddy Atlas and Kevin Rooney to train and nurture the young Tyson on the mental and physical aspects of the game. This was a turning point in Tyson's boxing mindset. Mastering the emotional and mental aspects of prizefighting is as difficult, if not more so, than perfecting the physical elements. In this, D'Amato created the perfect boxing synthesis — a mixture of blazing speed, crushing power, and scintillating defence, combined with supreme mental toughness. Mike Tyson was D'Amato's masterpiece.

When Tyson turned sixteen, tragedy struck. His mother died. He was now legally an orphan. According to Tyson, "I never saw my mother happy with me and proud of me for doing something: she only knew me as a wild kid running the streets, coming home with new clothes that she knew

I didn't pay for. I never got a chance to talk to her or know about her. Professionally, it has no effect, but it's crushing emotionally and personally."[6] D'Amato legally became Tyson's adoptive father at this point. As with people in every walk of life, Tyson's profound family losses and rough upbringing shaped him both in and outside of the ring. Tyson obviously had trust issues long before he ever entertained the idea of becoming a fighter. Losing his mother at such a young age, and never developing a relationship with either his birth father or stepfather, impressed upon him a realization that he could only count on himself. In the sleazy, criminal-controlled world of professional boxing, having trust issues is a smart safety mechanism to possess.

—————— The Rematch — Holyfield-Tyson II ——————

Many problems arose prior to the Holyfield-Tyson rematch. Tyson's representatives, John Horne and Rory Holloway, the Beavis and Butt-Head of boxing management, asked the Nevada State Athletic Commission to select a referee other than Mitch Halpern, who had done an excellent job of officiating the first Holyfield-Tyson fight. They felt that Tyson would be "psychologically damaged" by allowing Halpern to referee the rematch. This was, in a word, preposterous. Halpern was an outstanding referee. Did he make mistakes during their first bout? Sure, he did, but very few, and fewer than most referees make in fights of a similar magnitude. This was gamesmanship. Horne and Holloway stated that "Mike Tyson is totally convinced that this man cannot be fair with him in this fight."[7]

Tyson's co-managers ludicrously blamed his loss to Holyfield in their first fight on the referee, rather than on their own incompetence in Tyson's corner — they and Tyson were incapable of accepting that Holyfield was simply the better man that night. Accepting defeat gracefully is the first step back on the road to victory, and they could not do that. Even more shocking is that, for the first time in his career, Tyson was publicly depending on the referee and not himself for success in a fight.

The Nevada State Athletic Commission smartly rejected Horne and Holloway's outlandish protest as being utterly without merit. However, Halpern outsmarted Horne, Holloway, and Tyson by surprisingly recusing himself from the fight as he did not want to be the centre of attention. It was a wise move on his part. Inadvertently, through their incredibly short-sighted blunder, Horne and Holloway had put even more pressure on Tyson to achieve a spectacular knockout victory over Holyfield in their rematch. Now, Tyson would have no excuses if he lost. Halpern was replaced by Mills Lane.

The rematch did not start out well for Tyson. In the first few seconds of the opening round, Tyson came forward with a left jab and a straight right hand. The jab missed, but his short right hand landed. Holyfield easily shrugged it off. Holyfield smartly started to create some distance by jabbing Tyson repeatedly from long range. And just like in their first brawl, Holyfield was outmuscling Tyson in the clinches. Tyson continued to come forward, throwing straight right-hand leads rather than setting his shots up with his jab. He had abandoned the basic fundamentals of boxing. Holyfield saw Tyson's right-hand leads coming and easily ducked under them. Tyson would have been more successful throwing combinations rather than one punch at a time. He was looking for a Hail Mary punch, which is something impatient fighters resort to when they have run out of other options.

In the first round, Holyfield caught Tyson with a very low left hand to the testicles. This was not the first time he had hit Tyson low. Holyfield had done so in their first bout numerous times. Although referee Lane immediately told Holyfield to keep his punches up, the champion continued to hit Tyson low in their rematch. Holyfield also kept leading with his head. Tyson did not want to be on the receiving end of another head-butt, as he had been in their first fight.

With 1:09 left in the opening round, Holyfield caught Tyson moving backwards with a perfectly timed, hard overhand right on the side of the head. Tyson did not fight well going in reverse — he had proven that in their original encounter. Then, with forty-one seconds left in the round, Holyfield caught an oncoming Tyson with a short, crisp right hand to the head. Tyson's legs buckled momentarily. Tyson was being heavily outpunched by Holyfield. Tyson responded in kind with a few hard left hooks, but Holyfield remained unfazed. Holyfield was again proving to be the stronger, more assertive fighter. Muhammad Ali's trainer, Angelo Dundee, used to say that if you hit your opponent with your best punch and nothing happens, then you must concede the knockout and rely on your boxing skills to win the match. Tyson had thrown his boxing skills out the window, preferring instead to look for that one home run punch, which never came.

At the beginning of round two, Tyson threw a right hand as Holyfield was starting to throw a left hook. As Tyson leaned into the punch, Holyfield ducked under it and their heads clashed. A deep, long gash appeared over Tyson's right eye. Head-butts were a problem in both of their fights primarily because of the difference in their respective heights. Holyfield had a tendency to lead with his head, which is what Horne and Holloway should have focused on rather than replacing the referee. Lennox Lewis would later make the same complaint about Holyfield after their two fights.

Referee Lane called time and informed ringside officials that the cut was caused by an accidental head-butt. Tyson knew that because of the cut, his right eye would eventually swell shut, making him susceptible to Holyfield's punishing left hands. This was a bad omen for Tyson. A terrible cut in a vulnerable place so early in the fight only added to Tyson's mounting frustrations. The challenger was rapidly losing focus; his anger had started to consume him.

Right after Lane called time in, Holyfield immediately came forward and butted Tyson directly on the cut over his right eye. The second head-butt staggered Tyson. Holyfield was making good use of his shoulders, forearms, and elbows while attacking Tyson. Tyson looked at referee Lane helplessly, but no specific warning was given to Holyfield other than Lane imploring both combatants to "keep it clean!" Holyfield was mauling and fouling Tyson and beating him to the punch. He was using Tyson's own style to beat him down. On those rare occasions when Tyson managed to land a punch, Holyfield clinched him and walked him back to the ropes. Tyson was barely treading water.

The bell clanged to begin round three and Tyson emerged from his corner with renewed malevolence in his eyes. He wanted to make Holyfield pay for bullying him during the first two rounds. Ironically, in light of what was about to happen, Tyson walked out for round three sans mouthpiece. He went back to his corner to retrieve it. He started the round out well, pressing the attack and looking like the Tyson of old, landing hard left and right hands on Holyfield. Then Holyfield started to clutch and grab him again. Holyfield was constantly hitting Tyson on the break. Just 1:12 into the third round, Holyfield landed a very low left hook to Tyson's groin again. Lane admonished Holyfield to keep his punches up. Tyson responded by landing a three-punch combination to the champion's head, forcing Holyfield to clinch. Excessive holding was part of Holyfield's overall game plan, designed to smother and blunt Tyson's attack while frustrating the hell out of him.

The fight went quickly downhill from there when, with about 1:15 left in the round, Holyfield caught Tyson with another very low left hook. Once again Lane told Holyfield to keep his punches up. Holyfield made no effort to comply. With just under a minute left in the round, Tyson caught Holyfield on the chin with a vicious left hook. Holyfield took it well and pushed Tyson back to the ropes. With just forty seconds remaining in round three, a supremely discouraged Tyson bit off a large chunk of Holyfield's right ear. Holyfield jumped in the air in pain and disbelief. It took a few seconds for Tyson's ear bite to fully register with both fans and the Showtime broadcast team.

Holyfield had walked over to his corner to show his seconds what had happened when Tyson ran at him from behind and pushed him into the ropes. Holyfield's trainers, Don Turner and Tommy Brooks, two extremely well-respected men within the boxing community, asked Lane to immediately disqualify Tyson. Lane called time, sending both men to their corners. Lane then conferred with Nevada State Athletic Commission chairman Marc Ratner. Lane told Ratner that Tyson was disqualified for a flagrant foul, according to the NSAC rulebook. Ratner asked Lane if Holyfield could continue. Lane posed this question to the ringside doctor, Flip Homansky, who said Holyfield could continue fighting. Lane then deducted two points from Tyson. Tyson told Lane that Holyfield's bloody ear came from a punch. Lane responded to Tyson's claim with one word: "BULLSHIT!"

Lane warned Tyson that if it happened again, he would be disqualified. Lane called time in, and with just twenty-two seconds left in round three, Tyson bit off a chunk of Holyfield's left ear. The two men continued warring until the round ended. During the one-minute rest period, Lane disqualified Tyson for his second flagrant foul. He told Tyson, "It's over! You're gone!" A riot ensued in the ring with Tyson trying to get at Holyfield. The ring was dense with police officers and security guards, many of whom Tyson took a swing at. Holyfield's corner smartly hustled him out of the ring to his dressing room.

Controversy

Unlike most boxing controversies, this dispute seemed one-sided. Tyson committed two flagrant fouls in the last minute of the third round, leaving referee Lane with no choice but to disqualify him. One flagrant foul is enough to get a fighter disqualified. Two flagrant fouls are a no-brainer. Everyone in attendance believed they saw Tyson become totally unhinged from reality. Were Tyson's actions those of an unhinged man, or were they calculated with malice aforethought? In other words, did Tyson deliberately try to get himself disqualified? Specifically, what prompted Tyson to twice bite Holyfield's ears? Should Tyson have been disqualified after the first bite? Did Tyson purposely forget his mouthpiece to start the third round? Was Tyson acting out of frustration because of his inability to dominate Holyfield? Finally, were Tyson's ear bites a reaction to Holyfield's fouls (particularly head-butts) being ignored?

The Decision

Given his comments after the fight and at his inquiry before the NSAC on June 30, 1997, it is unlikely that Tyson began round three looking to specifically bite Holyfield's right ear. However, we can't say that categorically because we simply don't know what was in Tyson's mind at that moment. In all probability, the opportunity presented itself and Tyson took it by spitting out his mouthpiece and chomping down on Holyfield's left ear. Tyson claimed he did not know why he acted in such a disgraceful manner. But to veteran boxing insiders, the answer as to why Tyson snapped and bit Holyfield's ear was obvious: *fear*. Tyson was afraid to lose by knockout to

Holyfield for the second time. It was fear that prompted Tyson's terrible, odious actions, not frustration. Ultimately, Tyson ignored the sage advice of his mentor and adoptive father, Cus D'Amato. D'Amato firmly impressed upon Tyson that both men in a fight experience the same fears in the ring; however, it is the man who can best control his fears who emerges triumphant. Tyson let his fear get the better of him.

Fear made Tyson look for an easy escape route once he realized that Holyfield was even stronger and more dominant than in their first bout. The first bite might have been a spur-of-the-moment action, but the second bite was obviously deliberate — it occurred immediately after Lane had told Tyson that if he did it again, the fight would be over. The second bite proves that Tyson was completely unhinged and looking for an easy way out. After the fight, Holyfield needed eight stitches in his right ear.

Referee Lane rightfully felt Tyson should have been disqualified after the first bite, and he most definitely would have done so had NSAC executive director Ratner not intervened. Ratner knew that boxing's prestige and financial future were at stake. There had also been two million pay-per-view buys for the fight, generating over one hundred million dollars. To end the fight early would disappoint boxing fans worldwide and conceivably hurt future boxing pay-per-view revenues.

Interestingly, Tyson's former trainer, Teddy Atlas, presciently told reporters the night before the fight that Tyson "will try to get lucky, naturally," but that if he can't land a knockout punch early, "he's going to try to disqualify himself, either by elbowing, or throwing a low blow, butting or biting."[8] Atlas, who knew Tyson well, believed "Iron Mike" was a bully at heart, much like his fistic predecessor, Sonny Liston, who took the easy way out in his first fight with Cassius Clay, by spitting out his mouthpiece and quitting on his stool after the sixth round. Liston was a feared head-breaker for the Mob and a quintessential bully who greatly relied on intimidation as much as his physicality to defeat his opponents. The same description applied to Tyson, excluding the part about Mob employment. Atlas's prediction was eerily accurate — when Tyson realized he could not intimidate or physically impose his will upon Holyfield, he looked for an easy way out via disqualification.

Tyson's claim that he did not know why he had acted in such an egregious manner is understandable. The process Tyson experienced in the ring was not intellectual but emotional. He completely lost his focus. Disciplined, fully focused fighters don't react emotionally in the squared circle, and they certainly don't bite their opponents. Only scared and desperate fighters act this way.

Tyson was certainly frustrated by Holyfield's numerous foul tactics in both of their fights and what he perceived as Lane's inability to keep Holyfield in check during their rematch. Tyson's perceptions in that regard were incorrect as Lane did issue warnings to Holyfield. For instance, when Holyfield hit Tyson low for the second time in the fight, Lane told him that was his second low blow and to keep his punches up. After the head-butt by Holyfield in round two, which opened the cut over Tyson's right eye, Lane admonished the champion to watch his head. Lane also warned Holyfield to stop holding Tyson. Tyson complained to Lane for the three rounds the fight lasted that Holyfield was constantly hitting on the break, which was true. Lane repeatedly told both men to break clean. So, in fact, Lane was keeping a close eye on Holyfield's array of fouls and warning him throughout the fight.

Tyson was entirely responsible for his own disqualification. He reacted in anger, which stems from fear. In this case, Tyson's fear was losing to Holyfield again.

Significance

The immediate significance of this fight is that Tyson would be forever remembered as the guy who bit Holyfield twice rather than as the youngest world heavyweight champion of all time. The NSAC fined Tyson three million dollars, which was 10 percent of his purse. This was the most the NSAC could penalize him according to Nevada law. Tyson's boxing licence was suspended for fifteen months. It was reinstated in October of 1998. The fight gave boxing another black eye and much bad press, but after three hundred years, the sport was well used to, and cared little about, such adverse media coverage. Holyfield vs. Tyson II was, at the time, the highest-grossing boxing match in history. The live gate was $17,277,000. Domestic pay-per-view buys were more than 1.99 million and generated an amount of $99,822,000.

More significantly, this was the last time Hall of Fame promoter and convicted felon (manslaughter) Don King ever promoted a Mike Tyson fight. Don King and Bob Arum were the two biggest and most successful boxing promoters from the late 1960s onwards. King achieved his lofty status in boxing courtesy of the Cleveland mafia. King had stolen millions of dollars from Tyson by padding his expense accounts over the years. King also embezzled millions of dollars from almost every fighter he promoted. In 1998, Tyson sued DK Productions for one hundred million dollars. The suit was settled out of court in 2004 when King agreed to pay Tyson fourteen million dollars. Tyson never saw a dime of the settlement as the entire amount went to the IRS to repay unpaid back taxes. This, too, is a sad but frequent occurrence that runs through boxing history. In 1997, *Ring* magazine named Tyson-Holyfield II as the second-dirtiest fight in boxing history.

The only thing worse than Tyson's actions were the odious comments of his co-manager, John Horne, after the fight. The splendidly obtuse Horne reputedly said, "Mike got a cut over his eye three inches long. Evander has a little nip on his ear that don't mean nothing, and that's the bottom line. He jumped around like a little bitch." Horne's post-fight comments proved author Maurice Switzer's old adage to be true: It is better to remain silent and be thought a fool than to speak and remove all doubt.

Mike Tyson had ten more fights before officially retiring from boxing on June 11, 2005, after being stopped in six rounds by unheralded Kevin McBride. In these bouts, Tyson experienced five wins, three losses, and two no-contests. His final record stands at fifty wins and six losses with two no-contests and forty-four wins by way of knockout. He was inducted into the International Boxing Hall of Fame in 2011.

Evander Holyfield was inducted into the International Boxing Hall of Fame in 2017. His final record consisted of forty-four wins, ten losses, and two draws. Twenty-nine of his wins came via knockout. After his second bout with Tyson, Holyfield fought an amazing twenty more times, albeit often inadvisably. Holyfield fought well past his prime in a futile attempt to regain past glory. In his final twenty bouts, he sported a record of ten wins, seven losses, two draws and one no-contest.

The excitement and history that Mike Tyson and Evander Holyfield brought to heavyweight boxing during their careers cannot be measured by mere ring statistics. Tyson got even non-boxing fans to start tuning in to his fights. Many of these uninitiated fight enthusiasts became boxing fans for life after watching Tyson fight. No fighter in recent memory in any weight division brought more excitement to boxing or sports in general than Tyson. He was absolutely must-see pay-per-view and certainly left boxing in better financial shape than when he entered it.

Evander Holyfield was a gentleman both in and out of the ring. He was also in more great fights than any other fighter of his generation. He was boxing's everyman. His appeal to the common boxing fan is the reason for his continuing popularity. Everyone faces tremendous obstacles in their lives. We have often been told we will never succeed at whatever we do. Holyfield calmly disregarded such unfounded criticisms while achieving everlasting fame in his chosen profession.

Both Holyfield and Tyson attained fame and fortune on their own terms and through their own efforts. The untold thousands of hours they put into perfecting their craft was evident every time they stepped into the ring. If they had never fought each other, they would still be remembered forever. But they did fight each other, and without a doubt, their two clashes have placed them on a higher plane in boxing annals, alongside Dempsey-Tunney, Louis-Schmeling, and Ali-Frazier. The Holyfield-Tyson wars added two new chapters to the continually unfolding history of professional boxing. Both of these chapters were provocative and memorable. Of course, the lasting significance of their two fights is, ultimately, left for the fans to decide.

ACKNOWLEDGEMENTS

I would like to graciously acknowledge the following people for their generous time, encouragement, suggestions, proofreading skills, advice, insights, and kindness: Russ Anber, Colleen Aycock, Gene Aguilera, Al Bernstein, Steve Buffery, Tyler Buxton, Morgan Campbell, Nigel Collins, William Dettloff, Angelo Dundee, Jimmy Dundee, Dr. Len Eisen, Lewis Eisen, Mark Eisen, Marvin Elkind, Doug Fischer, Tony Gee, James Gentle, Rick Glaser, Thomas Hauser, Graham Houston, Hank Kaplan, George Kimball, Lennox Lewis, Steve Lott, Don MacDonald, Don Majeski, Louis Manfra, Clay Moyle, Adam J. Pollock, Simon Rakoff, Michael Rosenthal, Ron Ross, Wayne Turmel, and Les Woods. My sincere apologies to anyone I may have left out.

Special thanks to Tony Gee for his tireless attention, hard work, and magnificent editing skills, which are displayed in the first chapter of this book. Without him, there would be no first chapter.

Special thanks to the generosity and kindness of Craig Hamilton and Louis Manfra, without whom there would be no photos in this book.

Special thanks to Gregory Joseph Speciale for use of his wonderful un-published manuscript on the extraordinary boxing trainer Jimmy DeForest.

Special thanks to Kwame Scott Fraser for his masterful editing.

Special thanks to Paul Harrietha, Ph.D., for keeping me calm and focused.

Very special thanks to my wife, Cynthia Leithwood, for always looking after me and for watching boxing every Saturday night.

Very special thanks to my daughter, Esther, for always believing in me and for filling my life with joy every day from the very moment she was born.

NOTES

CHAPTER 1: PETER COCKRAN VS. BILL DARTS

1   *Bath Chronicle*, December 19, 1770.

2   Pierce Egan, *Boxiana; or Sketches of Ancient and Modern Pugilism, from the Days of the Renowned Broughton and Slack, to the Championship of Cribb*, Vol. 1 (London: George Virtue, 1830), 75.

3   Henry Downes Miles, *Pugilistica: The History of British Boxing*, Vol. 1 (London: Weldon, 1880), 45.

4   Tony Gee, personal communication.

5   Ibid.

6   A "whip round" was an impromptu collection of money from spectators at the fight.

7   Tony Gee, "Fresh Light on the 'New Rules' of 1838," *IBRO Journal* (December 2021), 14–16.

8   *Aris's Birmingham Gazette*, June 1, 1772.

9   *Bingley's Journal*, May 30–June 6, 1772.

10 *Public Advertiser*, June 5, 1772.

11 *Newcastle Courant*, June 20, 1772.

12 Tony Gee, personal communication.

13 Henry Downes Miles, *Pugilistica: The History of British Boxing*, Vol. 1 (London: Weldon, 1880), 85.

14 *Morning Post*, April 24, 1775.

15 Tony Gee, personal communication.

16 Ibid.

CHAPTER 2: JOE GANS VS. TERRY MCGOVERN

1 *The First Black Boxing Champions: Essays on Fighters of the 1800s to the 1920s,* ed. Collen Aycock and Mark Scott (McFarland, 2011), 79.

2 Ibid.

3 Colleen Aycock and Mark Scott, *Joe Gans — A Biography of the First African American World Boxing Champion* (McFarland, 2008), 23.

4 *The First Black Boxing Champions: Essays on Fighters of the 1800s to the 1920s,* ed. Colleen Aycock and Mark Scott (McFarland, 2011), 79–80.

5 Collen Aycock and Mark Scott, *Joe Gans — A Biography of the First African American World Boxing Champion* (McFarland, 2008), 8.

6 Wikipedia, "Terry McGovern (boxer)," en.wikipedia.org/wiki/Terry _McGovern_(boxer).

7 Arne K. Lang, *The Nelson-Wolgast Fight and the San Francisco Boxing Scene, 1900–1914* (McFarland, 2012), 97.

8 Collen Aycock and Mark Scott, *Joe Gans — A Biography of the First African American World Boxing Champion* (McFarland, 2008), 71.

9 George Siler, "Mayor Forbids Boxing Planned," *Chicago Tribune*, December 25, 1901, 6.

10 BoxRec, "Terry McGovern vs. Joe Gans," boxrec.com/en/event/12127.

11 Arne K. Lang, *Clash of the Little Giants* (McFarland, 2022).

CHAPTER 3: JACK JOHNSON VS. TOMMY BURNS

1 Dan McCaffery, *Tommy Burns: Canada's Unknown World Heavyweight Champion* (Lorimer, 2000), 10.

2 Ibid., 31.

3 BoxRec, "Jack Johnson Boxing Debut," boxrec.com/en/event/495327/19078.

4 Christopher J. LaForce, *The Choynski Chronicles: A Biography of Hall of Fame Boxer Jewish Joe Choynski* (Win by KO, 2013), 520–21.

5 Tommy Burns, *Scientific Boxing and Self Defence* (London: Health and Strength, 1908).

6 Lou Eisen, "George Dixon," *Boxing Monthly*, June 2019.

7 BoxRec, "Joe Walcott vs. Rube Ferns," boxrec.com/en/event/97617/166954.

8 Nat Fleischer, "Black Dynamite, Vol III. The Three Colored Aces: Story of George Dixon, Joe Gans and Joe Walcott and Several Contemporaries," *Ring*, 1938, 153.

9 *Milwaukee Free Press*, April 23, 1909.

10 BoxRec, "Tommy Burns vs. Jack Johnson," boxrec.com/media/index.php /Tommy_Burns_vs._Jack_Johnson.

11 Geoffrey C. Ward, *Unforgivable Blackness* (Knopf Doubleday, 2006), 123.

12 BoxRec, "Tommy Burns vs. Jack Johnson," boxrec.com/media/index.php /Tommy_Burns_vs._Jack_Johnson.

13 Personal communication with boxing historian and film archivist Steve Lott.

CHAPTER 4: JESS WILLARD VS. JACK JOHNSON

1 Arly Allen with the assistance of James Willard Mace, *Jess Willard: Heavyweight Champion of the World* (McFarland, 2017), 35.

2 Ibid., 36.

3 Ibid., 38.

4 Ibid., 44–46.

5 Ibid., 44–45.

6 Totally History, "Jack Johnson," http://totallyhistory.com/jack-johnson/.

7 *New York Times*, Thursday, May 16, 1963.

8 Ibid.

9 Ibid.

10 Jimmy DeForest's unpublished manuscript.

11 Ibid.

12 Ibid.

13 Ibid.

14 BoxRec, "Jess Willard vs. Jack Johnson," boxrec.com/media/index.php /Jack_Johnson_vs._Jess_Willard.

15 Geoffrey C. Ward, *Unforgivable Blackness* (Knopf Doubleday, 2006), 368–69.

16 Ibid.

17 Graeme Kent, *The Great White Hopes: The Quest to Defeat Jack Johnson* (Sutton, 2006), 219.

CHAPTER 5: JACK DEMPSEY VS. JESS WILLARD

1 Arly Allen with the assistance of James Willard Mace, *Jess Willard: Heavyweight Champion of the World* (McFarland, 2017), 11.

2 Roger Kahn, *A Flame of Pure Fire: Jack Dempsey and the Roaring '20s* (Houghton Mifflin Harcourt, 1999), 92.

3 Arly Allen with the assistance of James Willard Mace, *Jess Willard: Heavyweight Champion of the World* (McFarland, 2017), 42.

4   Ibid.

5   BoxRec, "Jess Willard vs. Jack Dempsey," boxrec.com/media/index.php/Jess
     _Willard_vs._Jack_Dempsey.

6   Arly Allen with the assistance of James Willard Mace, *Jess Willard:
     Heavyweight Champion of the World* (McFarland, 2017), 247.

7   Roger Kahn, *A Flame of Pure Fire: Jack Dempsey and the Roaring '20s*
     (Houghton Mifflin Harcourt, 1999), 92.

8   BoxRec, "Jess Willard vs. Floyd Johnson," boxrec.com/wiki/index.php/Jess
     _Willard_vs._Floyd_Johnson.

9   BoxRec, "Jess Willard vs. Luis Angel Firpo," boxrec.com/wiki/index.php/Jess
     _Willard_vs._Luis_Angel_Firpo.

CHAPTER 6: JACK DEMPSEY VS. GENE TUNNEY II

1   Roger Kahn, *A Flame of Pure Fire: Jack Dempsey and the Roaring '20s*
     (Houghton Mifflin Harcourt, 1999), 122.

2   Ibid., 121.

3   Ibid., 126–27.

4   Ibid., 132.

5   BoxRec, "Jess Willard vs. Jack Dempsey," boxrec.com/wiki/index.php/Jess
     _Willard_vs._Jack_Dempsey.

6   Roger Kahn, *A Flame of Pure Fire: Jack Dempsey and the Roaring '20s*
     (Houghton Mifflin Harcourt, 1999), 188.

7   Wikipedia, "Gene Tunney, Boxer," en.wikipedia.org/wiki/Gene_Tunney.

8   Jack Cavanaugh, *Tunney — Boxing's Brainiest Champ and His Upset of the
     Great Jack Dempsey* (Ballantine Books, 2009), 4.

9   Ibid., 48–49.

10   Roger Kahn, *A Flame of Pure Fire: Jack Dempsey and the Roaring '20s*
     (Houghton Mifflin Harcourt, 1999), 208.

11   Ibid., 208.

12   Wikipedia, "The Long Count Fight," en.wikipedia.org/wiki/The_Long
     _Count_Fight.

13   Roger Kahn, *A Flame of Pure Fire: Jack Dempsey and the Roaring '20s*
     (Houghton Mifflin Harcourt, 1999), 417.

14   Ibid., 413.

15   BoxRec, "Jack Dempsey vs. Luis Angel Firpo," boxrec.com/wiki/index.php
     /Jack_Dempsey_vs._Luis_Angel_Firpo.

CHAPTER 7: PRIMO CARNERA VS. ERNIE SCHAAF

1 George Kimball, "Ambling Alp Movie a Mountain of Myth," *The Irish Times*, May 15, 2008, irishtimes.com/sport/ambling-alp-movie-a-mountain -of-myth-1.924797.

2 Frederic Mullally, *Primo — The Story of 'Man Mountain' Carnera, World Heavyweight Champion* (Robson Books, 1995), 12.

3 Ibid., 12.

4 Ibid., 14.

5 Ibid., 12.

6 Ibid., 16.

7 BoxRec, "Paul Journee, Boxer," boxrec.com/en/proboxer/017597.

8 Ibid.

9 Patrick Coleman, *Fallen and Forgotten: The Ernie Schaaf Story*.

10 Ibid.

11 BoxRec, "Ernie Schaaf," boxrec.com/en/proboxer/12071.

12 Patrick Coleman, *Fallen and Forgotten: The Ernie Schaaf Story*.

13 BoxRec, "Primo Carnera vs. Ernie Schaaf," boxrec.com/en/event/56640 /91601.

14 Patrick Coleman, *Fallen and Forgotten: The Ernie Schaaf Story*.

15 Autopsy on Ernie Schaaf by Dr. Charles Norris, chief medical examiner, and Dr. Benjamin Morgan Vance, assistant medical examiner, February 1933.

16 *The New York Times*, February 18, 1933.

CHAPTER 8: EMILE GRIFFITH VS. BENNY "KID" PARET III

1 Fred Eisenstadt, "Benny 'Kid' Paret Profile," *Ring*, May 1960, 18–19.

2 BoxRec, "Benny Kid Paret," boxrec.com/en/proboxer/10925.

3 Ron Ross, *Nine … Ten … and Out! The Two Worlds of Emile Griffith* (Lisa Ross, 2008).

4 Ibid.

5 BoxRec, "Benny Kid Paret vs. Bobby Shell," boxrec.com/en/event/65159 /108890.

6 BoxRec, "Benny Paret vs. Federico Thompson (1st meeting)," boxrec.com/wiki /index.php/Benny_Paret_vs._Federico_Thompson_(1st_meeting).

7 BoxRec, "Benny (Kid) Paret vs. Don Jordan," boxrec.com/wiki/index.php /Benny_(Kid)_Paret_vs._Don_Jordan.

8 Luis F. Sanchez, *Atlanta Journal Constitution*, April 14, 2017.

9 BoxRec, "Benny Paret vs. Emile Griffith (1st meeting)," boxrec.com/wiki /index.php/Benny_Paret_vs._Emile_Griffith_(1st_meeting).

10 Ron Berger and Dan Klores, dirs. *Ring of Fire: The Emile Griffith Story* (Bravo and USA Network, 2005).

11 Gary Smith, "The Shadow Boxer," *Sports Illustrated*, April 18, 2005.

12 *Orlando Sentinel*, March 25, 1962, 11.

13 Alan H. Levy, *Floyd Patterson: A Boxer and a Gentleman* (McFarland, 2008), 145.

14 BoxRec, "Emile Griffith vs. Luis Manuel Rodriguez," boxrec.com/wiki/index .php/Emile_Griffith_vs._Luis_Manuel_Rodriguez_(2nd_meeting).

15 BoxRec, "Davey Moore vs. Sugar Ramos," boxrec.com/wiki/index.php/Davey _Moore_vs._Sugar_Ramos.

16 Ibid.

17 *Oakland Tribune*, March 25, 1962.

18 Personal communication with Angelo Dundee on set of *Cinderella Man*, August 2004.

19 Ron Berger and Dan Klores, dirs. *Ring of Fire: The Emile Griffith Story* (Bravo and USA Network, 2005).

20 *Lima Citizen*, April 3, 1962.

21 *Fresno Bee*, April 4, 1962.

22 Jim McCulley, *New York Daily News*, April 4, 1962.

23 Ibid.

24 "Paret Near Death: 'It's Up to the Almighty Now,'" *Daily Independent Journal*, March 26, 1962, 13.

25 *Lima Citizen*, April 3, 1962.

CHAPTER 9: MUHAMMAD ALI VS. SONNY LISTON II

1 Angelo Dundee with Bert Randolph Sugar, *My View from the Corner: A Life in Boxing* (McGraw Hill, 2009), 13.

2 Robert H. Boyle, *Sports Illustrated*, September 7, 1964.

3 Ibid.

4 BoxRec, "Muhammad Ali vs. Sonny Liston (2nd meeting)," boxrec.com/wiki /index.php/Muhammad_Ali_vs._Sonny_Liston_(2nd_meeting).

5 Robert H. Boyle, *Sports Illustrated*, September 7, 1964.

6 BoxRec, "Muhammad Ali vs. Sonny Liston (2nd meeting)," boxrec.com/wiki /index.php/Muhammad_Ali_vs._Sonny_Liston_(2nd_meeting).

7 Randy Roberts and Johnny Smith, *Blood Brothers: The Fatal Friendship Between Muhammad Ali and Malcolm X* (Basic Books, 2016), 225.

8 BoxRec, "Muhammad Ali vs. Sonny Liston (2nd meeting)," boxrec.com/wiki /index.php/Muhammad_Ali_vs._Sonny_Liston_(2nd_meeting).

9 Ibid.

10 Wikipedia, "Malcolm X," en.wikipedia.org/wiki/Malcolm_X.

11 Personal communication with Angelo Dundee on the set of *Cinderella Man*, August 2004.

12 Freedom Forum Institute, "Muhammad Ali: 'I Am America,'" freedomforum .org/i-am-america/.

13 Paul Gallender, *Sonny Liston: The Real Story Behind the Ali–Liston Fights* (CreateSpace Independent Publishing, 2014), 144–45.

14 *Sportsworld*, "February 25, 1964: The Championship," aired 1978–94 on NBC.

15 Randy Roberts and Johnny Smith, *Blood Brothers: The Fatal Friendship Between Muhammad Ali and Malcolm X* (Basic Books, 2016), 206.

16 BoxRec, "Muhammad Ali vs. Sonny Liston (2nd meeting)," boxrec.com/wiki /index.php/Muhammad_Ali_vs._Sonny_Liston_(2nd_meeting).

17 CBS Sports, "The Fix Was In: FBI Suspected Ali–Liston Bout in '64 was Rigged," cbssports.com/general/news/the-fix-was-in-fbi-suspected-ali-liston -bout-in-64-was-rigged/.

18 Antoine Fuqua, dir. *What's My Name: Muhammad Ali* (HBO, 2019).

19 CBS Sports, "The Fix Was In: FBI Suspected Ali–Liston Bout in '64 was Rigged," cbssports.com/general/news/the-fix-was-in-fbi-suspected-ali-liston -bout-in-64-was-rigged/.

CHAPTER 10: KEN BUCHANAN VS. ROBERTO DURÁN

1 BoxRec, "Ken Buchanan vs. Roberto Duran," boxrec.com/wiki/index.php/Ken _Buchanan_vs._Roberto_Duran.

2 BoxRec, "Ismael Laguna vs. Ken Buchanan (1st fight)," boxrec.com/en/event /40740/62963.

3 BoxRec, "Ismael Laguna vs. Ken Buchanan (2nd fight)," boxrec.com/en/event /40736/62959.

4 BoxRec, "Ken Buchanan vs. Ruben Navarro," boxrec.com/en/event/60499 /99047.

5 Boxingbiographies.co.uk, "Ken Buchanan."

6 BoxRec, "Ken Buchanan vs. Brian Rocky Tonks," boxrec.com/en/event /60464/99010.

7 Christian Giudice, *Hands of Stone: The Life and Legend of Roberto Duran* (Milo Books, 2009), 13.

8 BoxRec, "Pero Carrasco," boxrec.com/en/proboxer/16028.

9 Scott Turman, "Luck Is the Residue of Design," April 13, 2020, scottturman.com /luck-is-the-residue-of-design/.

10 N.Y. Comp. Codes R. & Regs. Tit. 19 § 211.48 — Injuries Sustained by Fouls, law.cornell.edu/regulations/new-york/19-NYCRR-211.48.

11 Ibid.

12   BoxRec, "Ken Buchanan vs. Roberto Duran," boxrec.com/wiki/index.php/Ken _Buchanan_vs._Roberto_Duran.

13   Ibid.

14   "Fighting Talk," Promotions, boxingcelebrities.co.uk/duran_buchanan_video .htm.

CHAPTER 11: MIKE TYSON VS. EVANDER HOLYFIELD II

1   David Scott, *Charlotte Observer*, December 3, 2013.

2   "Mike Tyson, Interview," *Details*, July 9, 2010.

3   Rob Tannenbaum, "Mike Tyson on Ditching Club Life and Getting Sober," *Rolling Stone*, December 4, 2013.

4   Quotefancy, "Top 280 Mike Tyson Quotes (2024 Update)," quotefancy.com /mike-tyson-quotes/page/4.

5   "Mike Tyson, Interview," *Details*, July 9, 2010.

6   Jabber Head, "Mike Tyson: His Childhood and Early Years," *Bleacher Report*, November 21, 2010, bleacherreport.com/articles/523260-boxing -mike-tyson-and-the-early-years.

7   BoxRec, "Evander Holyfield vs. Mike Tyson (2nd meeting)," boxrec.com/wiki /index.php/Evander_Holyfield_vs._Mike_Tyson_(2nd_meeting).

8   Colin Linneweber, "5 of Boxing's Most Controversial Fights Ever," CBS News, April 21, 2015, cbsnews.com/sanfrancisco/news/5-of-boxings-most -controversial-fights-ever/.

SELECTED BIBLIOGRAPHY

Allen, Arly, with the assistance of James Willard Mace. *Jess Willard: Heavyweight Champion of the World (1915–1919)*. Jefferson, North Carolina: McFarland, 2017.

Aycock, Colleen, and Mark Scott. *The First Black Boxing Champions: Essays on Fighters of the 1800s to the 1920s*. Jefferson, North Carolina: McFarland, 2021.

———. *Joe Gans — A Biography of the First African American World Boxing Champion*. Jefferson, North Carolina: McFarland, 2008.

Bak, Richard. *Joe Louis: The Great Black Hope*. Lebanon, Indiana: Da Capo Press, 1998.

Burns, Tommy. *Scientific Boxing and Self Defence*. London: Health and Strength, 1908.

Cavanaugh, Jack. *Tunney — Boxing's Brainiest Champ and His Upset of the Great Jack Dempsey*. New York City: Ballantine Books, 2009.

Dundee, Angelo, and Bert Sugar. *My View from the Corner — A Life in Boxing*. New York: McGraw Hill, 2009.

Egan, Pierce. *Boxiana; or Sketches of Ancient and Modern Pugilism, from the Days of the Renowned Broughton and Slack, to the Championship of Cribb*, Vol. 1. London: George Virtue, 1830.

Fewtrell, Thomas. *Boxing Reviewed; or, the Science of Manual Defence*. United Kingdom: Gale Ecco, Print Editions, June 2, 2010.

Gallender, Paul. *Sonny Liston — The Real Story Behind the Liston-Ali Fights*. Pacific Grove, California: Park Place Publications, 2012.

Gee, Tony. *Up to Scratch — Bareknuckle Fighting and Heroes of the Prize-Ring*. Great Britain: Queen Anne Press, 2015.

Giudice, Christian. *Hands of Stone — The Life and Legend of Roberto Duran*. United Kingdom: Milo Books, 2009.

Idel, Moshe. *Golem: Jewish Magical and Mystical Traditions on the Artificial Anthropoid*. Albany, New York: Cambridge University Press, 2009.

Kahn, Roger. *A Flame of Pure Fire: Jack Dempsey and the Roaring '20s*. New York: Harcourt, 1999.

Kent, Graeme. *The Great White Hopes: The Quest to Defeat Jack Johnson*. Great Britain: Sutton, 2006.

Kram, Mark Jr. *Smokin' Joe: The Life of Joe Frazier*. New York: Harper Collins, 2020.

LaForce, Christopher J. *The Choynski Chronicles: A Biography of Hall of Fame Boxer Jewish Joe Choynski*. Win by KO, 2013.

Lang, Arne K. *Clash of the Little Giants*. Jefferson, North Carolina: McFarland, 2022.

———. *The Nelson–Wolgast Fight and the San Francisco Boxing Scene, 1900–1914*. Jefferson, North Carolina: McFarland, 2012.

Levy, Alan H. *Floyd Patterson: A Boxer and a Gentleman*. Jefferson, North Carolina: McFarland, 2008.

Liebling, A.J. *The Sweet Science*. New York: Farrar, Straus and Giroux, 2004.

McCaffery, Dan. *Tommy Burns: Canada's Unknown World Heavyweight Champion*. Toronto, Canada: Lorimer, 2000.

Miles, Henry Downes. *Pugilistica: The History of British Boxing*, Vol. 1. London: Weldon, 1880.

Mitchell, Kevin. *Jacobs Beach: The Mob, the Garden and the Golden Age of Boxing*. London: Yellow Jersey Press, 2009.

Mullally, Frederic. *Primo — The Story of 'Man Mountain' Carnera, World Heavyweight Champion*. England: Robson Books, 1995.

Roberts, Randy, and Johnny Smith. *Blood Brothers: The Fatal Friendship Between Muhammad Ali and Malcolm X*. New York: Basic Books, 2016.

Thomas, Dylan. *The Poems of Dylan Thomas,* edited by John Goodby. New York: New Directions, 2017.

Ward, Geoffrey. *Unforgiveable Blackness: The Rise and Fall of Jack Johnson.* New York: Alfred A. Knopf, 2006.

IMAGE CREDITS

ABOUT THE AUTHOR

Louis Joshua Eisen was born December 1, 1960, in Toronto, Canada. One month earlier, John F. Kennedy became the thirty-fifth president of the United States. On August 25, 1960, American Cassius Clay captured the light-heavyweight boxing gold medal at the Rome Olympics.

Lou grew to love the fighters, trainers, and writers involved in the hurt business. His interest in boxing became a consuming passion.

On September 22, 1973, Lou went to Toronto's Maple Leaf Gardens to see the Clyde Gray–José Nápoles welterweight title fight. After the bout, Lou met Angelo Dundee, Nápoles' trainer. Lou wanted to be a boxer, but Dundee suggested he write about boxing instead. And so it began.

Read more of Lou's writing on boxing history on his Substack page *Once Upon a Time in the Prize Ring*, which takes an in-depth look at great fights and fighters from boxing's glorious past.